The Crisis Gambit

By

Dean diCiacca

A chess piece can slide across the board unencumbered or it can fall in a trap and break its very back- author's warning.

The Crisis Gambit

Preface

A crisis happens to everyone in the course of life and there is no escape. The brave, the young, the rich, the poor, the deserving and the undeserving, are all tested. Eventually all of us will face a crisis that will push us to the verge. That crisis can rampage the mind of your next-door neighbor or it can take place in London, Beijing, or Moscow. This global problem can result in school shootings, murder, and suicide. By employing inventiveness and ingenuity we can help others put down that gun, step away from that bridge or drop that knife. A crisis is an enduringly human condition that has yet to be dissected by a field expert with over 34 years of experience, until now.

Crisis counselors, phone counselors, mental health professionals, police officers, clergy, EMTs, firefighters, teachers, and medical personnel, are typical first responders. These first responders and those I overlooked, will find strategy on these pages. The human brain has approximately 86 to 100 billion neurons (Herculano-Houzel, 2020), when a crisis enters our life, some of us fail to access the full potential of those billions of neurons. Discrepancies in logic, distortion in reality will occur and without guidance can lead to a tragic outcome.

I have approached crisis counseling like a detective analyzing a locked room murder mystery. I have wrestle between an obvious trail of clues and clandestine explanations with obsessive acuity. With painstaking effort, I have pieced together the chain of events that create a crisis.

This book will reveal how a crisis is formed, how it is fueled, how it burns and how it is extinguished. Murder, suicide, and violence coupled with the "low-hanging fruit" of guns (Adams, 2007) is a topic discussed daily in our country and throughout the world. Unfortunately for some of us, it has reached our schools, our neighborhoods, our doorstep, infiltrated our homes, and even linger within far hidden recesses of our brain. *The Crisis Gambit* is designed to prevent the unthinkable. For others, this book will reveal a pathway to happier days and remove the echoes of lingering calamity.

Introduction

Crisis counseling is like the game of chess. The first move has 20 options. After each player makes a move, over 400 possible board configurations exist. After the fifth move, 4,865,609 configurations are possible (Shannon, 1950). Chess has several established strategies to navigate the myriad of possibilities. Players use well-known plays such as the Bird's Opening, the Queen's Gambit, and the Sicilian Defense to seek the best possible outcome. **Here you will learn how to use the Crisis Gambit as a new strategy.** Like chess the crisis counselor must match his/her skill to the issues presented. A gambit is defined as an opening move to gain a later advantage.

Leonardo DaVinci combined knowledge of several different sciences and academic disciplines to further his studies and his art. The 12th Librarian of the United States Congress wrote about the Italian polymath, "We are amazed by his reach in all directions," (Boorstin, 2001). DaVinci's marriage of disparate knowledge and the disciplines at large is the foundation used to create *The Crisis Gambit* equation. Never revealed until now, this new equation utilizes cross-disciplinary resources found in psychology, philosophy, architecture, movies, literature, radio, war, business, history, religion, art, music, and poetry.

The Rescue Legacy

For more than half a century, Rescue Mental Health and Addiction Services evolved into a 24/7 emergency services agency for Northwest Ohio. With a staff pool ranging from 90 to 110 individuals, it was also the training ground for students in Nursing, Psychiatry, Counseling, and Social Work. As a player, in those gallant years, there was an abundance of wisdom that exponentially passed profoundly from one dedicated individual to the next. With deep pride, those trained individuals have embarked on the world and even reached faraway places such as Japan, Scotland, and Australia. This book is an attempt to showcase some of the analytical skills used to tame the challenging, enigmatic crisis. Without Rescue Inc., the pages of this book would be barren. My hope will always be that Rescue Inc. continues to inspire, flourish, and remain a godsend for generations to come.

Table of Contents

Qualifications

This approach will employ knowledge I learned with boots on the ground as a crisis counselor, then as a working supervisor, and as the director of clinical operations, in the fray of mental health emergencies in Northwest, Ohio. My journey has surpassed 34 years and continues to grow. I have conservatively completed over 14,000 psychiatric evaluations using the DSM (Diagnostic and Statistical Manual of Mental Disorders).

Rescue Mental Health and Addiction Services provided Lifeline, Central Access, Recovery Helpline, and the Rescue crisis line. It furnished 24-hour service walk-in service, 365 days a year supplying a continuum of mental health treatment including: 16 Crisis stabilization adult beds, 8 Crisis stabilization adolescent beds, a 24-hour emergency services program, an urgent care medication assistance program, a community-based stabilization program, a health officer program, a criminal justice diversion program, a mobile response stabilization services (MRSS), DART liaison, and a 24-hour outreach program.

A Professor and a Nun

From English Professor Simone Yehuda's screenplay *Willing* (1982), I was given these catalyzing lines, "…there is a whole world to know, we must always grow, every moment, every hour, the world is a flower, a jewel, a breath to be taken in deeply and enjoyed until death." This is the impetus for actions and expanding our knowledge about crisis strategy. As an actor in this play, I learned to respect the power of words to move an audience and adopted her mantra to seek knowledge and growth in every moment.

From Sister Eileen K. Rice, O.P., as one of her students, I gained the impetus to use the full force of creative thought and couple it with work ethic. Sister Eileen, also known as the "bionic nun" had an unmatched diligence and was often seen reading and grading papers as she walked down Siena Heights University Drive, before losing her life to cancer at age 47. Fortunately, in her book *Idea Tasting* (Rice, 1995), this benchmark educator captured her class curriculums that required the pursuit of creative thought and its exploration on an exceptionally far and wide scale. The bionic nun was also a tireless student of knowledge, an unmatched renaissance woman even in the brightest halls of academia. She pushed herself to learn and grow daily. She pushed her students to read the work of great thinkers and writers. Once they come upon a new or unusual idea, explore it, write about it and stretch your mind.

An Old Movie Starring Sidney Poitier

If you are fortunate, you will see raw heroism on display in the movie *The Slender Thread* (Alexander, 1965). The actor, Sidney Poitier, portrays a young phone counselor thrown into an intense emotional situation. He has a caller on the crisis line, played by Ann Bancroft, who has overdosed and will certainly die unless he keeps her talking, gaining clues, giving authorities the time needed to make the trace and provide a medical rescue. Sometimes life is hanging by a thread, and sometimes only a first responder can keep that thread from breaking. Like this movie, *The Crisis Gambit* was designed to shed light on the process of crisis intervention. Unlike the movie, *The Crisis Gambit,* it will delve deep and seriously into the soul of a crisis.

How a Crisis is Formed

There are three basic components that create a crisis: the event, the perception of the event, and the reaction and coping ability (Kanel, 2007). During a crisis, we often think in black and white terms or irrationally as described by Albert Ellis (1994). These phrases come to mind: "I'll never win, I'll always have financial problems, my whole life is over, no one will ever love me, etc." Albert Ellis Rational Emotive Behavior Therapy (REBT) promoted replacing irrational thoughts with rational ones (Ellis, 2004). Since the dawn of time, humans have known that the way we think about an event creates our emotions or as Shakespeare's Hamlet (1604) said, "…nothing either good or bad, but thinking makes it so." Epictetus, born a slave in 50 AD is quoted, "Men are disturbed not by things, but by the view which they take of them (Epictetus, 2018)." Crisis counseling must understand this important principle. The emotional, and hasty Dr. Watson side of us often takes over in a crisis, rather than letting the logical reasoning Sherlock Holmes side take control (Konnikova 2013).

The Authentic Concept

Theoretical influences for *The Crisis Gambit* come from the father of behaviorism, the father of ethology, the father of American psychology, a Yale neuroscientist, and the London School of Economics co-founder; however, I will explain their impact in the following paragraph. I would like to give credit to five books. These books are important because they each created their own system to understand a problem; they developed their own authentic concept. *I'm OK – You're OK* written by Thomas Anthony Harris (1967), *Rethinking Narcissism* written by Dr. Craig Malkin (2015), a *The Bully at Work* by Drs. Gary Namie & Ruth Namie (2009), *The Ego and the Id* by Freud (2019) and *Zen and the Art of Motorcycle Maintenance* (Pirsig, 1974).

All five books are important for providing a method for becoming liberated through knowledge, but also the authors showcase creative uniqueness. These authors have unique thoughts for understanding roles, actions, and dialogs. These books help to understand what is right and what is wrong with certain behaviors. More importantly, they provide unique and original concepts. In the book by Thomas Anthony Harris, he was able to simplify and identify three ego states: the parent, the adult, and the child; he was able to make the founder of transactional analysis, Dr. Eric Berne, readable and practical. Dr. Gary and Dr. Ruth Namie show us the four bully boss theme types: the Screaming Mimi, the Constant Critic, the Two Headed Snake, and the Gatekeeper. Dr. Craig Malkin shows us the opposites and the land that exists between personality types on his Narcissist and Echo Scale. Freud's personality theory created in 1923, explains the role of the id, the ego, and superego that are building blocks for understanding personality and behavior. Pirsig concept of quality that runs through the thread of life and artistry that is accessible, this is the only book that can end with a long philosophical debate; however, it remains influential.

The Crisis Gambit is geared to help individuals and professionals manage a crisis. Being in crisis services for decades, I have learnt to throw everything imaginable at the crisis. When you pick up a crisis call, board a plane with an unruly passenger, walk into an emergency room on lockdown, or arrive at the scene of a domestic violence in progress, do you know what to do next? I have spent a great deal of time turning over stones looking for ways to help someone in crisis. Many great people walked the earth before we were even conceived. As humans we share a common experience that binds us together, we often share the same hardships or happiness as other people. Interwoven in the human experience are the keys of wisdom, we will better understand the how, when, and why change occurs if we tread over our historical past, listen to the thinkers that once crossed our past, live in our presence or are currently projecting our future.

The Importance of Crisis Counseling (Quintilian example of narration)

For the sake of the story to come (Moore, 1975), I need to define the word, "wicked". This word has several meanings and at this time I chose to select the definition: to act morally wrong (Merriam-Webster). This is a story of two men. This story takes place during

the 1960's. Both men were famous, and virtually anyone
who watched television or owned a radio in that period
knew these two men. From time to time, they would
visit a place thirty-eight miles West of Chicago, Illinois,
called Mooseheart, the Child City and School.
Mooseheart was an essential blessing for single parents
or orphaned children funded by the Moose Lodges that
dotted the landscape in the United States and Canada.

In the story of the two men, the first man was in
no hurry, he would often visit a hall at Mooseheart
called Baby Village, he would motivate the staff that
worked at this school and home for children by his mere
presence. He would not allow his visits to be filmed or
photographed. He would bring gifts and interact with the
workers and residents by sharing his valued time. The
children would rifle through his pockets for treats and
candy, they would jump on his expensive suits and
polished shoes. At the end of the day, he looked like he
was thrown down a hill during a windstorm. He would
then slip away with no fanfare and no record of the
event, only the people that witnessed this event could
barely believe what happened, someone so famous,
someone so important, would take the time to visit them.
And the well-known television star would visit secretly
time and time again. This is a story of two men, the
second man would also visit Mooseheart, people might
even say his star in Hollywood burned even brighter
than the first man. But the second man had a different
agenda; he was following his agent's demands.

He arrived in a long limousine and surrounded
himself with bodyguards and photographers. His breath
reeked of alcohol, he wore dark sunglasses, fancy
clothing, and expensive jewelry, he placed the small
poster child on his lap known as the "curly head," sat for
pictures, pushed the child off, brushed his pants and

disappeared faster than a summer breeze. A den mother working at baby village shook her head sideways and uttered the words, "Phony."

Over a thousand years ago, before the two men in the story were even born, there was a great thinker walking around antiquity, known as Socrates. In The Apology of Socrates as told by Plato (2003), the great thinker was put on trial. During his self-defense, Socrates said, "A man should not calculate his chances for life or death, he should determine if what he is doing is right or wrong, whether he is a good man or a wicked one."

In the story of the two men, it could be called a story of a good man and a wicked one. But the story does not end there. The first man in this story, was indeed a good man, of course we already knew this, his name proper was Danny Thomas (2002), the renowned actor and the founder of St. Jude's Children Hospitals. The wicked man is the focus of the story. The wicked man battled addiction for thirteen years, and in his darkest hour he stood with a bottle of painkillers and reached for a gun. By the grace of God, he heard a voice of a child playing in the distance. He loved making children laugh and that solitary voice was just enough to give him hope to fight out of his darkest moment. This second man became the man he was meant to be, he gave back to the community, and he saved countless suffering children (Clark, 2020). This second man, Jerry Lewis, became an example for humanity, a role model for hope and determination.

Whether you hear the voice of a child or reach a crisis counselor, that voice is critically important. If that voice is trained, the outcome has the best possible outcome. When a person's life is vanquished, all their future potential is lost, every hope, every dream, and every inventive idea is lost in that moment. When a person stares into the abyss, the draw toward death can be gripping. In this pivotal moment, a well-trained first responder is unmeasurable. At times they can become the only defense against a tragic outcome, a single and solitary voice, reaching into the darkness and pulling someone out.

Pawn Stars

I have seen an extensive number of individuals in crisis during my thirty years of service. Rick Harrison, a reality television personality, and co-owner of the world-famous Gold & Silver Pawn (store) which is featured on the television series Pawn Stars states at the beginning of his show he has been working for over twenty years in the industry, and one fact remains, "you'll never know what's gonna walk through that door," (Harrison, 2016). The truth of this statement is accurate for people that work in an emergency service, also called being at ground zero. A crisis counselor can face a complexity of conditions. Clients may present with symptoms for: Anxiety, Panic Disorders, Schizophrenia; Bipolar Disorder; Schizoaffective Disorder, Posttraumatic Stress Disorder; Major Depressive Disorder, Delusional Disorder, Personality Disorder, Substance Use Disorder. These examples are only a few of the conditions that a client may have when they come to a mental health agency accompanied by police, case manager, family, friend, or alone.

In any city, on any given day, at any given hour, crisis actualities can run the gamut that include life or death medical emergencies to just a breakdown in coping skills. I have seen clients pass out from overdoses, heart attacks, and seizures, I have seen a client light the security guard's hat on fire, I seen clients cut their wrists and cut staff that attempted to take the razor way, I have seen police thrown around like rag dolls, I have had clients hand over guns, knives, pills they intended to use, I have seen clients covered in someone else's blood and even gasoline. Mostly, I have seen friendly, sometimes scared, and mostly good-hearted people just searching for hope.

Traditionalists might say the three components to a crisis are: The event, the client's perception of the event, and the reaction to the event. Charles Dickens said, "We forge the chains we wear in life." We create our own limitations and our own chains. This program will reveal a new approach to crisis management. This approach will help to liberate individuals from their limitations and make them stronger.

What Constitutes a Crisis?

The United Nations had trouble combating terrorism in the1980's. The belief was to combat terrorism, you had to define it. A large part of their struggle for a definition was to differentiate between a freedom fighter and a terrorist. Eventually, a conditional definition was born. This includes treaties against hostage-taking, airplane hijacking and terrorism financing (Harris, 2003). I decided that I should employ this approach used by the United Nations and take it into the crisis arena. I would define a crisis and then combat it.

Defining a crisis is not going to be a straightforward process, a crisis means many things to each of us. In science and engineering, root cause analysis (RCA) is a method of problem solving used for finding the root causes of faults or problems (Wilson,

1993). Just the term root cause makes me think of one of the best questions to ask a person in crisis, "What chain of events occurred to put you in a crisis?" RCA was an indirect influence by giving my method a structure to problem solving and supplying the spark to create my own equation. The root cause of a crisis and its treatment can be divided into eight steps.

The Crisis Gambit Equation

Step one:

Address medical emergencies and safety protocols

The philosophy: "Nothing within the bounds of human nature is beyond the wit of man, or woman, to solve," author of *The Scotland Yard Puzzle Book* (McKay, 2020)

The Chain of Events (United Nations & Sidney Poitier movie)

a.) Safety vs. Freedom (**Ohio Rev. Code, Olmstead decision, Tarasoff**)

b.) Rapport & dynamics of numbers (**Battle of Pease River in 1836**) Build a relationship: A sentence does two things: convey a message and continue to negotiate a relationship (from *The Stuff of Thought* by Steven Pinker).

c.) Paraverbal Language, take notice of the tone, volume, and cadence of your speech (Fabius Quintilianus, book Institutio Oratoria circa 95 A.D.)

Step two: Four Core Motivators & The Motivational Triad (ethology & behaviorism) Lorenz & Watson

a.) Love-5 types, Eros, Philia, Storge, Agape, love of expression

b.) Anger: anger (the emotion), rage (targeted & propaganda), resentment (long-term) Rabbi Twerski

c.) Fear: socialized & memorized

d.) Hunger: physical and psychological. Motivational Triad: seek pleasure, avoid pain, extend the least amount of energy. Drive Reduction Theory to maintain balance or homeostasis (Hull & Spence)

Step Three: Modus Operandi Thermostat (Yale neuroscientist: Dr. Paul MacLean), crisis threshold, agents of socialization

a.) Rational State

b.) Emotional State

c.) Survival State (crowded hour syndrome)

Step four: The Reaction (imbalance) & The Bellwether Monitor

Step Five: Polestar Strategy & Occam's Razor (Franciscan friar c. 1287-1347)

Step Six: Problem Solving: generating alternatives, better than your former self

a.) Life instincts: pleasure, social & cultural

b.) Find your polymath: Franklin/Davinci traits: pragmatic conservative vs. idealistic liberal, active your Genius life force, develop gumption.

c.) Balance (**Vitruvius circa 27 B.C. stability, usefulness, beauty**), blueprint questions, 4 pillars of balance and the construction of hope. Identify areas of imbalance.

d.) Brainstorming (conscious) and incubation (unconscious). (**London School of Economics co-founder Graham Wallas**)

Step Seven: Goal Setting (the evolution of quality), patterns and routines. Realistic: negative forces are always present.

Step Eight: Vision Casting (construct and conceptualize your own evolution)

Developmental Level:

Before we apply the eight steps to a crisis, it is important to adjust to the language and educational level of our client. Development level is a major factor to consider when working with people in crisis. In Roman antiquity, the educator called Quintilian (Institutio Oratoria circa 95 A.D.) recognized that children learn differently at different ages. Quintilian thought speaking correctly was paramount, followed by reading and writing, before studying other subjects (Quintilian & Russell 2001). Piaget was the first known psychologist to make a systematic study of cognitive development, the age of an individual from childhood to adulthood is worth consideration (Chapman, 1999).

When we are children, we have concrete thinking patterns. When we move through adolescence to adulthood, we eventually increase our intellectual abilities and develop a more complex, hypothetical, and abstract understanding of the world. In "Indian Camp" by Ernest Hemingway (1996), the story illustrates that the young Nick, given his age, has no comprehension whatsoever about death. In the short story, Nick is witness to a suicide. A young native American Indian mother is screaming, while Nick's father, a doctor, is helping to deliver her child. The father of the child is so distraught by overhearing his wife's screams, he hangs himself. In the final scene, Nick is in a rowboat with his father; they are returning home, the final line of the story illustrates the young boy's cognitive ability, "he felt quite sure that he would never die." Pre-schoolers see death as temporary and reversible. Usually, between age nine and adolescents, most children begin to realize that all living things die and they too will die and it is not reversible. I have noticed that some clients that have anxiety disorders have not effectively processed the question about their mortality which is a natural stage of individual development. During interviews and counseling sessions with these clients, events involving trauma, chaos, or being raised in a dysfunctional family structure, have taken away the nurturing and supportive environment that has a better chance for producing an individual that has effectively adjusted to this paramount stage of individual development.

Crisis Threshold

In simple terms, as you live you learn things, the threshold for responding to different stimuli is different for different people, and age is naturally a contributing factor. When you journey through life you will face a series of events that will test your ability to cope. The humanist psychologist Carl Rogers (2011) wrote, *On Becoming a Person* in the 1960's which also suggests a similar opinion. If we allow ourselves to develop properly, we can become better at resolve, achieve self-actualization, expressing one's own capabilities and creativity (Rogers 2016). We are not born with wisdom and courage like the Greek hero, Odysseus, in Homer's *Odyssey*. These three stages identified by Erikson (Cherry, 2021): Industry vs. Inferiority, Identity vs. Role Confusion, and Intimacy vs. Isolation are problem areas for many adolescents and are areas for further discussion during treatment.

The three following scenarios will illustrate our understanding that our crisis threshold development changes as we navigate through life. In example one, I remember losing a battle with my nephew, Joshua, age three. We were in the car, running a little late and I was determined not to turn around. He continued to cry, yell, and scream, we had to go back and open the car door to let in his imaginary friend! A three-year-old is only beginning to understand the difference between reality and imagination.

In example two, my daughter, Natalya, was on the couch texting her friend Amelia, who was sitting at the other end of the couch! It is as though she was not able to communicate without her phone. A teenager losing cell phone privileges could be considered a traumatic event; it is often a vital connection to their social network. The fallout from cell phone related turmoil is undeniable. The *Trinidad Express* (Feb. 4, 2019) reported a sixteen-year-old girl committed suicide by drinking poison. Her mother took away her cell phone because her daughter posted revealing pictures on social media. *The Des Moines Register* (Jan. 27, 2019)

reported an Iowa kid freezes to death by running away
into a blizzard after his parents took away his cell phone.
The Chronicle Apr. 12, 2013) reported a teenager living
in Zimbabwe hanged herself from a tree branch at
around 10:15 A.M. while her sister was busy cooking in
the kitchen; her mother withheld her cell phone because
it was interfering with schoolwork.

      Health Insurance Portability and Accountability
Act (HIPAA) is a 1996 Federal law that restricts access
to individuals' private medical information. Having a cell
phone that can record and take pictures, makes it
impossible to adhere to this privacy law on a crisis unit.
Frequently adolescents refuse to stay on crisis
stabilization units because they refuse to relinquish their
cell phones. The addiction and emotional connection that
individuals have to social media and their cell phones is
alarming, but we cannot ignore how people think and
feel.

      In example three, an elderly man came to our
agency, and he was devastated with depression and had
intermittent suicidal thoughts because his daughter was
moving to Kentucky, his daughter was age 78 and he
was 101 years old. Years ago, I was playing a game
called *Therapy The Game* (2014). It was made by the
Pressman Toy Company, and to win the game, players
had to fill their couch up with clients by answering trivia
questions. I remember one question and the answer:
What makes elderly people the happiest? The answer
was the proximity to their children. According to the
National Center for Injury Prevention and Control
(NCICP), it is estimated that 50% of the elderly people
who commit suicide live alone.

      In the next illustration, I will show the difference
in cognitive development by age groups. When my

children were small, they used to have battles in the back seat of our SUV. Their testimonials would include, "he's looking at me," "she's touching me," etc. This was more than annoying. Having higher cognitive abilities than a preschooler and kindergartener, my wife and I simply produced "Quiet Town." "Quiet Town" was a place in Ohio created by librarians. So, when driving through this town, the length of the town varied-the longer the better, everyone in the car had to be quiet, encouraged to read a book, play a game silently or subject to arrest by library police. This peaceful parental bliss lasted a few years until my daughter uttered, "Hey, we're in Kentucky, Quiet Town is in Ohio." My wife looked at me with a frown, "Busted."

Agents of Socialization

At least six identified agents of socialization exist, they include family, friends, school, religion, work, and the mass media (Goffman, 2022). Of these agents, family is considered the primary agent of socialization, much of your personality is formed before age seven (Erikson, 1974). In the mental health field, it is common to trace phobias and learned coping skills to one parent if a strong bond exists. If a parent has trouble managing anxiety, has a phobia about bees, or has claustrophobia, some of these irrational coping skills can be passed on to their child. We are all influenced by those within our inter-circle and the six agents of socialization.

The impact of socialization can be seen when looking at African elephants. Many older bull elephants are being slaughtered by poachers for their ivory tusks. Elephants are an exceedingly social animal. According to Caitlin E. O'Connell, a professor at Stanford, young bull males are directly influenced by the lack of senior bulls in the elephant herd (Bale, 2015). This article explains that young bulls without guidance from older bulls become aggressive and exhibit delinquent behaviors. This illustration can be used to provoke thoughts about similar problems that exist in human circles. The family structure of everyone is a factor worth serious thought for understanding behavior.

As friends are an agent of socialization, a mentor has a special place in that category. A mentor is a person who teaches or helps a less experienced person. The word was first used in Homer's Odyssey as the name of a character. The word mentor was famously applied in the instruction of Alexander the Great. Alexander was a king that created one of the largest empires in the ancient world that stretched from Greece to India. Alexander's father chose the great thinker and teacher Aristotle to be his son's mentor (Green, 2013). Aristotle taught Alexander medicine, philosophy, morals, religion, logic and art, but hopefully he taught him to live a better life and become a better person.

Unfortunately, a person may have an acceptable attitude toward suicide based on their socialization that will make the job of saving a life harder. If your mentor, your parent, or even a celebrity you admired committed suicide, or a television show glamorizes the results of suicide, the task of reaching a safe alternative can be compromised. Social media, another agent of socialization, coverage of the Columbine shooter in 1999 has been shown to influence copycat shooters, which became known as the Columbine Effect (Muschert, 2014).

My daughter, Natalya, gave me the Enneagram (Wagner, 2021) to figure out my personality type. As a novelist and crisis counselor, it was interesting to find out how I share personality traits with two of my favorite writer's Agatha Christie and Conan Doyle. We are in a group called the "Investigator." Sure enough, being an "investigator," I had to determine how I am wired this way. It was the storyteller-mentors in my life that forced me to analyze and figure out the validity of their information. This makes a durable argument for at least some precipitating factors.

For part of my own socialization, I was exposed to three people that were superb story tellers and jokers: my stepfather, William Henry Moore, my uncle, Jim Bryce, and my mentor, Richard Proud. Each of these individuals had an enthusiastic sense of humor. They could tell a story or spin a yarn and I often took their stories hook, line, and sinker before being hit with the punchline. In the beginning I was gullible. When I was a kindergartener, I was convinced that chocolate milk came from a brown cow. My own children suffered the same fate, they were confused when their teachers told them your dad cannot kill a grizzly bear with his bare hands. My children were also told how tough my generation was. If I needed a pillow, I used a rock, if I needed clothes, I used a burlap sack, if I wanted a snack, I had toast on a stick. According to my parents, Abraham Lincoln walked 20 miles daily to get to school, but they did not tell me, as he was late every day. Without knowing it, unconsciously, I am a product of my environment and the agents of socialization.

My son, Nicholas, picked up some of these personality traits and often resembled Mark Twain's Huckleberry Finn, "He told the truth mainly" (1952). When my son was 16, he said when I begin a story with the introduction, "When I was your age," that is his que to stop listening. The agents of socialization have a profound impact on who we can become.

Step One of The Crisis Gambit:

When to Act (safety)

When you meet a person in a crisis, you will be faced with a decision to act. When do I call 911 to help a friend, a family member, or a fellow human being? Some of you reading this program might be health officers, police officers, physicians, and nurse practitioners with the power to place someone on an Application for Emergency Admission. Clinicians in the field call this a "pink slip". This is an act of making an individual in need go through a mental health evaluation that could result in a hospital level of care.

Marcus Tullius Cicero in 63 B.C. said, "Let the welfare of people be the supreme law." As a crisis counselor many of your decisions can have a significant impact on someone's life. The goal for any ethical mental health professional is to advocate for self-development, self-reliance and to keep independence. When you have a client walk-in to your agency or call your crisis line, your goal is to supply a level of care. You want to provide consumers with immediate relief from distress and help them keep stability in their lives.

I recommend three laws to consider how you arrive at your decision to act:

One, "Ohio Revised code 5122-29-10 "Persons with mental health conditions can and should be treated in the least restrictive environment and in a manner designed to preserve their dignity and autonomy and to maximize the opportunities for recovery."

Olmstead Decision

Two, the Supreme Court ruled in its 1999 Olmstead decision that under the Americans with Disabilities Act (ADA), public services for people with disabilities must be provided in the most integrated setting possible, giving them the opportunity to live independently in the community and not be segregated in institutional settings.

Tarasoff

Three, Tarasoff 1976 case (Tarasoff v. Regents of University of California, 17 Cal.3d 425, 131 Cal.Rptr. 14, 551 P.2d 334; 1976) established "the duty to warn", The Tarasoff case is based on the 1969 murder of a university student named Tatiana Tarasoff. An Indian graduate student at the University of California, Berkeley who had met Tarasoff at a folk dancing class on campus became obsessed with the victim before killing her and shared some of this information with his therapist. The law allows confidentially to be broken to warn a potential victim. Ohio is a "duty to protect" state, meaning: does the client have the intent and ability to carry out the threat. "Duty to warn" seen in the Tarasoff ruling refers specifically to a duty to warn an identified victim, whereas the term "duty to protect" is broader and allows for alternative means of protection from violence, such as notifying the police or initiating hospitalization" Rule 5122-3-12 | Duty to protect. Ohio Administrative Code.

Two Rules

Along with the three laws, I believe it is important to also follow two rules. Rule #1: You should never promise an outcome. "When schemes are laid in advance, it is surprising how often the circumstances fit in with them." -Sir William Osler (QuoetsWiki.com.) You lose objectivity and try to keep a promise rather than complete an honest evaluation. Often a parent, spouse or guardian will tell you a story about their loved one and you are convinced by their account that their loved one should be placed in a psychiatric hospital at the bare minimum. During the evaluation, you discover the client only requires out-patient counseling. Unfortunately, when husbands and wives are separating or fighting for child custody, they will create outlandish claims about their partner, the child's grandparents, that even includes false domestic violence and even false sexual abuse. You must hold off your final judgment until all parties have been interviewed.

Rule # 2: You should never assume you know what a person is going through. In the Aesop's fable the Horse and Goats, three goats made fun of a terrified horse running away from something unseen. The horse replied, "O' you hopeless fools, if you only knew who was chasing me!" In this situation the horse was running away from a lion. Never suspect what a person is going through, listen carefully. Cynthia Ann Parker was kidnapped at age nine by Comanche Indians and rescued twenty-five years later at the Battle of Pease River in 1836 by the U.S. Calvary and Texas Rangers. She never wanted to be rescued; she had married an American Indian brave and had three children; she had become a true Comanche. John Wayne starred in a Western film directed by John Ford called *The Searchers* in1956 that commemorates Parker's remarkable event (Eckstein,

2006). The life of Cynthia Ann Parker illustrates that a tragic result can happen when your voice is not heard, to her the rescue felt like a death sentence (Meyer, 2012).

Professor Bob

When I was being trained as a therapist, these words of wisdom still hold up. "It is important to let your client tell their story, let them vent." The late psychologist Bob Brady, my professor at Siena Heights University said, "If a client has a real problem, you will not have to look for it, give them an opportunity to talk and they will hit you over the head with it." So, once a client vents and starts losing some steam then present them with the question: "Tell me the chain of events that led you to this point?"

Freedom vs. Safety

Most state laws can detain an individual for an initial 72 hours to determine the validity of a homicidal or suicidal threat. When the 72 hours hold is used, there must be significant symptoms and circumstances present that fail to guarantee the safety to self and others. You will have to tackle the dilemma of freedom versus safety. As a mental health provider, you must protect your client's rights. When freedom and liberty are jeopardized, the consequences are far reaching. I look at the lines in a book by Alex Haley (1976) considered one of the most important U.S. works of the twentieth century. In the book Roots the father of Kunta Kinte, looks outward toward a slave ship disappearing into the vastness of the ocean, and along with other fathers they begin to chant, "To take away a man's son is to take away his immortality, to take away a man's son is to take away his immortality." To take away a man or woman's freedom also carries a significant burden. We are Americans and part of our fabric was stitched by the sacrifice of others so we might live in a free and just society. Nathan Hale (Quotes.net.) gave his life for liberty and said, "I only regret that I have but one life to lose for my country." Patrick Henry gave that death affirmation (Currier, 1876) "Give me liberty, or give me death!"

The act of being a first responder may require you to work out a safety plan with your client. If the threat of suicide is imminent, or if your client's mental illness has caused a substantial and grossly impaired judgement you must act quickly. Essentially, when you make a decision that takes away someone's freedom, it carries a burden of responsibility. Clients wanting to stay home to attend to their children, their pets, protect their homes from crime, or maintain the pride and dignity that comes from going to work, or staying close to loved ones, are all valid reasons why a pink slip is written with caution.

Lifeline

In 2009 my agency joined the National Suicide Prevention Lifeline. This direct line has a dedicated ringtone. Crisis agencies must adhere to a set of guidelines for assessing suicidality and imminent risk. This includes asking a minimum of three prompt questions: Are you thinking of suicide? Have you thought about suicide in the last two months? Have you ever attempted to kill yourself? (preventsuicidepa.org, 2018). There is no beating around the bush with these three questions. After you develop rapport and build trust, these three questions can provide you with clarity about the situation at hand and if you need to take safety measures.

Rapport

You start by building a rapport and gain the client's perception of the event. You must choose your words carefully. In most situations, words are exchanged before a fight breaks out. If you greet someone with the wrong words, your window to help can be shut down instantly. Ralph Waldo Emerson said, "Every man I meet is my superior in some way." A client in a crisis has superior knowledge and the only resource we have for explaining their viewpoint. Use these examples of paraphrasing, I.E, "So, you are saying..." "I understand you to say …" "I'm hearing that you feel …" "I want to see if I understand you correctly?" When you paraphrase or summarize an event, your client will see you as an interested ally.

You are not there to win an argument against someone in crisis, you are there to help them solve the problem. You could even lay out some places that you agree with your client's position. An example might be that you agree that going through a divorce is a tremendous stressor. Someone you thought was going to live with you for the rest of your life is now done an about-face and now is acting like an enemy. The more you elaborate or summarize your client's viewpoint the more they feel heard. You are laying the foundation for your client to accept a new idea, and the likelihood that they will look at a new perspective. When you and your client are on the same page, you introduce hope. Hope often dies in a suicidal person, hope never dies in an effective first responder.

Desiderata

I treated a client from an extremely abusive and dysfunctional family. His parents would not reveal that they had any love for him. He appeared obsessed with gaining their approval. He had a successful career, supportive wife, children, and friends. However, he was not able to turn the corner without some form of parental validation. His answer came from the non-judgmental, unconditional positive regard captured in these lines from the poem Desiderata, (Ehrmann, 1927). "You are a child of the universe no less than the trees and the stars; you have a right to be here." Morgan Freeman was interviewed by Oprah Winfrey in 2012 and expressed how advice from this remarkable poem shaped his life (Bonfiglio, 2012). Desiderata was written by Max Ehrmann (1872-1945) in 1927. The poem only achieved fame decades after it was penned and after Ehrmann's death. Leonard Nimoy who played "Spock" on Star Trek, recited the poem on his 1968 album (Nimoy, 2015). In 1972, Canadian Prime Minister Pierre Trudeau lost his election and reassured the nation by quoting Desiderata (Valpy, 2004).

Mr. Rogers and the Crocodile Hunter

Sometimes, people inspire us the right way. My mother was like this in every type of weather. Mr. Rogers, our "neighbor" from PBS, or even Steve Irwin "The Crocodile Hunter" had an undeniable grace that made us all want to be better as human beings. The positive energy and kindness from people like these radiated embers of hope and promise, making us want to reach higher. No matter how traumatic an event sounds, a crisis counselor cannot fold and must stay the course. Your client should understand that they have formed a therapeutic alliance, a coping strategy can be found for any problem. "When you think you have exhausted all possibilities, remember this: you haven't." – Thomas Edison.

Stay Gold

"Stay Gold" is a reference to a poem by Robert Frost (1949). I was introduced to the poem because it was used in Francis Ford Coppola's movie *The Outsiders* (Coppola,1987). To "Stay Gold" in the movie was meant to hold on to all things good and innocence, the beginning of every day holds this promise. A person that falls into pessimism is no longer an asset to your agency and they are hurting their own potential. Finding counter moves, developing strategies, and building your skill set will keep you golden. The art of counseling has millions of counter moves.

The Dynamics of Numbers

The human body has five basic senses that include: sight, hearing, smell, taste, and touch. According to experts the human brain has substantial real estate dedicated to the sense of sight, as this was part of human evolution (Huberman, 2022). Avoiding predators and gathering food were essential skills needed by ancient humans and it required sight. So, the way things look cannot be overlooked. When you have an interaction with an employee, student, or a person in crisis you must beware of numbers. Too many people can cause a calm person to feel threatened. I had a performance meeting with an employee, on one side. On the other side, was me, a human resources director, and another administrator. Unfortunately, our good employee crumbled under the critique of three against one. It was not the result anyone was looking for. If you are dealing with a mob or large group of people, ask for one or two people to remove themselves from the group and talk with you and your co-worker in private.

Another situation happened to a man suffering from the symptoms of a schizoaffective disorder with elevated paranoia. He was in our lobby and had broken a chair and the television remote control. I could see the expression on his face was that of rage and anger. I gingerly entered the room, keeping my escape route open. I told him I was there to help. I told him, he was clearly stronger than me and I was not going to produce a challenge against his strength. I made it clear; I wanted to help and presented him with several options. I remained non-confrontational in my voice and posture. As the conversation progressed, he stopped yelling and began to shadow my calm voice. I told him he appeared angry at the world, and most people were afraid of him because of his enormous size, muscular frame, and angry demeanor. The conversation was going well, and it even progressed to him wanting to be his former self that opened doors for his mother and protected his sister at the playground, but not someone who randomly threatened people. He agreed to see if our nurse could reach our doctor on call for a medication order to help him manage his auditory hallucinations, not a guarantee, but probable. So far, so good, and then two staff clinicians enter the room wanting to give me support in this potentially dangerous situation. The calm client exploded, me and the two other staff bolted out of the room. Our cameras showed him destroying the lobby. Unfortunately, he then assaulted two police officers and it took six officers to take him to jail. You must beware of the dynamics of numbers

Paraverbal Language

Psychological acoustics or psychoacoustics is the study of the relation between sound and the behavior of humans and other animals. Here we are basically, looking at sound and its effect on people. Think of the movie *Dumb and Dumber,* "The Most Annoying Sound in the World" scene (1994), one of the characters belts out his impression of a continuous buzzer while traveling down the road. The noise makes the newly acquired hitchhiker annoyed and irritated to a point of anger.

One of the best-known and misquoted proverbs about psychoacoustics comes from English playwright and poet William Congreve (1670-1729) - "Music hath the charms to soothe the savage breast." This quote is meant to mean that music can calm an angry or aggressive person (Congreve, n.d.). If you have trouble with road rage, and have a trigger, make yourself find a calming tune on your car radio as your first protocol. As a first responder a calm voice will have an impact on the people you engage. When a client is in a frantic state, it is important to stay calm, even though it may feel like they are yelling at you. They will begin to shadow your behavior; it is an axiom that behavior influences behavior. Voice inflection is the pitch and tone patterns in a person's voice. If you watch your inflection and your voice can stay on an even keel, your client will mimic your behavior. Yawning is a simple example of someone being influenced by another person's behavior.

How you say something is more important than what you say. In a study by Mehrabian and Wiener, (1967), subjects listened to nine recorded words, three conveying liking, three conveying neutrality, and three conveying disliking. The experiment finding was that tone carried more meaning than the individual words themselves.

A Sentence Does Two Things

"So, every sentence has to do two things at once: convey a message and continue to negotiate that relationship," from *The Stuff of Thought* by Steven Pinker. I agree with Pinker citing the following examples. When your mother tells her son, "You may want to clean your room before Friday." Or a young man tells a young woman, "You have a fine-looking dog, maybe he can go for a walk sometime with my dog." The mother's message is a threat to cancel weekend plans. The young man's message is an invitation, in hopes of gaining a romantic partnership. One can argue most forms of communications convey a message that is said to garner a certain type of relationship. Humans are highly equipped to negotiate a relationship. Both sides attempt to win, build, or solidify trust. You may find that you will tailor your words differently to your partner, siblings or mother. High-stakes conditions that accompany a crisis, require that a professional establishes trust quickly without the luxury of giving it time to develop.

Quintilian

When you approach someone in a crisis it is important to consider paraverbal language according to the Crisis Prevention Institute (CPI), the tone, volume and cadence of your speech will affect the response from the listener. *The Crisis Gambit* will strive to teach students some of Quintilian techniques learned by promoting narration, imitation, repetition, and memorization. Writing and research were critical for making a good speaker. According to Quintilian, if you do the work, your speech will not be empty and lack substance.

Marcus Fabius Quintilianus, the Roman educator, master orator, teacher of rhetoric usually referred to as Quintilian was right. He said it is no easy task to create an orator in his book Institutio Oratoria (circa 95 A.D.) or translated to Institutes of Oratory. Quintilian advanced students only once they learned the skill, unlike today when students advance by grade or age as a group. He also said the moral character of a teacher is paramount, and a teacher must be truthful about a student's progress. Quintilian would not let students applaud each other, this could be a false reward, only the teacher that is the master of rhetoric is the qualified judge. Quintilian also was conscious of not being too harsh or too critical of his students to hinder their learning and expression, a teacher must be truthful and friendly at the same time. Good speakers are concerned about paraverbal language, and it will take real effort to master.

Art of the Interview (Quintilian example of imitation)

If you want to improve your paraverbal language, turn on your radio to a talk show and listen to a host interviewing a guest, take notice of the open and probing questions, take notice of the tone, the volume, and the cadence of the host. Two radio personalities stand out for their interviewing skills and their amassing of knowledge: John Batchelor of WABC AM 770 (O'Connor, 2006) in New York and the late J.P. McCarthy of WJR AM 760 in Detroit (Whorf,1995). Although these are two brilliant talk radio hosts, their preparations for their interviews are clear. What sets them apart from most interviewers is that they possess a wealth of knowledge and information to add to a conversation.

Often a crisis counselor feels like a professional interviewer. By studying transcripts and videos of these two radio hosts, some patterns appeared that will help strengthen your interviewing skills. They make their guests comfortable, introduce icebreakers, no matter how deep the subject of discussion, their voices appear casually comfortable. They made their guest and everyone listening feel like one of their trusted friends. They build a rapport in a skillful way, ask open-ended questions like what, how, and where; and listen attentively. They have a skill for making a genuine connection with their guests.

J.P. McCarthy gave the most astounding interview I ever heard in 1986. I was a graduate student working in the student union. A radio guest named Eva Hart, age 81, a survivor of the RMS Titanic tragedy, was on the air. She was only seven when the ship sank. I can tell you, it felt like the world had stopped, and I was transported back to the ship during its ill-fated voyage. Later, I would learn that people pulled their cars over to the side of the road to hear every word of her story.

Fortunately, the master interviewer was asking the right questions to make us feel like a part of history (Shields, 1995).

Batchelor was off the air for a while and a patron of the show described him as a "fine wine or a box of chocolates, something worth savoring," his soothing voice coupled with insight feels like a rare commodity. If you can review recorded conversations of your voice, you can use these two radio personalities as a benchmark. We can all work on sounding casually comfortable like J.P. McCarthy and soothing like wine or chocolate like John Batchelor.

Step Two: identify the four core motivators

The second step of *The Crisis Gambit* was inspired by the writings of four people: Konrad Zacharias Lorenz known as the father of ethology (Manning, 1977) and John B. Watson is known as the father of behaviorism (Watson, 1997), and psychologists Clark Hull and Kenneth Spence for their work with Drive Reduction Theory (Mélon,1996). Ethology is the scientific study of animal behavior. Behaviorism can be described as the study of persons and animal behavior. Drive Reduction Theory states that the body is constantly working to maintain homeostasis or remain in balance. I concluded that humans and animals have four core motivators of the same name. These four core motivators can also be physical or psychological. In *The Crisis Gambit*, they supply fuel to feed a crisis. At least one of these core motivators is found in all crisis events. The four core motivators of a crisis are called love, anger, fear, and hunger.

Fuel

In the science of firefighting experts discuss the fire-tetrahedron. A chemical reaction must occur between four elements for a fire to occur. Those elements are oxygen, heat, fuel, and combustion (firesafe.org). If you remove one element from the tetrahedron the fire will cease. In step two of *The Crisis Gambit,* if a crisis does not have a disruption in one of these powerful core motivators: love, anger, fear, or hunger, the crisis will not occur. I will illustrate this point. A news broadcast comes over the airwaves of your radio and announces that Joe Smith was killed in an auto accident. This broadcast does not likely have the fuel to produce a crisis; however, if you are married to Joe Smith the fuel to produce a crisis is activated.

Konrad Lorenz, a 1973 Nobel Prize recipient, said, "Animals have an inner drive to carry out instinctive behaviors (Burkhardt, 2005)." A dog is born with the instinct to hunt, he may plunge into freezing water, jump through a thorny bush to chase a rabbit. According to the Drive Reduction Theory, people are motivated to take certain actions to reduce the internal tension that is caused by unmet needs. For example, you might be motivated to drink a glass of water to reduce the internal state of thirst (Cherry, 2021). Drive Reduction Theory gained traction under Clark Hull. (Hull,1943). Hull conducted an experiment with rats. One group of rats was allowed to eat every three hours by going down a hall where the food was available. The other group had a scheduled feeding every 12 hours. Hull's experiment showed that rats fed less often had greater drive. The father of American psychology, William James suggested that every instinct is an impulse or a reflex action. And, thus, human beings cannot help behaving in a specific way when acting on their instincts. I believe hunger is the core motivator for the dog's reason to hunt and hunger again is the core motivator for a human's need to drink a glass of water.

When the father of behaviorism, John B. Watson (Oelze, 2021), left academia after having a scandalous affair with a student, the American psychologist went to work in the field of advertising and took some of his knowledge of psychology with him. He is quoted as saying for advertising to be effective, "[…] it should appeal to three innate emotions: love, fear and rage (Todd,1994)." He names three of the four crisis core motivators I placed in *The Crisis Gambit*. Watson does not mention hunger in this quote; however, Hunger Marketing is a whole category in advertising strategy. This potent motivator plays on people's desire to get something others desperately want (Fender, 2019). Hunger can be both a physical and a psychological need.

The identification of core motivators is still a way to strengthen the rapport that was covered in step one. Tony Robbins, the benchmark for motivational speakers, said, "Rapport is created by a feeling of commonality," (Gagnon, n.d.). By explaining these powerful motivators, we now realize we are more alike than different and share this commonality. On the Canadian television comedy, *The Red & Green Show*, the main character makes a rapport building statement to his viewing audience, "[…] I'm pulling for you, we're all in this together," (MacPhee, 2011).

Love

The first core element, love, plays a powerful role in a crisis. This Swedish proverb captures the importance of this motivator, "Guld blindar manga, karleken blindar alla," translates to, "Gold blinds some, love blinds all," (Proverbial, 2022). During a breakup, it is interesting that a person might say they feel like they are going to die without their lost love. The novelist, Haruki Murakami (Peterson, 2020) said, "[…] I thought I could imagine how much this would hurt, but I was wrong." As we historically advanced as humans, socialization was a primary survival trait, banishment from a tribe meant certain death; being removed from a loved one (or taking away a cell phone from a teenager) can feel like banishment. When we dissolve a relationship, it challenges our basic instinct to survive. Love is a requirement for survival of the species. Nothing can capture the feeling of love gone wrong than the movie *Casablanca*. Rick Blaine, who owns a nightclub in Casablanca, Morocco, discovers his old flame is back. Humphrey Bogart delivers the line, "Of all the gin joints in all the towns in all the world, she walks into mine," (Epstein, 1942). This enables us to feel some of the pain love can leave in its wake. Emily Dickinson wrote, "[…] the sweeping up the heart, and putting love away, we shall not want to use again, until eternity," (Dickinson, 1927).

When we feel unloved by people we cherish, it can lead to the false belief we have no worth. An ironic twist is that people naturally avoid pain and seek pleasure. People that do care about you, do not want to see you depressed so they may unconsciously avoid contact with you, only to add to your isolation and depression. In the Alan Parsons Project song (Parsons, 1977), "Breakdown" the song lyrics capture this avoidant behavior: "Anybody else could see what's wrong with me, but they walk away and just pretend."

The Golden Gate Bridge in California is the number one suicide site in the United States (Yangtze River Bridge in China is the world's #1). It averages 35 deaths yearly and one of the prevailing motivations is feeling unwanted or unloved. In 2016 alone, 39 people are reported to have died there. Bridge patrol officers also conducted 184 successful interventions (Schmidt, 2017).

Goldwater Disclaimer

Arizona Senator Barry Goldwater, a conservative Republican, was running against incumbent President Lyndon Johnson. Psychiatrists were polled and rendered opinions about Goldwater's mental health. The Goldwater rule (2017) states it is unethical for psychiatrists to give a professional opinion about public figures whom they have not examined in person. This is a reasonable assertion for any mental health professional, not just a psychiatrist. This program will look at the lives of some famous people that I have never engaged in face-to-face contact with, and it is never proper to render a professional diagnosis; however, I will use famous people to illustrate points, gathered from media sources and supply references to that information.

Agape, Philia, Eros, Storge

The Ancient Greeks had four words to describe this core motivator called love. Agape means self-sacrificial love, Philia means brotherly love, Eros expresses romantic and sexual love and Storge expresses unconditional love and affection as seen especially between parents and children (Wilcox, 2019).

Eros

Edwin Howard Armstrong is known as the inventor of FM radio broadcasting that he patented in 1933. Television was considered the next big thing, so it took a while for FM radio to grab the industry. The inventor, facing financial ruin, struck his wife and she moved in with her sister. He wrote a two-page suicide before jumping out of his 13th floor apartment window in Manhattan in 1954. He was heartbroken at being unable to see her and expressed his deepest regret for hurting her. In his suicide note, he called her, "the dearest thing in his life." The suicide note was printed in The New York Times (Lessing, 1969).

Eros & Storge

Television audiences know him as the "Dog Whisperer," Caesar Millan. His wife was divorcing him, and he would be separated from his two children. In a state of clouded judgment, he overdosed on pills (Post Wire, 2012). Being without the people we love can throw anyone into a crisis. I believed that the "Dog Whisperer" and Anthony Bourdain, the international travel celebrity chef had a great deal of stress to accept and process. Both men would eventually become divorced, and both had considered suicide and one of them did not survive (Lockie, 2018). They were exposed to the belief of losing, not one, but two types of love, Eros and Storge. In simple terms they both felt the stress of losing a romantic partner and being separated from the love of their child or children. With my significant years as a crisis counselor, I have noticed a pattern:

losing two types of love (or the threat of losing) is an even greater shock to the system. Anthony Bourdain may not have fully recovered from the divorce from his daughter's mother, while entering another failing relationship. Unfortunately, the wife of an NBA legend, Vanessa Laine Bryant, lost both her husband and thirteen-year-old daughter in a helicopter accident had to endure this actual type of loss (Beacham, 2020).

The pain of losing a child appears aptly captured by Sir William Osler, the father of modern medicine. He wrote in his diary after hearing that his only son was killed in World War I. "The War Office telephoned at 9 in the evening that he was dead. A sweeter laddie never lived, with a gentle and loving nature. We are heartbroken, but thankful to have the precious memory of his loving life (…) call no man happy until he dies (Barton, 2019)."

Philia

Philia or brotherly love is also love between friends and sisters. The power of friendship is on display in the short movie, *Skinny and Fatty* (Terao, 1969). In this black and white film, two Japanese schoolboys are bullied as individuals. Together, they form an alliance, develop a strong bond to take on life's challenges. In the beginning of the film, Fatty is ridiculed for not being able to climb a bamboo pole in gym class like all the other boys, his extra weight makes this task appear all but impossible. In a sad twist, Skinny must move away to another town, but writes Fatty a letter and tells him to stay confident and remain determined. In the end Fatty climbs to the top of the pole and the whole school is cheering for him. This film meets my criteria for friendship. A friend is someone who wants the best for you.

The power of friendship is felt clearly in the songs and poems within our society. "Wish you were here," by Pink Floyd (2002) is a song with a deep message. David Gilmore and Roger Waters, the creators of this song, effectively captures the pain and grief of losing their band member to mental illness. At New Year all over the world, Robert Burn's poem (1927), 'Auld Lang Syne', a sincere expression about a long-standing friendship or Philia is sung. The poem by James Whitcomb Riley (1915), "Out to old Aunt Mary's," captures the bond between brothers that exists through shared experiences. An elderly brother reminisces about his time with his brother in their youth during days of lost sunshine.

One of the most significant stories to celebrate the loyalty between friends was the bond between two cattle ranchers Oliver Loving and Charles Goodnight. In 1867, Loving was mortally wounded during a cattle drive by Native-Americans of the Comanche Nations. Goodnight stayed by his good friend's side for over two weeks until his death. It was said he carried a picture of his friend long after his death and returned a year later to move Loving's body from New Mexico back to Texas, keeping his friend's dying wish (Hedstrom-Page, 2007). Best friends can develop unbreakable bonds, treasured memories, and priceless comfort.

Agape

Agape can be defined as showing moral nature and character that exhibits goodwill to others. Agape or self-sacrificial love is captured aptly in the life of Johnny Appleseed. He entered the world with the proper name of John Chapman. His father encouraged Johnny to learn about nursery work and agriculture to solidify a source of income during the United States expansion era. In a shrewd business move, he predicted the calendar movements of homesteaders going west and their migration patterns. He planted orchards before settlers arrived in each area. When settlers eventually arrived, he would sell the apples as a food source and teach others how to take over the orchard for a price. When he matured, he no longer cared about making money. He was concerned about planting apples to help others and appeared genuinely concerned about making the world a better place for strangers he would never meet (Means, 2014). It fittingly says on his tombstone in Fort Wayne, Indiana, "He lived for others."

Beyond the Greeks

The Ancient Greeks named four types of love. Eros or romantic love, Philia, or friendship, Storge or parent-child love, Agape means self-sacrificial love or helping others (Wilcox, 2019). I believe they should have had five types. A quote by the poet Ralph Waldo Emerson may lend us insight: "A man is only half himself; the other half is his expression." Many people put their passions even above friends and family. I am not passing judgment on those people; I am just saying this type of love is a reality. A small sample of the great passions that people might have been animals, painting, writing, filming, building, sports, hunting, fishing, hiking, flying, dance, theater, rewarding work. The theory on natural instincts supports my position. Under cultural instincts, people have the impulses to gain wisdom, discover, and express themselves artistically, among others.

Ernest Hemingway may have killed himself for not being able to write, doing the thing he loved.

Hemingway lost some of his ability to think or write after receiving electroshock therapy (ECT) which seriously damaged his short-term memory. Alcohol use and head injuries throughout his life were other contributing factors; his family members have mentioned a decline in his physical capabilities that also added to the writer's turmoil (Meyers,1999). Inaugural Committee Member, Kay Halle, asked Hemingway to write a message to President Kennedy as a surprise after his inaugural ceremonies. His wife, Mary Welsh, reported the author was tormented by struggling to construct this complimentary message (Chandler, 2018). Although theories will abound around suicide victims, Hemingway had a need to express his ideas by writing. As a young man in high school Hemingway called himself the "junior" Ring Lardner showing his desire to be like the American sports columnist and short-story writer he idolized and would in time, significantly surpass in stature (Lardner, n.d.). Freud concluded that the fulfillment of a childhood dream is one of life's greatest achievements. Freud was inspired by archeologist Schliemann who found the lost city of Troy in Northern Turkey after reading Homer's Iliad as a boy (Kaus, 1992). Hemingway had a desire to be a great writer in his early years, being unable to hold on to this ability could only add to his depression. There have been five alleged suicides in the Hemingway family over four generations: Hemingway's father, Clarence; his siblings Ursula, Leicester, and himself; and his granddaughter Margaux (Meyers, 1999). *The Crisis Gambit* will help others not to choose that path. In summary, love is a massive motivator and there are five types of love in *The Crisis Gambit* equation.

Anger

Let us look at examples for the motivation called anger. Nature can provide us with undeniable beauty. On Queen Charlotte's Island, off the west coast of Northern British Columbia there once was an unusual evergreen, the world's only golden Sitka spruce tree. This type of spruce is the world's largest and longest-lived species; it can live for more than 800 years. This magical tree appears like finding a unicorn in the real world and attracted boatloads of tourists to its remote location. The tree was sacred to the Haida Gwaii Indians. Imagine seeing a golden tree in a sea of green, this tree was so rare it was given its own scientific name. In 1997 Grant Hadwin cut down the world's only giant golden spruce tree, angering Canadians and anyone with an affinity for nature. Hadwin was angry at the logging industry and its over reach and unfortunately lost his life while trying to return to the island to face trial (The Golden Spruce by John Vaillant 2005).

Anger Propaganda

The motivation of anger is often used to gain a result. Nations at war sling insults at each other and often accuse each other of committing deplorable and heinous acts. The adversary is demonized by being called negative words: barbarian, cannibal, heathen, Nazi, and other derogatory or racial terms. According to Aristotle, the three pillars of rhetoric are: Ethos, Pathos, and Logos (Kennedy, 1991). Pathos is the persuasive technique used to stir emotions, making your enemy sound like a monster is an example. Usually, men are more aggressive than women, if you look at completed suicides and the number of men in prison for violent crimes, it supports this position. According to the CDC, the suicide rate among males in 2020 was 4 times higher than the rate among females. According to the Statista Research Department, murder offenders in the United States who were male were almost seven times the number of female murder offenders in the same year. When you watch The Bachelor on T.V. you will see women who resulted to character assassination (Davis, 1950), or harming someone's reputations, as a method to show their aggressive toward other candidates, men tend to show physical aggressiveness when angered, but again men are not off the hook, propaganda used in war or politics can come from both genders.

A sergeant in the army would not give an order to kill a combatant and then tell his subordinates that your adversary is the father of three, he has elderly parents that depend on him, he leads food drives and helps at a local homeless shelter. Civil War Union General, Lew Wallace- "Sympathy is in great degree a result of the mood we are in at the moment: anger forbids this emotion," (Wallace, 2020). In the movie, *Outlaw Josey Wales*, Clint Eastwood's character motivates three women in a frontier cabin to protect themselves when he is gone. He tells them, "Ya gotta get mean."

During an episode of *Thursday Night Football* (Bernstein, 2020), a Cleveland Browns football player, Myles Garrett, ripped the helmet off of an opposing player, Pittsburgh Steelers' quarterback Mason Rudolph. Garrett then used the helmet as a weapon and hit Rudolph in the head. Anger can cause the career of any successful athlete to come into jeopardy, on any given day. Woody Haze, the head football coach at Ohio State, also succumbed to a fit of rage and struck an opposing team's player, abruptly ending his illustrious career (Picaro, 2020). Both events show how anger can quickly cloud judgment. In 2022, I saw the University of Michigan's head basketball coach strike the opponent Wisconsin team's assistant coach. Also, during the 2022 Oscars, Will Smith became angered by comedian Chris Rock's joke about his wife's hair. She suffers from alopecia, a medical disorder that causes the hair to fall out. The bellwether monitor explained in *The Crisis Gambit* could have prevented these events.

Twerski's Three Types of Anger

The feeling of anger has three phases according to Hasidic Rabbi Abraham Twerski: "anger, rage, and resentment" (Twerski, 2017). Twerski is influential by showing anger can come in degrees. In *The Crisis Gambit*, targeted anger is considered an important situation to address. If you use propaganda on yourself, you have a better chance of acting out your anger. If you label someone by calling them a bitch or a bastard. You are using propaganda to convince yourself. Your propaganda has made them a target. Targeted anger can produce rage or resentment.

In October of 2019, *The Zebra* conducted a national survey of American drivers to determine their perception of the "road rage" phenomenon. The survey found that 82% of drivers in the U.S. admit to having road rage or driving aggressively at least once in the past year. Over a seven-year period, AAA found over 12,500 injuries could be linked to road rage and could also be linked to 218 deaths (Covington 2021). When a person states they lost control, anger is often the motivator. Resentment is an extreme form of anger that lasts the greatest amount of time. Resentment does not go away quickly like the first two phases of anger. Resentment, and hate are hard to differentiate, life is too short to invest the time and energy hating anyone. Carrying resentment is only taking you farther away from enjoying the present. Wisdom from the philosopher king and ruler of the Roman Empire, Marcus Aurelius (121-180 A.D.) in Meditations instructs us not to resent anyone; in that obstacle there is an opportunity. Like Aurelius, *The Crisis Gambit* will preach that "another path is always open."

Anger Control

Crisis counseling can show how a person can have control over their anger by gaining insight. One exercise I use is to imagine yourself in a line with ten other people. The line consists of diverse types of people, they vary from a little old lady, a young kid, a Catholic priest, a construction worker, a biker, etc. Now, imagine you are in line at the grocery store, at a baseball game, or riding your bike. In the routine of your life, one of the ten people now approaches you, they call you a name you find offensive. You now imagine how you would respond. Each of the ten characters says the same phrase, but you never react to them the same way. Why is this? It is because you always have a choice. The drill illustrates that you have control over your reaction to anger. Will Smith slapped Chris Rock at the Oscars in 2022. Would Will Smith Slap Dwayne "The Rock" Johnson under the same circumstances? Pre-planning and future psychodrama should be taught to students during driver's education to avert road rage.

While we are still on the topic of control and anger, there is a pertinent question to ask yourself that comes from a military idiom. "Is this the hill you want to die on?" When you get cheated out of two cents at the coffee shop, is it worth your valuable time to fight and argue your point? The most valuable lesson for controlling your anger may come from Epictetus (2021) who is quoted, "Some things are in our control and others not." An example is that your neighbor parks his car on the street in front of your house. The law is clearly on your neighbor's side, learning the limits of what is within your control can clearly prevent you from further anger and turmoil or being filmed and called a 'Karen' on social media.

Blinded by Anger:

Client's that suffer from Intermittent Explosive Disorders often can be described as act now, think later. When the emotional and survival parts of the brain are working, it can hinder or even appear to shut off parts of the top of our brain, the part of the brain that handles reasoning, planning and problem solving. By performing diagnostic assessments for years, its' common to have clients with Intermittent Explosive Disorders to also have (comorbidity) the presence of borderline intellectual functioning or an intellectual disability. Talking to a client and often a child in this state is all but impossible, allowing them to pace, yell into a pillow, squeeze stress balls may provide a better release. My colleague, Ms. Jodie, devised an unconventional, yet brilliant idea. By allowing an adolescent to vandalize their room with toilet paper, she averted a more serious outburst. It is critical that parents properly socialize their children and guide their angry outbursts as unacceptable behavior.

Many children go through their terrible twos, due to the frustration of not being able to fully express themselves verbally, they act out by throwing tantrums. If this type of behavior is allowed, without consequence, the child will go on to develop more serious anger problems into their later years.

Resentment

Anger is not always a short-term motivator in the resentment stage; it can lead to planned and calculated violence. When someone holds onto anger it turns into resentment that can last hours, weeks or even years. Workplace violence comes to mind as a significant example. Known as 'Mad Bomber,' George Peter Metesky, a mechanic and electrician terrorized New York City for sixteen years feeling he was unfairly fired from his job in the 1950's (Cannell, 2018). Another example, John Robert Neumann was fired in April from his job at an Orlando factory and returned in June killing five of his former colleagues (Randall, 2017).

Fear

Many things motivate us, and some things more than others. "Sometimes called the most powerful motivator of all is fear" (Wilson, 2009). This primal instinct served us as cave dwellers, and it keeps us alive today. If we survive an unpleasant experience, we learn how to avoid it in the future. "Our most vivid memories are born in fear. Adrenaline etches them into our brains,"

(Wilson, 2009). The amygdala is a part of the brain that everyone has next to our brain stem, and it provides us with our fight, flight or freeze response to keep us away from danger. The worst component of fear is that it can keep us from learning or taking on a new challenge, the unknown can be scary.

The brain has two halves: the right hemisphere and the left hemisphere, they overlap in functions, creative people may network these two sides better than less creative people. However, according to one study, the left hemisphere specializes more in what is known to you and the right hemisphere is for analyzing and deciphering things that are not known to you. This conclusion comes from studying brain damaged individuals (Goldberg, 2002). In a crisis, the unknown can make us freeze, the world is either chaos or order, unexplored or explored, explained or unexplained. A good example for describing fear and the unknown is a person who cannot swim. Fear and chaos are ever present, until a person learns to swim. On a lesser level, this situation happened to me after golfing. When I opened the trunk to my car, I was dumbstruck after looking at my new golf shoes, they appeared to have aged significantly. In my bewildered state, I felt frozen. It took me a minute to piece together that my golfing friend had the same size, brand, and color of shoes as my new shoes and left his in my car. People suffering from Alzheimer's unfortunately, must deal with many unexplained and confusing events on a regular basis.

Fear is categorized into two types: socialized and memorized. Socialized fear comes from the agents of socialization that include family, friends, school, work, religion, and mass media. An example of socialized fear would be your mother is afraid of bugs so you too could be afraid of bugs even though a bug has never harmed you. Another example would be, your agents of socialization tell you that all people from a political group or a certain ethnic background are no good, so you avoid diversity in your life, restricting your full potential, losing an avenue for friendship, and unlimited growth. Memorized fear is driven by avoiding pain. When we burn our hand on the stove, get bit by a dog, or stung by a bee, we will avoid or approach these items with caution.

The Cyberbully

Sadly, the fear of being bullied again, going through another terrible experience can lead to suicide. Fear remains a potent motivator. Often cyberbullies are the cause of shame. Monica Lewinsky's parents were fearful that their young daughter might kill herself as she was publicly shamed by the media and on the internet after falling in love with the President of the United States between 1995 and 1997. She reported her parents were so worried for her safety, her mother would not let her shower unless she left the door open (Lewinsky, 2015). In 2010, a young music student at Rutgers University, eighteen-year-old Tyler Clementi posted on Facebook: "Jumping off the gw [George Washington] bridge sorry." His suicide was in response to someone breaching his privacy and streaming a video to the public of him having an encounter with another man (CBSNewYork/AP, 2019).

Ryan Halligan, age 13, was an American student from Essex Junction, Vermont. Halligan was allegedly repeatedly sent homophobic instant messages, and was "threatened, taunted and insulted incessantly". He hung himself with the tie from a bathrobe. In 2003, there were no laws against cyberbullying, and no one was charged with a crime (Khalid, 2015). In all three cases: Monica Lewinsky, Tyler Clementi, and Ryan Halligan were all bullied by media sources; unfortunately, only one of the three of them survived.

We are hardwired to be fearful, but through skill we can keep fear from being the driving force in our actions. Fear may never go completely away, but we can learn to put it in the back seat. Mark Twain said, "I am an old man and have known a great many troubles, but most of them have never happened." Unfortunately, fear can also keep us in our comfort zone and prevent us from learning or exploring the world around us. We are afraid of the unknown, fear of looking bad, and fear of messing up. However, when we move out of our comfort zone, face some of our fears, this is a prelude to learning. *The Crisis Gambit* considers both socialized fear and memorized fear.

Hunger

The core motivator, hunger, can be both physical and psychological. We can hunger for things that make us feel better like food, clothing, shelter, drugs, or alcohol. Victor Hugo is one of the greatest and maybe the best-known French writer of all time. His most famous works are the novels Les Misérables (1845) and The Hunchback of Notre-Dame (1831.) In Les Misérables, Hugo depicts a character's nineteen-year-long struggle to lead a normal life. He served a prison sentence for stealing bread to feed his sister's children (Robb, 1999). The novel shows how a good person can be pushed to the edge, during a time of economic depression. The motivation is hunger. Many clients enter mental health centers and emergency rooms in search of food. Cornell researchers found that young people, ages fifteen to sixteen that struggle having enough to eat, are five times more likely to try suicide, compared with well-fed adolescents (Lang, 2002).

One travesty that exists in the mental health system is the cost of staying in a psychiatric unit. Imagine, if a hungry client was able to supplement his ability to buy food with money that is used by Medicaid. Community stabilization residential programs have significantly lower cost than a hospital level of care. States should always consider community residential treatment over a hospital level of care first. The money saved can increase support to combat hunger. In the article, "I Wish I knew About the Cost of Mental Health Care Before Being Hospitalized" (Catel, 2019). In this article a woman reported being charged $3,500 per day in a psychiatric hospital and staff wanted to keep her for 30 days. Finally, her parents were able to get her released on day 13. Financial stress can contribute to depression and 30 days at $3,500 equals $105,000. When people run out of money, lose the ability to buy food, psychiatric units fill to capacity between the 15th and 30th of every month and less in the first ten days of a month.

Psychological hunger can be tied to hunger marketing, wanting things that other people have or do. When Tom Sawyer (Twain, 1896) had to paint his Aunt Polly's picket fence, he cleverly enlisted his friends to perform the work. Yes, he swindled them, by convincing them that painting the fence was fun and a privilege. If you look at the core motivator, hunger, people hunger to feel important, to achieve something valued, to become part of group inclusion. They may have benefited from

Tom Sawyer's trickery, they bonded with friends and completed something that felt like fun.

Work and financial resources are tied to hunger, simply put, food, clothing, and shelter cost money. The number of people committing suicide after losing their job is significant. The founder of Victoria Secret committed suicide by jumping off the Golden Gate Bridge, he had many financial setbacks and failed business ventures (Schmidt, 2017). The University of Zurich attributed 45,000 or one in five suicides a year worldwide to unemployment (Cummins, 2015). Often a person in a stressful situation goes into survival mode and begins compulsively overeating. Survival threats trigger instincts and reflexes that we are consciously unaware of. Unfortunately, the flight response of the amygdala can be activated to escape the pain of hunger, and result in suicide.

Suicides in France 1840'S

History can reveal many secrets relevant in today's world. Below is a categorical study of suicides that occurred in France during the 1840's. The human experience is the commonality we all share. I'm struck at how problems of the past still ring true today. At the heart of these suicides are core motivators. Here Brierre de Boismont (1797-1881) gives the classification of 4,595 cases of suicide that occurred in France (The Project

Gutenberg eBook of Suicide, by W. Wynn Westcott, London, Published by H.K. Lewis,1885):

652 Mental illness (term changed) about one-seventh of all cases. 405 Other diseases of the body, incurable, or with intolerable pain. 556 Motive unknown. 530 Alcoholism. 361 Domestic troubles. 311 Sorrow, disappointment. 306 Disappointed love. 282 Poverty and misery 277 Reverse of fortune, and cupidity (greed for money) 237 Ennui (boredom). 145 Hypochondriac and hysterical. 134 Remorse, and fear of law. 121 Misconduct. 56 Indolence (laziness). 55 Delirium and acute disease. 54 Jealousy. 44 Gambling. 43 Want of occupation. 26 Pride and vanity, notoriety.

Core Motivators

All of us are influenced by four powerful core motivators called love, anger, fear, and hunger. When explaining why someone acted a certain way, it is not unusual to see one of these motivators in the following phrases: He did it for love, he did it out of anger, he acted out of fear, I could not help it, I was hungry. Understanding core motivators in a crisis, will help us later in the problem-solving stages of the STE. For now, simply put, if you are angry at someone, if you love someone, or if you fear someone, you will act a certain way. If your basic needs cannot be met and you are starving, this can elicit a certain response.

When we combine two motivators together a radical response can occur. People sometimes are extremely angry while going through a divorce, and they are subjected to the forces of love and anger, therefore divorce is a higher risk factor than the death of a spouse. In some cases, divorce can have all four motivators: Loss of a loved one(s), anger at the person causing the rejection, loss of income and status, fear of starting a new life. Hunger is tied to survival issues that involve securing food, clothing, and shelter. In the article, "Divorce is a Factor for Suicide, Especially for Men" (Sullivan 2019), the author points to Emile Durkheim's studies that show suicide rates are 2.4 times greater for men involved in divorce. The author then points to Dr. Kposowa work that noted that there were huge differences between genders. In fact, the data showed that, compared to divorced women, divorced men were nine times more likely to die by suicide (Sullivan, 2019).

Step Three: Modus Operandi

This step will shed some light why we fail in human interactions. Well make mistakes from time to time and say, "I cannot believe I said that." "Why did I do that?" "Damn, I'm such an idiot." If your brain is operating in an emotional or crisis state, you will likely show poor judgment until trained otherwise. Not to worry, this section will explain the modus operandi.

The Inspirational Dr. Paul D. MacLean

The third root cause in the sequence of *The Crisis Gambit* is called modes of operation or modus operandi. Much of my inspiration for step three comes from Dr. Paul D. MacLean (1990). He was an American physician and neuroscientist who researched the functions of the brain at Yale Medical School and the National Institute of Mental Health. In the 1950's he produced a controversial theory that humans have not one brain, but three. In MacLean's Triune Brain Model, he believed each of our three brains had a different function and purpose. He called the three parts of the brain: The Neocortex, the Limbic System, and the Reptilian Complex.

Modern neuroscientists may agree less with the MacLean's theories due to the advancements in neuroscience; however, the most crucial factor about MacLean's work is that he believed the brain had three command centers that sometimes appear to run independently of each other, and sometimes intertwined with each other which I call modes of operation. It is obvious that the brain changes modes during a crisis. I call the modes that the brain can go into rational state, emotional state, and survival state. In most cases our brain will favor one state over the other given the crisis.

Based on Dr. MacLean's work (1990), three levels to our brain exist. In a loose geographical sketch, we could say the brain has three parts: the top, the middle, and the bottom. On the top, is the Prefrontal Lobes (Rational State) responsible for learning and planning. In the middle, is the Limbic Brain (Emotional State). It handles emotions and memory which help to determine if I am wanted or loved. On the bottom, the Brain Stem controls the flow of messages between the brain and body. Dr. MacLean believed that the human brain had older "preserved" brain structures for basic survival functions. The survival brain had three common goals, "Can I eat it? Will it eat me? Can I mate with it?"

The Amygdala

The amygdala forms part of the limbic system, but it's best known for our fight, flight, or freeze response (Survival State). Often when humans face a survival threat, it triggers an emotional and instinctual reflex, it happens naturally and so quickly we might not even realize it is happening. The survival state is mostly reactive. When people are lying and are given a question, they cannot hide the non-verbal cues or reflexes that materialize before they can think of a clandestine response.

The Freeze Response

People can show a condition called the Dominique Strauss-Kahn or freezing the upper body. This condition is attributed to the controversial figure Dominique Gaston André Strauss-Kahn (n.d.). He is a French politician, former managing director of the International Monetary Fund (IMF). Strauss-Kahn's involvement in several financial and sexual scandals put him on the witness stand. He showed this unique physical response while testifying. People go into a survival state to avoid a fearful consequence and act like a deer in highlight. Humans can also freeze when facing a threat. Social anxiety is the fear of being evaluated. Social anxiety can result in selective mutism (inability to speak), stage fright is a common example.

I recall a significant freeze response I saw, but it remains a vivid memory. My brother, David, was nine and I was a year younger. He was carrying our dad's metal tackle box up a steep long dirt trail to the cabin on Smith Lake in Southwest, Michigan. The path he took was created out of dirt plateaus framed by railroad ties, creating steps up the trail. I was walking behind him carrying fishing poles. In David's path was a hissing coiled snake showing its fangs. He froze, going into a survival state, he could have certainly just moved out of the way by stepping backwards. I was not able to think clearly either. I could have just pulled him backwards out of harm's way. I yelled and ran up the hill a long way to get dad. I was running away from the problem showing a flight response. Dad grabbed a rake and journeyed a long way to the bottom of the hill and killed the snake with a rake. Dad showed a fight response but operating from a more rational state than my brother and I. David snapped out of his frozen trance after the threat was removed.

It is interesting on social media when people post videotaped pranks, if someone jumps out to startle an unsuspecting victim, they will elicit a fight, flight, or freeze response. Another story illustrating the freeze response comes from my friend Rodney. He was in Northern Michigan with friends on a black bear hunt. Each of the four friends had a tree stand and created bait drenched in honey to draw the bears out, after four hours the four hunters would meet at the designated rendezvous. Eric never appeared; his concerned friends fired three shots into the air and listened for reply shots. The air remained deadly silent. Fearing an accident, the team cautiously made a hike to Eric's tree stand. Amazed, they saw a black bear in the tree stand with Eric. The bear leaped from the tree and disappeared into the woods. Eric had stepped in his bait and the bear was licking the honey off his boots. The team was astonished, Eric remained frozen and unresponsive for several minutes. They eventually got him to take a shot of whiskey, helped him down from the stand, and walked him a round.

The DSM-5 manual has a condition called a Conversion Disorder or the Functional Neurological Symptom Disorder (American Psychiatric Association, 2017). In a brief explanation this is a disorder that happens to some people that endure a significant amount of distress in a key area of life. I had a client that was going through divorce and developed paralysis in his left arm. For many reasons divorce can generate catastrophic thinking like financial ruin, never finding another mate, etc. Step Two and Step Three of *The Crisis Gambit* shows us that fear is a core motivator that can place someone's mind into a survival state. Fear can trigger an involuntary freeze response to the whole body or in this case a partial body response.

The Three Modes

Dr. Paul D. MacLean's work would lead to looking at the brain as having three command centers or states that I call modes of operation. In summary, they are called the Rational State, Emotional State and Survival State. The modus operandi completes step three in *The Crisis Gambit*. The modus operandi is like a thermostat for the intensity of a crisis. Little to no intensity comes from the rational state of the brain, medium intensity comes from the emotional state of the brain and high intensity comes from the survival state of the brain.

School Shootings

"Nothing within the bounds of human nature is beyond the wit of man, or woman, to solve," author of the Scotland Yard Puzzle Book (McKay, 2020). If there is a better statement to support the belief that things can change, I have yet to discover it. This quote is full of hope that is critical to finding a solution to gun violence. This book is not going to look at gun regulation as the answer, although the correlation appears obvious. In 2019 the U.S. Department of Homeland Security clearly linked gun accessibility as a factor. It found that 76% of school attacks came from the home of a parent or close relative (White, 2021) where the shooter could acquire the gun. Some call this the low hanging fruit argument and it appears like a reasonable position. However, this book is going to stay in its lane, because this is a book about mental health.

This may seem like a controversial view made by Tom Selleck on the Rosie O'Donnell show on May 19, 1999. Selleck participated in advertisements for the National Rifle Association and Rosie wanted him to admit that stronger gun laws would stop shootings. Selleck said, "Guns were much more accessible forty years ago. A kid could walk into a pawn shop or a hardware store and buy a high-capacity magazine weapon that could kill a lot of people and they didn't do it. The question we ought to be asking (…) in today's world, someone who is suicidal sits at home nurses their grievance develops a rage (…) but they take 20 people with them. (…) something changed in our culture (Levine, 2021)." I believe both Tom and Rosie are right. Society has clearly changed; an example would be the difference in violence that occurred at Woodstock in 1969 vs. Woodstock of 1999. As a crisis counselor, I will focus on the changes that can make a kid into a shooter and this is the cornerstone for containing this problem.

Earlier, we discussed crisis development and thresholds that occur as a person ages. Often school shootings can be attributed to the lack of coping skills. A teenager may have experienced fewer crisis events during their short life and had less opportunity to problem solve than older people. Erik Erikson also has three psychosocial stages that can occur in the psyche of young male shooters: Industry vs. Inferiority, Identity vs.

Confusion, and Intimacy vs. Isolation (Cherry, 2021).
Biological development is also a factor. One study done
by the National Institutes of Health found that the region
of the brain that inhibits risky behavior does not fully
form until age 25 (Sheehan, 2017).

There are elements responsible for school shootings:

Can Tom Selleck's question be answered, "What
changed in our culture?"

Some experts in the field of psychology have
theorized the Columbine Effect has influenced the trend
in high school shootings. Copycat events followed the
tragedy that took place in 1999. The Sandy Hook
Elementary School shooting in 2012 also influenced
others to target the youngest of our population. In 2011,
the band *Foster the People* wrote a song called "Pumped
up Kicks," which was played on American radio
stations. One line in the song, "All the other kids with
the pumped up kicks, you better run, better run outrun
my gun." All three events are examples of how the
thought of school shootings has entered into conscious
thought.

Evidence from psychology has looked at
conscious thought and how it affects human behavior, a
commonly held view assumes that conscious thought is
in charge of behavior (e.g.,Wegner, 2002). "We propose
that conscious thought enables coordination with the
social and cultural environment (Baumeister and
Masicampo, 2010). To answer Tom Selleck, culture has
been changed by events like the Columbine, Sandy
Hook, and songs on the radio. The mind is influenced by
conscious thought and also unconscious thought.

Evil is not a new event in the history of the world or its coverage in social media. In America, the famous Chicago lawyer, Clarence Darrow, delivered an astonishing 12-hour closing plea for mercy in the Leopold and Loeb trial of 1924. His eloquent plea helped spare the two accused men from the death penalty (americanrhetoric.com). In his closing argument Darrow explained how the American Civil influenced behavior, "--it changed the world. For four long years the civilized world was engaged in killing men." "(...) How long will it take the calloused hearts of men before the scars of hatred and cruelty shall be removed?" "(...) No one needs to tell me that crime has no cause. It has a {s} definite {a} cause as any other disease, and I know that out of the hatred and bitterness of the Civil War, crime increased as America had never seen before."

One solution to prevent school shootings, community shootings and violence toward women, is the untraceable crisis line. In this suggested pilot program, a completely confidential crisis line will be manned by *The Crisis Gambit* trained crisis counselors. A crisis agency cannot have a recording that states, "This phone call may be recorded for quality assurance." If a caller is aware their voice is being recorded, some people immediately end the phone call and others may never call you. The law must guarantee that a threatening or dangerous person has a place to call. Current laws require mental health professionals to inform an organization when a patient may be at danger to oneself and others. This untraceable crisis line is an attempt to reach the unreachable. I have had several clients in jail, going to jail, or facing charges say the same thing, "If I just would have talked to someone first." The breach in confidentiality is well presented in the article "Who's

Listening When You Call a Crisis Hotline?" (<u>Calou</u>, Y., Zeavin, H., 2022).

Prevention is the key, this grant proposal program will use explicit billboard advertising to flush out callers, forgiveness programs for gun owners. Even if a caller has several guns and made plans, it is not too late to abort or dismantle, but we must create a safe haven, not punitive consequences to gain access or treatment for that caller. A consumer in this program will receive case management treatment that will utilize diversion over arrest. Other components could include developing: a mentoring program, and the power of music program: including rappers for the DMZ, teenagers for peace, the metro park's non-aggression program, Bellwether trained officer interaction, group meetings at area churches and mental health organizations. The *Crisis Gambit* programming is put into our schools that explain how the brain works, how core motivators generate behavior and propaganda anger elicits violence. **Humans have an evolutionary need to form a group, but this leads to irrational thinking or the** "us and them" philosophy that makes violence possible. Friends are an agent of socialization that drives behavior.

Highly successful rappers still involve themselves or lose their lives in gang activity. This statement is supported by the article, "Here Are the Longest Prison Bids in Hip-Hop History" (www.xxl.mag.com) Feb. 3, 2023). Showing examples of people in prison can be a deterrent, school shooters sentenced to life in prison include the Parkland shooter (www.cnn.com), Colorado school Shooter (www.npr.org), Forest High School shooter sentenced to 30 years (www.sao5.org). In a

G.Q. magazine article (Hannaford, 2018) called, "We asked 12 mass killers: 'What would have stopped you?' Some common themes that ignited the event included: angry at two teachers and mother not letting him live with biological father, depression, anger, isolation, money, family problems, my behavior at work not being reported, beatings from father, being ignored, going through divorce, doing drugs and alcohol, nightmares, paranoid, loneliness, fear. These mass shooters also revealed ideas that they believe may have stopped them included: mental health treatment, access to counseling, better parents, locked up guns, no access to a gun, sleep, letting church back in schools.

Imagination Used Correctly is a Strength

A few pages ago, I wrote about suicide in France during the 1840's conducted by Brierre de Boismont (1797-1881). Of the 4,595 cases of suicide that occurred, 237 were due to ennui or better known as boredom. If you watch castaways on the survival show called "Alone." you will notice the creative survival experts that fair the best can entertain themselves. A child with an imagination is rarely bored. Idea tasting created by Eileen Rice is a class that all students in high school should take to engage their creative side, ideas will stretch your mind and improve your mental health.

A key to stopping school shootings is acknowledging that people fantasize and daydream. You don't have to watch the news if it upsets you. You've known people your whole life, absorbed in comic books, podcasts, nature, bogs, movies, books, writing, painting, dreaming. I call this the two-world syndrome. We all experience escapism, to slay a dragon, rescue a princess, to make something beautiful, to travel in outer space, to win the World Series. Using your own fiction or enjoying a famous author you can imagine a better world, where good in the end conquers evil. A key to understanding yourself is understanding that there are two worlds to live in and your imagination is one of your greatest strengths. According to novelist Neil Gaiman, "Imagination and reality are two separate worlds. "Everybody has a secret world inside of them. I mean everybody. (...) no matter how dull and boring they are on the outside. Inside them, they've all got unimaginable, magnificent, wonderful, stupid, amazing worlds… Not just one world. Hundreds of them. Thousands, maybe." Neil Gaiman who wrote this quote is the creator of *American Gods* and *Sandman*. The celebrated author also won the Bram Stoker award as well as the Newbery and Carnegie medals.

John Lennon wrote a song, "Across the Universe" that was later sung and performed by Fiona Apple. In this video, Fiona has headphones on and sings the lines to the song. The most important line in the chorus is, "Nothing's gonna change my world". The video shows men violently breaking the storefront glass window of a soda shop, throwing furniture, swinging bats and crowbars. Complete carnage and chaos ensue, all the while, Fiona calmly sings, "Nothing's gonna change my world, Nothing's gonna change my world…" Fiona remains completely unaffected by the violence around her and maintains a happy and calm demeanor. The video is an example of the strength of the human mind and the power we as individuals have to turn things off and control what we let in. In a perfect world we could have independent thinkers in politics. Politicians that independently see an issue and try to come up with the best possible solutions regardless of their political affiliations with the Republican or Democratic party. The strength of your imagination and the belief in a better world is up to you.

The Crowded Hour Syndrome

In a crisis our adrenal glands can be activated that heighten our awareness and prepare us for an oncoming threat. With our increased awareness and attention to detail, time appears to slow down. Gordon Lightfoot, often called Canada's greatest songwriter, captured this awareness in the song; "The Wreck of The Edmund Fitzgerald," "Does anyone know where the love of God goes when the waves turn the minutes to hours," (Lightfoot, 1976). In a crisis our senses are heightened, and every sound or motion is seen, heard, or felt, time feels like it is standing still, loved ones waiting for news suffer an unbearable wait. This must be the condition of my mother when she was waiting for news the day my father was killed in a mining accident.

According to an article by BBC Future, 70% of the people who had skirted close to death, reported the feeling that the event occurred in slow motion (Robson, 2014). Some researchers claim that intense emotions can lead us to recall more details. When a client states that they are feeling as time is stopped, they are getting close to making a decision that could result in suicide; they are on the brink of something dangerous. If they appear hypervigilant with details this could be a clear warning sign; detailed suicide notes are no joke.

A near death experience during the Spanish-American War for Teddy Roosevelt caused him to develop a hypervigilant memory full of intricate details. The book called *The Crowded Hour* by Clay Risen recounts Teddy Roosevelt's Battle of San Juan Hill in Cuba with the famed United States Cavalry nicknamed the Rough Riders. 144 Americans were killed in Cuba during this battle and Roosevelt produced the term the "crowded hour" to describe his experience. He was able to recount so many details and actions that were verified by witnesses with remarkable clarity. During his brush with death, adrenalin was coursing through his veins (Risen, 2019). During that hour on San Juan Hill, Roosevelt experienced the oncoming threat of death; a suicidal client can feel the same threat. Clients that are focused and make statements full of clarity have been one of the rarest types of suicidal clients to walk into your crisis center, but also one of the most dangerous.

Emotions Will Affect Your Language

Another example of how parts of our brains stop working is when we become emotional. When we act from an emotional state and drift farther from our rational state, our speech can be affected. It is common for a movie star or football coach to be quoted saying something offensive when they are attacked by the press. In a survival mode, a person can even lose their voice, with options like flight, fight, or freeze; it is likely the person was unconsciously using the freeze response, as it might be better to be quiet to avoid an aggressive predator.

Why do I use the word recipe coupled with modus operandi? Depending on the crisis, blurred lines between the three states of the brain will occur. Everyone is an individual and how they deal with a crisis will vary. The person in the survival state is farthest away from the rational state. Their reaction may result in a physical response or action. The emotional state is closer to the rational state and tends to stay more verbally oriented. As individuals some of us are thinkers, some of us are more emotional. A recipe is the better term, because a client can be 25% rational 50% emotional and 25% survival or a client can be 71% emotional and 29% rational. A person with an antisocial personality or someone with psychopathic traits that lack empathy and remorse for others can be violent and rationally justify their use of violence. They could appear 80% rational. A person who was not raised in a caring or loving environment, can also tend to lack a show of emotions. If your parent had a schizoid personality, someone who avoids interacting with others and avoids social activity, this also would produce a less emotive child.

People that suffer from a histrionic personality disorder are prone to be emotional and prone to have anger issues. This personality disorder is described as someone requiring attention, acting overdramatic, and making a mountain out of molehill. They appear to think in an extreme manner that makes them prone to becoming emotional. In their emotional state, they can be described as not thinking before acting, resulting in making rash decisions. Military personnel and first responders are trained heavily for this reason. Drills are beneficial because when battles, fires, or shoot-outs take place, trained individuals do not start thinking for a solution under duress. Planned reactions are rehearsed to elicit the best possible result. "Drill is the foundation of discipline in battle, and that its importance has been proven again and again (Powers, 2011)."

Bellwether Monitor

The bellwether was used by sheepherders to identify the location of their flock if they disappeared over a hill or were on the move. One goat was fitted with a bell. If the herd was calm and relaxed the bell was silent. If a wolf were lurking nearby, the restlessness of the flock would sound the bell and gain the sheepherder's attention.

I have been trained yearly in several types of crisis de-escalation systems; the most prominent and the current system used in our agency is called C.P.I. from the (Crisis Prevention Institute, 2011) . All systems are geared to manage aggressive or assaultive behaviors to avoid physical altercations. These systems strive to interact with potentially dangerous clients in the safest manner for staff and client(s). I feel even the most current systems lack the advantage of having more focus on identifying modes of operations. When a provider of care is not aware of his/her own modus operandi and how it can change instantly, poor decisions can result. When staff are unable to handle verbal insults, it shows a lack of scenario training, particularly in this area. My answer to this problem is to have a team leader or co-worker appointed as the bellwether monitor before the event and one staff member is appointed to watch the bellwether. Their sole purpose of the bellwether is to watch everyone's modus operandi. When the bellwether monitors orders a staff person to stand down for two minutes to regain control or leave the area, they are the law. Often the hot head is not willing to listen, and this is where the rest of the team must be trained to support the bellwether.

Soccer appears to have this element of safety incorporated into the game. I have seen parents out of control in the stands during a soccer match, the head referee will stop the game until the disruptive parent is warned or removed from the stadium. An emotional or belligerent first responders can add fuel to an existing fire, increasing the chance for a violent outburst, putting everyone at the scene at risk. Usually, two types of emotions surface in situations when a client must be restrained, staff can appear fearful or angry. The staff in a fearful state can also be dangerous because they forget their training. They are too afraid to help the group working to gain control over a situation. Fear can also trigger a flight, fight, or freeze response. Fearful staff could be assigned a role that has less direct contact with the client, like getting a room ready, getting keys ready, getting the client something to eat or drink, or getting ready to call for outside back up. The bellwether should be welcomed by any agency concerned with public safety, it is a critical component to protecting its members and the population they serve.

In summary, step three of *The Crisis Gambit* is called modus operandi. Your brain is triggered by the perception of an event and fueled by motivators. This results in your brain operating from a command center in various degrees called: Rational State, Emotional State and Survival State. Knowledge of how the brain works and functions is paramount to *The Crisis Gambit*. When we train to be a bellwether, we will also better understand the potential pitfalls that our own behavior may slip into.

Step Four: Reaction Phase

***The Triage: Vague Threat vs. Potential Threat vs.
Serious Threat***

Step four is the reaction phase of *The Crisis
Gambit*. This is the emotion and the resulting behavior.
Before applying the equation to real examples, I want to
point out some cautionary information. Statistical
information can help us in triage situations. If I have two
suicidal callers and only have time to speak to one caller,
how can I ethically choose a course of action?
Unfortunately, this is a true situation that can happen.
911 operators and emergency room physicians know that
medical emergencies all vary by degree. Crisis teams
also must consider a vague threat vs. potential threat vs.
serious threat.

Suicide Notes

Known as the "Mysore Study," suicide notes
from 22 people who committed suicide were examined
and published in the Indian Journal of Psychiatry. Most
suicide notes show a consistent theme that included
apology/shame/guilt 90% (Namratha, 2015). In the
Canadian Journal of Psychiatry, suicide notes and
themes were also analyzed. The themes of 42 suicide
notes from the Northern Ireland were examined and the
commonest themes were "apology/shame" at 74%.
(Furqan, 20 18.) When someone is angry at themselves
and fearful people will not love them, they can develop
shame and guilt. The motivators: love, anger, fear, and
hunger combined are forces behind many completed
suicides. People that suffer from substance use disorders
and gambling disorders have components that involve
apology, shame, and guilt.

Scenario

Now let us look at the scenarios using the first three steps to arrive at step four. The crisis event will be that Joe's girlfriend broke up with him. He perceives this to be an awful, terrible, and catastrophic event. He says I cannot live without her. Using *The Crisis Gambit*, we can understand the root cause of his reaction. Joe's motivator involves Love. Joe's modus operandi is in the survival state. His reaction is at considerable risk for harming himself. His rejection from his social group is like banishment from a tribe and he loses the ability to mate or secure survival of the species. The unconscious mind is powerful; most people do not understand why we fall so hard. Our culture promotes idealism and often people do not live up to those ideas like: Romeo and Juliet, or songs on the radio like, "Always and Forever" by Heatwave (Temperton, 1976) or "Thinking Out Loud" by Ed Sheeran (Sheeran, 2015) are indeed examples of perfect love. I wish I had written the line by the country singer, Alan Jackson, "You're where I belong, like red on a rose," (Jackson, 2006). In the novel Madame Bovary (Flaubert,1856) based on true events, we learn that a young bride can never find the unrealistic love she reads about in romance novels that eventually leads to suicide.

Imprinting

Another thought on love is inspired again from Konrad Lorenz, he is recognized as one of the founding fathers of the field of ethology, the study of animal behavior. His most significant work as it relates to love is his discovery of the principle of attachment, or imprinting, through which some species form bonds between a newborn animal and its caregiver (Burkhardt,

2005). I find that this obsessional, imprinting connection is like a love relationship. A lot of patients that fall in love, have a significant problem of letting go of that first real love. A puppy raised with sheep will grow up believing he is part of the flock through imprinting and protecting them from predators. Barbara Braams drafted an article in the Leiden Psychology Blog: "Adolescents in Love, What Makes a First Love Special" (Braams, 2013). She describes an experiment that involves showing a person a picture of their first love and the resulting brain activity that has similar intensity to using cocaine or other euphoria-inducing drugs. This imprinting is the same reason why my brother likes 60's music, sister likes the 70's and I like the 80's. I am thirteen years younger than my oldest brother and my sister is somewhere in between. Knowledge is power, how love scientifically affects us can change behavior.

Joe's behavior is like most people with a broken heart, he becomes withdrawn and slips into a dark depression, he feels his pain will never go way, he lost his soulmate, he thinks about suicide. Love is an enormously powerful motivator, and you will find that talking with someone with a broken heart takes considerable creative effort. No matter how logically you explain the need to look at other ideas, your client is stuck in a survival or emotional state and will have a challenging time letting go.

Lame Blame Phenomenon

Another dark defense mechanism exists in love scenarios. Often the person that breaks up with their partner also wants to protect their own ego. Even if their partner was loyal and attentive, they do not want to take ownership for the breakup. They will try to convince themselves and make their ex-partner believe they caused the breakup. This is done by pointing out any faults, real or imagined under a microscope. They point out all their ex-partner's shortcomings, so now their ex-partner feels even more worthless and depressed. I call this the lame blame phenomenon.

Gaslighting

A more deception, narcissistic tactic is called gaslighting, and it can trace its origin to the movie Gaslight (1944). The stars of the movie were Charles Boyer and Ingrid Bergman, and the movie received two academy awards, including Bergman for best actress. In the movie the husband slowly manipulates his wife to believe she is insane (Hoberman, 2019). The husband would turn on a gaslight and search in the attic for the family's treasured jewels. The wife would see the gaslight on, but the husband convinces her that it was a figment of her imagination that she was losing her mind.

Svengali Effect

The Svengali effect is another manipulation technique. The name comes from a fictional character, and the villain of the romantic novel Trilby (1894) by George du Maurier. The name Svengali became synonymous with an authority figure or mentor who exerts undue, usually evil influence over another person. The character also employs some techniques of hypnosis. Sociopaths, in a relationship can use their charms, money or experience to get what they want or impose their influence or political will. This is also the reason why; teachers must have a moral compass. This is critically important with young children, and according to Erikson (1974), much of the personality is formed by age seven.

Using the same crisis event, Joe's girlfriend once again breaks up with him. This time Joe has two motivators involved and they are love and anger. How Joe reacts to the situation is much different, his modus operandi is in the survival and emotional states, and this overrides his rational state from working properly. He thinks that his ex-girl betrayed him and now she becomes an enemy without a name, she is a "demonic bitch" as far as he is concerned. He is angry at everyone and negative about the world, he has chosen to fight over flight or freeze. His negative attitudes are affecting his behavior in other parts of his life and his behavior has soured some of his work relationships. He could still be suicidal because he believed he will make his ex-girlfriend feel responsible and sorry for his suicide. We are human, and although we may or may not act on them, thoughts and feelings exist.

Sometimes, people become violent or homicidal toward their partners or ex-partners and want to inflict pain regardless of the consequences. Trace Atkins's then-wife shot the country singer in the heart and lungs. Surprisingly, Trace survived, and his wife granted him a divorce and Trace never filed charges (Geromeap, 2007). The three-time winner of the Masters Golf tournament, Sir Nick Faldo broke up with a twenty-year-old golfing student who then trashed his Porsche 959 with a golf club (O'Neill, 2002).

Demonizing Enemies

It is common for us to demonize our believed enemies. Soldiers have gone to war making their enemies sound like monsters, devils, and terrorists. Road rage has a challenging time working if you call your adversary Susan, a nurse who helps people through medical emergencies. To have road rage toward a driver, the words son-of-a-bitch are more likely to spill from your lips. In Toledo on 3/10/2020 a thirty-six-year-old man by the name of Soto posted alarming and threatening statements on social media full of rage against the mother of his children. Our staff were alerted to this man's post in hope he would reach out to our agency, unfortunately he never contacted us, and the police were not able to track him down. Later that day, Mr. Soto non-fatally stabbed his ex-girlfriend and her friend (State v. Soto, 2021).

In these two situations the event is the same; however, using a different motivator completely changes the reaction. When love is the motivator in a crisis the tendency is toward harming oneself, this is a flight response from the pain of a broken heart. When anger is the motivator in a crisis, wanting to fight, lash out or hurt others becomes the tendency. Both situations are dangerous until a rational state of thinking is reestablished. Understanding the motivators in your situation will help you to understand where the fuel is that feeds your crisis.

Three Heroes

Here are three extraordinary examples of people that have been able to deal effectively with their anger: Nelson Mandela invited his prior jailers to his inauguration, he was jailed for twenty-seven years, "I knew if I continued to hate them, they would still have me" (Mero Pen, 2020). Christian evangelist Louis Zamperini, an Olympic distance runner, and World II War prisoner of war, was tortured and then forgave his captors. He was rightfully given the honor of carrying the Olympic torch in 1998 on its way to the games in Nagano, Japan (Graham, 2018). The third example is a story about my father who was a Warrant Officer in the British Airforce in World War II. He was shot down over Germany and spent over three years in a German prison camp. I heard a story that when he immigrated from Scotland to Canada in the 1950's he was upset to see a German man on the same bus he was taking to Timmins, Ontario. My father was then killed in a mining accident in 1962. Days after his death, my father's German friend, Gunther, visited our family. My mother told how, Gunther took off his bowler hat and consoled my mother with tears in his eyes and said, "Going to the mines with Domenic was like going to a picnic." My father and Gunther planned to fish together that coming Sunday. These three examples show three people returning to rational thinking, allowing their lives to go forwards. One man gains true freedom, one man gains strength in his faith, and one man gains a friend.

Step Five: Strategy

The primary focus of step five is to develop a strategy and navigate through a sea of troubles. From the dictionary, "a problem is defined as a matter or situation regarded as unwelcome or harmful and needing to be dealt with and overcome." Sailors plot a course by referring to the polestar known as both the North Star and Polaris. The polestar is important for navigation because it sits directly over the North Pole and appears to stand almost motionless, while other stars in the Northern Hemisphere move around it (McClure, 2019).

When you find the polestar in the litany of your problems, you are giving your ability to solve a problem direction and purpose. It would be inefficient and confusing to try to tackle multiple problems all at the same time. Your first order of business is to find the premier problem, the polestar. That problem is just waiting for you to deal with it, to overcome it, and it will remain in a fixed position unless you navigate to it.

The Underlying Polestar

These four murky situations will force you to find a polestar. The world is full of dilemmas: The Catch-22, Malthusian Trap, Between a Rock and Hard Place (Ammer, 2003), and the King Sisyphus Predicament. Imagine these scenarios if applied to some of life's difficult dilemmas and then the use of strategy to make a change. The goal is to help your client break their crisis into manageable parts and focus their attention on the premier problem.

Catch-22 Scenario

The Catch-22 scenario is taken from the novel of the same name by Joseph Heller. In the novel a pilot wants to stop flying dangerous missions, by admitting himself to the hospital. To get into the hospital he would have to say he was mentally unstable, but if he admits to being mentally unstable, he is considered sane, because anyone who flies in such dangerous assignments is considered mentally unstable (Heller, 1961). The Catch-22 will feel like damned if I do or damned if I do not.

Like choosing between jumping into a pit full of lions or a pit full of rattlesnakes. Step two of *The Crisis Gambit* will help you identify the motivation or fuel to create a crisis? Is it love, anger, fear, or hunger? In this situation the answer is fear. The polestar problem for the pilot is personal safety.

The Malthusian Trap

Robert Malthus was an English clergyman, economist, and historian born in 1766. The Malthusian Trap or population trap is a condition whereby excess population would stop growing due to a shortage of food supplies leading to starvation. However, when a society shows an abundance of food the standard of living improves, this also causes an increase in population. The population grows bringing it back to its original lower standard of living, with shortages in resources (Dolan, 2000). Today only a small percentage of Americans have budgeted to make it to retirement. Some Americans upon getting a raise in salary, immediately buy a more expensive house and a more expensive car keeping their ability to solve their debt out of reach. Where is the motivation or fuel to create a crisis? The motivation in the Malthusian Trap is hunger. For people to get out of the Malthusian Trap is to obtain and hold on to resources. It may benefit your client to invest the future and compare immediate gratification to future financial security. The polestar goal is to maintain security and avoid hunger.

Between a rock and a hard place scenario

This phrase can be traced to Homer's account of the hero Odysseus (Griffin, 2008). The hero in the story had two poor options in his path, a man-eating monster or a ship destroying whirlpool. He cannot retreat backwards because his ship and crew are running out of resources. Where is the motivation or fuel to create a crisis? Is it love, anger, fear, or hunger? In this situation the answer is fear and hunger. The polestar problem has been found. The crew must move forward to avoid starvation. Odysseus must make a decision that will harm his crew the least.

If you are deciding to live near your parents or your partner's parents this can be especially difficult if one family lives in Tennessee and the other lives in Michigan. Odysseus weighed his options and sacrificed six men to the man-eating monster, Skylla, over losing the lives of everyone and the ship to a whirlpool, called Charybdis. The sacrifices made or gained by moving to a certain location must be examined. Looking at the pros and cons of a problem can help you to find a solution. The polestar problem is identified as which place could offer the most growth or benefit.

The King Sisyphus Predicament

In Greek mythology, King Sisyphus (Encyclopedia of Greek Mythology) was punished by Zeus for his hubristic belief that his cleverness surpassed even that of a god by cheating death twice. Sisyphus's chore was to push a giant boulder to the top of a giant hill. However, Zeus enchanted the boulder to roll away just before reaching the top. Sisyphus is described as involved in a never-ending activity. Today a person going through multiple attempts at substance use rehab and failing can feel like a never-ending process. In this situation where is the motivator? Sisyphus keeps getting angry and frustrated by failing over and over. The motivator is anger. Sisyphus must develop an innovative approach. Most of all, Sisyphus cannot perform the same task over and over and expect a different result. The polestar problem is to get out of this hellish situation. If we were talking about someone with an addiction problem, the polestar problem might be identified as leaving the hell of addiction. It is time to rewrite the story and give it a better ending.

The Strategy of War

Carl von Clausewitz was a Prussian general who fought against Napoleon during the years 1813-1815. He is most noted for authoring the book called *On War*, published in 1832. *On War* is regarded by military experts as essential reading on strategy and even today it is required reading at The United States Military Academy, better known as West Point. Clausewitz wrote, "Strategy is the necessary response to the inescapable reality of limited resources. No entity, regardless of size, has unlimited resources. Strategy, therefore, is about making choices on how we will concentrate our limited resources to achieve a competitive advantage" (Clausewitz, 1989). For a crisis counselor, this can be a reality check for your client, you must work with available resources.

You may ask your client this question," I heard you talk about several problems. Which one would you like to talk about first? No effective military leader would enter a battle without strategic planning. Breaking a problem into pieces is a method for gaining control. A client saying that their "whole life" is in turmoil or "everything is ruined" is too large of a statement to handle. They are just asking for sensory overload; you can do nothing but listen. Give them a chance to vent and wait for the moment to ask them to focus on the problem that is causing the most stress. This technique is why *The Crisis Gambit* has polestar identification. Clausewitz makes the thought of war sound comprehendible when he wrote, "War is nothing but a duel on an extensive level."

When you are developing a goal sometimes the results are future oriented and take time to realize. One of the best leaders to use long-term strategy was Napoleon Bonaparte, the Emperor of France. He established a vast empire by improving the lives of those he conquered and thus improving his chance for gaining their loyalty. When he conquered a territory, he built roads and canals to improve trade and planted wheat to strengthen food supplies. Ears of wheat, an emblem of prosperity and generosity, evoking rebirth, and peace, were among the symbols taken up by Napoleon (Wheat, 2021). Your client may not solve their problem immediately by talking with you; however, they can lay a foundation that will improve their chance for reaching post-trauma growth. Abraham Lincoln understood strategy when he said, "Give me six hours to chop down a tree and I will spend the first four sharpening the ax," (Quotespedia).

Beginning in the third century and extending into the fifth century, China was involved in the warring states period. The Chinese philosopher, Confucius, lived at the end of this period and proved himself to be a brilliant strategist and laid a foundation for success. Warlords sent their kingdom's most beautiful women to marry the neighboring warlords. Future peace is more likely to occur as a warlord is less likely to attack his wife and his children's relatives living in another territory. This strategy was used against Confucius by the ruling class that feared his social reforms policies. These women may have been great heroes that knowingly sacrificed their lives to protect peace and thus saving the lives of thousands (Weebly, 2022).

Public Figures and Public Platforms

Presidential debates, job interviews and beauty pageants require strategy. The older candidate, Ronald Reagan, stole the stage when a moderator asked him if his age would be a factor for his presidency (1984 Presidential Debates). The President showed his brilliance when he replied, "…I am not going to exploit for political purposes my opponent's youth and inexperience." Lloyd Bentsen used Dan Quayle's words against him in a Vice-Presidential debate. Quayle compared himself to having just as much political experience as JFK before he became president (Halloran, 2008). Bentsen was considered the winner of this debate when he said, "Senator, I served with Jack Kennedy, I knew Jack Kennedy, Jack Kennedy was a friend of mine. Senator, you're no Jack Kennedy!"

During the Miss Universe of 2000, Lara Dutta, Miss. India was given this question, "Right now there is protest going on right outside here calling the Miss Universe Pageant disrespectful of women. Convince them they are wrong? Miss Dutta replied (Tanushree, 2019), "Pageants like Miss Universe gives us young women a platform to foray into the fields that we want to forge ahead, be it entrepreneurship, be it the armed forces, be it politics. It gives us a platform to voice our choices and opinions and makes us strong and independent that we are today."

Alan Roger Mulally, the Executive Vice President of Boeing and CEO of Boeing Commercial Airplanes joined Ford Motor Company in 2006. He may have had one of the best replies in an interview. There was doubt that a CEO from an airplane company could run a car company and this is his legendary reply (Miller, 2015), "An automobile has about 10,000 moving parts, right? An airplane has two million, and it has to stay up in the air."

Anxiety

Anxiety is a necessary tool all of us use to survive, it floods our body with adrenaline to give us power to act. People that have clinical anxiety are not able to manage their anxiety effectively. There are many types of anxiety, I will address three types: catastrophic anxiety, social phobia, and phobia. The fuel behind anxiety is fear.

The Grocery List

The strategy for breaking things down into pieces will work for most of your patients, but sometimes a person suffering from an obsessive-compulsive disorder, or an anxiety disorder still wants to talk about every detail and every problem. A tool to help someone suffering from anxiety is using what I call the grocery list. Constant worry is a stressful condition. Think about this, if you did not make a grocery list, all day your mind could become cluttered with the task of remembering: What do I have to get from the grocery store? I must get eggs, butter, milk, dog food, chocolate chip cookies and spaghetti sauce. Your client can also write down all their problems on a sheet of paper, choose their best course of action at that moment. Once your problems are written down and you decide what you can achieve today, you rid yourself from the need to think and re-think. The grocery list has helped shoppers everywhere and it can help people that struggle with anxiety. The list can keep you in the here and now, enjoying these moments without all the distractions of what could happen.

Poems

Another activity for someone suffering from severe anxiety is to memorize poems and songs. My grandmother was born on a farm in Scotland in 1900 and she had absorbed an incredible array of poems that she could recite from beginning to end, her favorites included "The Slave's Dream" by Henry Wadsworth Longfellow (1842), and "O Captain! My Captain!" by Walt Whitman (1865). These poems kept her mind active in her golden years and provided our family with treasured memories of her prowess. My uncle Jim would carry on the family tradition by reciting "The Highwayman" by Alfred Noyes (1906). When I am bored at a meeting or at a redundant workshop, I will non-verbally recite "The Cremation of Sam McGee" by Robert W. Service (1907). The concentration required to memorize a long poem can only take you away from your current problems and engage the part of your brain that thinks rationally. When I am in a road rage situation, I start reciting a poem because it requires me to employ the rational part of my brain. As seen in Step three, the modus operandi, or the states your brain will have a direct impact on your behavioral response. It is clear if you are engrossed in a movie, you are not thinking about your anxiety. If you learn a poem, you can take it anywhere.

Catastrophic Anxiety

Darwin borrowed a phrase from Herbert Spencer (1864), "survival of the fittest". I do not believe it is the strong that survived in early civilization, but those who were cautious and showed a resilience for adaptation. Logically, the coward with anxiety had a better chance of avoiding the multitude of predators that roamed early civilization. There was no modern medicine to patch you up once you were injured or sick. Carl Sagan shared his belief in evolution, in The Dragons of Eden (1977). He said humans often dream about falling and have this natural fear. He explains that he believes this is because humans are related to primates that lived in trees and this is a required survival trait, anxiety is part of our DNA. My premise is that we are naturally cautious and fearful and have all experienced an episode of anxiety; however, uncontrolled anxiety is unhealthy.

The underlying cause of anxiety is not feeling safe or having unresolved fear. This is often caused by past trauma, disorders like social phobia, agoraphobia, PTSD and generalized anxiety disorders all have this component. I have noticed that anxiety can be extremely deep seated. Sometimes, a client that was raised in a chaotic environment skips natural steps of development. World Vision International also supports this position (Morris, 2013). Most people in early adolescence deal with questions about their mortality unless their life is disrupted by chaos. In a Hemingway (1972) short story, the main adolescent character, Nick, is alone in a tent at night. It becomes deathly quiet, and Nick thinks about the line from a hymn he heard in church, "Someday the silver cord will break." It is still a fine example of a stage of development that most of us go through in adolescents and the realization that no one will live forever. This emptiness or fear of death overwhelms Nick. The silver cord stands for our life in the story called "Three Shots." In the story, Nick fires three shots, so his father and uncle will return, he does not want to be alone. He lies and tells them he heard an animal.

A person that ruminates about their fear of death, fear of embarrassment, or fear of failure is stuck disproportionately in the survival and emotional states of the brain. They often obsess over all the terrible things that have happened to them or might happen. The little voice in their head continues to criticize themselves. Anxiety is fear for oneself according to Wilhelm Stekel (n.d.). The cure for anxiety is changing your focus and thinking about others. This point can be illustrated in the animal kingdom. Most higher functioning animals, forgo their own fears to protect their young. A black bear may naturally run away from a car; however, if the bear has her cubs in tow, her reaction may be completely different. There are several benefits to telling you to think about others. Many people that suffer from social anxiety are completely absorbed about how they are being judged by others. They listen to negative self-talk like: "People are watching you look awkward." or "You are going to fail, people will see you stumble, this is gonna be a horrible, terrible, and an embarrassing situation for you." You must place your focus on what other people are saying and doing to break this ineffective pattern of behavior. Simply put, focus your attention on other people and give it your full attention. If you can practice giving up self-conscience you can reach a point of total freedom.

To battle anxiety, it is also helpful to join a group of people and avoid isolating yourself. Homo Erectus, an archaic human species hunted in coordinated groups, and cared for the injured and sick. Banishment from a tribe was a terrible punishment for a fragile ancient human and meant certain death unless the banished individual could join another tribe. Isolating yourself from others might be described as a self-imposed banishment and goes against what made ourselves and our human ancestors successful at surviving. Think-tanks were established because a collective group is better at solving a problem than a sole individual. C.S. Lewis (1942) - "Two heads are better than one, not because either is infallible, but because they are unlikely to go wrong in the same direction."

Cooperation is clearly a survival technique that helped settlers branch out into the unexplored west and relieve some anxiety. In the great American expansion movement, wagon trains would form a circle to defend themselves from Native American Indians. Larger groups had a better chance of weathering an attack. The Sioux, Apache, Comanche, and Cheyenne sometimes joined forces to ward off attacks from European expansionists. Schools of fish are formed to defend themselves from large predators, it is believed they look like one big predator as they swim in synchronicity (The Maritime Aquarium, Neighbor, 2013). It is hard to argue with the adage, "There is safety in numbers." Calling a crisis phone line will keep you from being alone in your quest to manage anxiety.

In The Wilderness Hunter written by Teddy Roosevelt (1927); the former president goes on to explain that the Greyhound is the most fearless dog. When hunting bears, the Greyhound will not retreat like other dogs. Imagine being out in an unprotected woodland or prairie, having a dog like a greyhound. Dogs have a keener sense of smell, maybe 40 times greater than us (phoenixvetcenter.com). Their night vision is considered likely to be five times better according to Paul Miller, clinical professor of comparative ophthalmology at University of Wisconsin-Madison (sciencedaily.com). Your canine friend would cut your anxiety in half and then some. The power of animal friends to help manage anxiety is well documented. My cousin Davey in Toronto told me his friend is a detective for the local police force and said dog owners rarely, if ever, deal with home burglaries.

What a person has done, is often a cause for anxiety. When we find fear as a motivator, anxiety is often a resulting emotion. Often anxiety is caused by doing something in conflict with our value system. I believe sometimes soldiers that develop posttraumatic stress disorder are subject to this experience. People that kill other people often feel anxiety or guilt. A soldier that is protecting his country's interest may have to kill someone, and if the soldier is Christian, it could be a morally difficult decision. Many Christians adhere to the Sixth Commandment: "Thou shalt not kill" (Exodus, 20:13 KJV). As discussed earlier, the inventor of the FM radio struck his wife and wrote a suicide note that clearly expressed his shame and guilt before jumping out of his apartment window (N Y T).

Memories

Our brains are equipped to handle traumatic events with REM sleep. It is true that we do not remember everything we did yesterday, we want to remember what we feel is important. If I am like most people, I am not good at remembering what I had for dinner or lunch a few days ago. REM sleep is linked to erasing things our brain needs to erase, our brain is built to forget unnecessary information ("To Remember, the Brain Must Actively Forget" by Dalmeet Singh Chawla July 24, 2018). Selective forgetfulness can help us work through traumatic experiences. Our memories always change and warp over time. Memory casting is a way to alter your memory of traumatic events. If you were in a situation where you almost drowned, a helpful approach would be to think of the event, but this time think of the event with you surrounded by boats and thousands of life preservers. Look at pictures of boats and life preservers before sleeping and the safety you are exposed to at this time in your life. Highly charged emotional events are etched into our memory so we must think about the event with a calmer and controlled experience. Cast the frightful memories of an event away by altering the narrative.

The more emotional the event, the greater the memory. If you are in a car accident, it is an emotional event. It usually is less emotional if you are seeing the car accident and even less would be hearing about it. If you can incorporate a safe distance from a past traumatic event, you can alter your dreams, and change memories to a manageable level. Creativity is taking what we already know and seeing if we can piece it together in a new pattern or innovative approach.

For you to tackle PTSD an innovative approach must be developed. Memory is the keystone for learning; however, our memory changes every time we take in added information and experiences, our memories are not an exact record of our past. Short term memory is interesting in the court of law. Lawyers often try to show a defendant is lying if they are not able to recall the exact details of an earlier testimony. It seems absurd to believe that everyone has an exact memory. Memories are not objective or unbiased; they change to fit the narrative we have about who we are or how we perceive ourselves. By having worked a crisis line, and having several chronic callers, it is undeniable that alcohol use affects memory retention, which is another concern for legal testimony.

Wendy Suzuki, a Professor of Neuroscience and Psychology at the New York University, tells us (Huberman, 2022), "Four things make something memorable: (1) novelty; (2) repetition; (3) association; (4) emotional resonance." If you are constantly reliving a traumatic event, therapy is beneficial to breaking that cycle of repetition. Author, psychologist Carl Rogers (2016), was masterful for helping people through traumatic events. His first step of psychotherapy includes active listening. The therapist is then strapped with the task of summarizing the events to the agreement of his client. This process allows both parties, client, and therapist to work back and forth clarifying the traumatic event. The summary process can shorten the memory to the basics and tend to leave out the horrific details. This process can give the client a summarized version or shorten new memory of an event that has caused them turmoil.

Personal Safety

At the beginning of this chapter, I said that the world is full of dilemmas: The Catch-22, A workplace Catch-22, Malthusian Trap, Between a Rock and Hard Place Scenario and the King Sisyphus Predicament. When we break a problem down, the focus of our actions become apparent. In the Catch-22 our goal is to achieve personal safety. In the workplace Catch-22 our goal is to get a job. In the Malthusian Trap the primary concerns are financial security. The Between a Rock and a Hard Place Scenario that was applied to where a family should live, the primary goal was to find the place that helps the family the most. In the King Sisyphus Predicament or addiction predicament, our goal is self-improvement that can only be achieved by leaving a dreadful place or through sobriety. When the goal is clear, then you can organize your steps to reach that goal.

The theme of every one of these dilemmas is self-improvement, one way or another. This can be done by looking into the future and weighing immediate gratification over future security. Looking at the pros and cons of a problem can help you to find a solution. In the King Sisyphus Predicament, we cannot perform the same task and expect a different result. We do not have to play by the rules, we do not have to limit our options, people in a crisis are always limited by the false belief that there are no other choices. A crisis counselor can advocate changing the rules: Sisyphus can choose a different bolder, the pilot can sabotage his plane to get a rest. Odysseus and his soldiers can fight the man-eating monster or set a trap, so the monster falls into the whirlpool. The Malthusian Trap was defeated by not living in a fixed area, but by moving to an area where people can grow, and a place where the land and agriculture can continue to develop.

The Malthusian Trap was also beaten by smart farming. The Dust Bowl of the 1930s was a period of severe dust storms that damaged the ecology and agriculture of the American and Canadian prairies (Worster, 2014). This led to the Great Depression. Yesterday's farmers were living in fear of grasshoppers, corn eating crows, windstorms, climate change, and the demands to feed a growing population. Smart farming made farmers much more resistant to the problems of the past which led to boosting crop and livestock yields. New farming methods used crop rotation that prevented soil erosion, supported soil fertility, and promoted moisture retention. Milestones in farm machinery, like the gas tractor, milking machine, corn picker and cotton harvester are only the tip of the iceberg to the war on hunger and poverty. Smart farming technology is a way to defeat the Malthusian Trap. Farmers, topsoil conservationists, and conservation agronomists are involved in regenerative agriculture. This movement has an aim to balance our planet, manage greenhouse gasses, feed the world, turn desert back to fertile ground (Tickell, 2020).

The most crucial decision a person can make is to be better. We must plan to get better. We face challenges that will give us tools to handle future events. If you can know more than you did the day before, when you were in a trap, a predicament, or in a struggle, you put yourself on the right track for self-improvement. Crisis situations have elements of chaos and overload, you must learn to strategize and identify the polestar.

In Step five we want to strategize and narrow our focus. Jamaican American chess grandmaster, author, and commentator, Maurice Ashley states that as the game progresses, pieces disappear (Marshall, 2016), "The game progresses to a relatively simple position-one in which only a few options remain". Taking problems off the board is a way to achieve strategy. By finding the premier problem in step five, we can then move toward generating solutions in step six.

True at First Light Phenomenon

Many of life's dilemmas appear daunting. There is a "True at First Light Phenomenon," that exists in a crisis. A person's thinking and perception of a crisis will make it feel true. True at First Light comes from a book written posthumously by Hemingway (2004). He wrote "In Africa a thing is true at first light and a lie by noon…" Hemingway makes reference to a lake he sees across the salt plain in the morning, "… it is there absolutely true, beautiful and believable." When hc walks across the plain to the lake, no such lake is there. Crisis counseling is all about exposing the truth about unbearable circumstances. Was the crisis really an inescapable circumstance, an impossible dilemma, or an insurmountable trap.

Occam's Razor

Occam's razor is the problem-solving principle that the simplest explanation is usually the right one (Duignan, 2022). The idea is attributed to English Franciscan friar William of Ockham (c. 1287–1347). Telling a lie takes much more time than telling the truth, the person telling the lie usually needs time to think of a good excuse. When you can isolate the polestar problem you can focus on the real problem. We have heard excuses for drinking like my wife left me, I had a troubled childhood, or I am under stress at work. If you admit you have a drinking problem, now you can take steps to reach sobriety. You are being honest with yourself.

Step Six: Problem Solving

Step Six: Problem Solving, what can we change & generating alternatives, brainstorming (conscious) and incubation (unconscious). Generating Alternatives or presenting innovative ideas to a client is necessary to promote change. Sister Eileen Rice introduced me to this pivotal quote by Emerson (1844), "The mind, once stretched by a new idea, never returns to its original dimensions." This is a key to getting a suicidal person to turn the corner. The presentation of new ideas is fundamental to The Crisis Gambit. In chapter one I spoke about Max Ehrmann's Desiderata, the ideas presented in this poem could change your view of the world. This poem was used to illustrate an unconditional positive guard for us and others, however, he also expresses one man's inspirational guide to navigating through life. He warns that comparing yourself to others can only make you vain and bitter. His advice relieves stress by not involving yourself in fruitless comparisons. For example, we as people can be rich or poor and this does not make us any better or less than our fellow beings. The writer Kurt Vonnegut Jr. (2020), once wrote that "Rich people are poor people with money." Teddy Roosevelt (McCarthy, 2015) explained that a wealthy person is not automatically an asset of any real worth and can be viewed as a false standard of success. "But it is the way in which it has been earned or used, not the mere fact of wealth." Admiration should not fall on the reward, instead it should focus on the deed rewarded. A wealthy person can be an asset; however, he can also be an unworthy citizen of the community. Albert Einstein can be quoted, "Try not to become a man of success, rather become a man of value."

You vs. Your Former Self

French Novelist Gustave Flaubert explains how ridiculous and unethical a class system is, when he wrote the world's greatest tragic novel, Madame Bovary published in 1857. Flaubert began keeping a record of idiotic thoughts that were promoted by newspapers. Flaubert took a stand against class stratification, he believed in equality, and despised the pompous behavior and ideas of the self-important upper class, his main character falling into an almost complete morale deterioration. His novel also showed the carefree lifestyle of male characters in contrast to the limited freedom of his female characters. Throughout history, different classes of people have different degrees of power and access to resources. Let us not forget, in history, there are other stories where the most unfortunate people rise to the top.

The best comparison is you against your former self. There is a quote you may have heard, "A shadow of your former self (Ghost, 2020)." According to the Merriam-Webster Dictionary, this means someone or something that is not as strong, powerful, or useful as it once was. Or Merriam-Webster defines this idiom: "a much weaker and frailer person that one formerly was." In *The Crisis Gambit*, we are going forward not backwards. The question is how you can be stronger than your former self or stronger than yesterday?

A Fish Out of Water

We know the analogy about people feeling like a fish out of water. It can be a person put in an unfamiliar environment or a person attempting or doing something in which they have had no training. When a person is fearful about giving a speech because they have little success and little to no practice, this can make them feel like a fish out of water. The key is to find your stronger self. When I was younger, I played tennis and held the number one position on my high school and collegiate teams. I could whack a tennis ball, and I had a massive amount of confidence in that arena. During high school, I was attacked by a large dog while walking home after tennis practice, with my tennis racket as a shield the dog was never remotely close to being able to deliver a bite. When I am required to give a speech, in an uncomfortable situation, I tap into the confidence I had as the "tennis star." If you were a good bowler, good at cards, or a great volleyball player, tap into that strength and confidence when you approach your boss for a raise. All of us have talent, take that talent with you into your next fish out of water experience.

Franklin's Two Virtues

Presenting new ideas to promote personal change can be found in American history. Ben Franklin, who is honored on the one-hundred-dollar bill, was an over achiever and created thirteen virtues to live by and improve himself; these virtues would then become an ingrained part of his character (Franklin, 1791). It might be interesting to put thirteen virtues on a list and walk around with them in your pocket for a month. I imagine that if everyone at your agency practiced his description of sincerity, it would all but halt gossip. Under his definition, if you practice sincerity, you strive to keep from criticizing others in a hurtful way, but instead, it strives to elevate other people in a positive manner. Justice is another virtue outlined by Franklin, which instructs us not to harm others for our own benefit. No matter how difficult, try to find a way so everyone involved in your interactions will find some genuine benefit. When completing employee evaluations, I have always made Franklin's two virtues: sincerity and justice permanent goals.

The Seven Deadly Sins

If your client is a humanist, Franklin's 13 virtues could help them improve your former self. If your client or you have a Christian ideology, looking at the seven deadly sins could help you outline areas for improvement. The deadly sins are pride, greed, lust, anger, gluttony, envy, and sloth. Greed is also called covetousness, which is defined in the Bible as the inordinate desire of riches. Religion is a powerful motivator, material things and behavior for acquiring an overabundance of things could be applied to someone that suffers from a hoarding disorder. Reviewing this deadly sin could help change someone's perspective of their behaviors.

Equality

Earlier I wrote, if we do not receive love from people we cherish, it can lead to the false belief that we have no worth. A good parent must walk a line between keeping their child safe or making their child stronger. I have always been a fan of Transactional Analysis, and the book by Thomas Anthony Harris called I'm OK, You're OK (1967) and the insight it provides. If a parent is over nurturing, they could produce a man-child, a Peter Pan, or a temperamental prima donna. Family members will rally around the dependent adult family member and only continue to foster the lack of individual strength. If the parent is too critical and demanding, neglectful, and non-supportive, a person could grow up to develop anxiety, a low self-esteem and lack confidence. Unfortunately, people raised by a dysfunctional and abusive family may never receive the normal praise that good parents bestow upon their children. This type of validation must come from other sources. This quote from the poem Desiderata (Ehrmann, 1927) is a powerful response, "You are a child of the universe no less than the trees and the stars; you have a right to be here." Even Thomas Jefferson wrote in the Declaration of Independence, "We hold these truths to be self-evident, that all men are created equal…" The Reverend Martin Luther King Jr. read these words and supported the true meaning of its creed (Younge, 2003).

The authors of the Declaration of Independence began to lay the foundation for a special and unique form of government. Unfortunately, not all people were enjoying the same equality when this document was written. Deep down in all ethical people, a voice tells us what is right and what is horribly wrong, and this statement is worth striving for. A proclamation for equality that all men and all women are created equal is of the highest order. If a government for the people and by the people had one keystone sentence, this is the sentence to build upon and to be sure with all clarity and all certainty it is a worthwhile effort. Abraham Lincoln said, "We are bound in honor to strive to bring ever nearer the day when, as far is humanly possible, we shall be able to realize the ideal that each man shall have an equal opportunity to show the stuff that is in him by the way in which he renders service, (…) but the reward must go to the man who does his work well." "Probably the best test of true love of liberty in any country is the

way in which minorities are treated in that country"-
Theodore Roosevelt.

Mr. Rogers and Dr. Suess

The children's television show called Mister
Rogers' Neighborhood ran from 1968 to 2001 was
paramount for building character and self-worth. Fred
Rogers stated (Miller. 2019), "As human beings, our job
in life is to help people realize how rare and valuable
each one of us really is..." Dr. Suess shared Mr. Rogers'
view when he wrote a popular children's book as a
source for understanding self-worth or equality. In Dr.
Seuss's Horton Hears a Who! Horton is an elephant and
the only one who can hear Whoville, a minuscule town
on a speck of dust. Dr. Suess wrote, "A person's a
person, no matter how small." In this way, this popular
children's book promotes a lesson of self-worth and
equality. Dr. Seuss's story was inspired by the sadness
he felt for the people killed by the bombs dropped on
Hiroshima and Nagasaki in World War II. (Thomas
Fensch, 2001).

The Time Advantage

The study of time can change your perspective.
If you are underwater for three minutes, it can feel like
an eternity. If you believe an average person lives about
eighty years, how many of those years are spent in high
school? If you took a time machine into the future by ten
years, what would you be doing? What would you like
to do? Looking outside of your microcosm you may see
that life is full of stepping stones. "Remember When,"
by country singer Alan Jackson (2013) is an example of

the journey some of us take throughout the course of a lifetime. The song tells a story about how life unfolds from falling in love, getting married, having children, having grandchild, and going all the way to the golden years. Place yourself on one of those stepping stones. As a crisis counselor, your client could be struggling through a dark period of their life. They must know, it is only a small part in the whole journey. One of the bloodiest battles of the American Civil War was the Battle of Gettysburg. In 1913, veterans of this conflict met on its 50th anniversary and shook hands (Quin, L., 2013). One can only imagine the profound change in perspective the old soldiers would experience. "Come what may, all bad fortune is to be conquered by endurance." -Virgil

In the scheme of things, a change in perspective can alter dangerous thinking. If you have a bully boss, and you read a book about four types of bully bosses (Namie, 2009), it will soon help you realize how negative traits of unethical and unprofessional conduct of such a boss can influence your mental health. By learning to find traits of an abuser, you can be liberated from victimization. You now know where the real source of the problem lies. You now have the tools to recognize manipulation. An organization that is willing to improve its management style should also make these four types of bosses known, in order that it might self-regulate its leadership team.

Breaking the Herd Mentality

A logical verse from Proverbs 13:20: "He who walks with wise men will be wise, but the companion of fools suffers harm." I want to point out that the company we keep can influence our behavior. Some refer to people as "sheeple " because we are so easily misled. Humans believe in witches, werewolves, astrology, and Bigfoot. I believe in Bigfoot because I saw him riding a bike at the corner of Sterns and Secor. Understanding when you are in a herd can change your perspective. If you are just going along with the flow, following the group, you will not be independent, you will not be that creative person that reaches their full potential.

"Three 12-year-old girls committed suicide from the Wapekeka First Nations district in Northwest Ontario" in 2017 (The Star, June 14, 2017). "Nine Japanese die in a suicide pact after meeting on the internet" (The Guardian, Oct. 12, 2004). Today, I see the power of mass media on a regular basis. I am surprised how it appears that so many people become polar opposites in politics. The United States has a herd dynamic. Friends I know on each side of the aisle appear to completely adopt every line item from their political party of choice. As discussed earlier, the agents of socialization are powerful and peer pressure and mass media can influence suicide pacts, and even suicide contagion.

In the 80's I read Mega Trends (Naisbitt, 1982) where the author gave the opinion of being completely for one party was committing intellectual suicide. Aristotle (n.d.) may agree when he said, "It is the mark of an educated mind to be able to entertain a thought without accepting it." Naisbitt and Aristotle suggest researching each viewpoint on a subject for yourself. His sentiments seem captured in the poem, "If" by Rudyard Kipling (1910). Lines in this poem offer us guidance on how to run independently from a herd, "If you can trust yourself when all men doubt you, if you can bear to hear the truth you've spoken twisted, if you can talk with crowds and keep your virtue." These lines promote thinking for yourself and learning to weather criticism, avoid going with the flow or the herd mentality. The song My Way (Francois. 1967) sung by Frank Sinatra and Elvis, can also offer fortitude if you consider these lines: "For what is a man, what has he got, if not himself, then he has not, to say the things he truly feels, and not the words of one who kneels." The key to breaking a suicide pack is breaking the herd mentality.

John Greenleaf Whittier (1807-1892) the poet from Massachusetts suffered violence for being the editor for several anti-slavery newspapers. Angry mobs pelted him with rocks and eggs and the building he worked in was burnt to the ground (City of Whittier video 2015). He went against the herd mentality when he wrote Our Countrymen in Chains (1837), a poem that described the inhumane dread of slavery. In The Pennsylvania Freeman he wrote, "If the light of discussion upon any subject, a rite made common to all by the Constitution of the United States, may be invaded with impunity, all freedom among us is abolished and we are the slaves of the very worst of all tyrants, the mob."

Papageno Effect

The Papageno effect is a necessary method to combat negative media attention given to suicide. In the study of suicides and its contagion effects is known as the Werther effect (Niederkrotenthaler, 2010). The Papageno effect comes from a character in Mozart's Opera *The Magic Flute*. In the opera, Papageno believed suicide was the only way to end his pain and suffering from a broken heart. Three characters intervene and show Papageno alternatives to solve his problems and save his life. When media puts out a tragic story of suicide it is necessary to show alternatives and statistics about people that were having suicidal thoughts and plans but were matched with interventions that put them back into a rational modus operandi and did not end their lives.

Climbing the Corporate Ladder

Many people spend a great deal of time climbing the corporate ladder and become disenchanted when things do not go their way, and this can be a source of their emotional stress. For some people, the most crucial factors in their life occur away from work. This could mean any type of individual growth that could include travel, time with family and exploring hobbies. All situations are subject to individual preference. It's doubtful for people to look back on their life and say I wish I would have spent more time at work.

Getting to the top may come with drawbacks. Benjamin Franklin said (Krupp, 2015), "Lost time is never found again." All of us want to be considered important and needed. According to Anthony Robbins, "one of the six core human needs is identified as significance (Gagnon n.d.)." A lot of people seek out a career that has linear narrative, each step has a better title and more pay. Other people choose the direction of their passion, the activity that supplies greater rewards.

Evil in the Workplace is Evolutionary

Some added thoughts on climbing the corporate ladder: Others may treat you like an enemy, because they perceive you as a threat to their need to reach that top rung. There is a natural inclination to see co-workers as competitors. In the business world, if you understand another person's need to feel significant, you can then understand where their behavior comes from. Heed warnings from Salvoj Zizek- "I never underestimate evil and envy." I am amazed at the evil that exists at times, but especially when I see the joy that some people take when destroying others (Aerial View, 2019). Co-workers will talk behind someone's back and sabotage their achievements, the action of competition results in behavior that avoids working together. Avoiding your co-worker is one of the worst tactics motivated by internal competition. Nietzsche pointed out; human nature is fundamentally flawed. A worker with misplaced ambitions may put their needs above everyone else; selfish ambition always causes division. I have seen this darker side, when their needs are not immediately met, they will spend a great deal of time filing complaints, and drawing up grievances and even manufacturing lies against an individual that has stood in their way to achieve their false entitled superiority. A workplace without teamwork can be toxic and lack the beauty that teamwork and collaboration can achieve. Human history is full of characters that were greedy and selfish. The caveman was stingy for evolutionary reasons. The daily news will give accounts of people that cheat, steal and plot. To believe these things cannot happen at your work is like an ostrich putting its head in the sand. "You should never punish employees for speaking up, they're the one that will reveal your agency's blind spots (Bates, 2021)." Tony Bates was also talking about technology and gives a significant case study of Eastman Kodak Company not listening to an employee that created the digital camera. Kodak did not embrace this blind spot; it did not embrace future technology and the consumer's wants. This blind spot caused Kodak to crumble into chapter 11 bankruptcy, in an ever-changing world of technology, while the digital camera and the smartphone embracing Instagram flourished.

Examples of Evil: The story of Joseph and the song "Strange Fruit"

In the book of Genesis, Joseph was favored by his father, and the jealousy of his brothers caused him to be thrown in a pit, sold into slavery, his identity stolen, and forgotten by those he helped. I have never heard the account of evil captured more in the song "Strange Fruit" sung by Billie Holiday in 1939. The song was written and composed by Abel Meeropol (1937). The choice of words in the lyrics, the slow haunting jazz virtuoso voice of Holiday, as she sings to a slow-moving solitary trumpet and stripped-down string quartet, and piano keys played decidedly gently, the listener hears in the opening lines of the song. The song progresses from "Southern trees bear a strange fruit" to shocking lines of "the bulging eyes and twisted mouth;" the story ever so slowly reveals the horrors of lynching black Americans in the southern states. Evil people do exist, they sometimes find employment at your agency or firm.

Teamwork at Work

The key to an ideal work environment was captured in 1936, with How to Win Friends & Influence People, Dale Carnegie (2006). I have worked in places where I was surrounded by friends and it felt great. Work can be fun when you enter an agency that promotes teamwork and camaraderie. Your work cannot make you a friend or give you an honest teammate, you are the only one that can make friends. There are two fundamental ways to win friends and influence others.

One, be genuinely interested in other people. You will waste time if you are trying to get people interested in you, which could take years. Two, you must praise others as much as possible. When I look back on my career, the people that have given me praise or recognized my work will always be the best people I have worked for. The value of friendship cannot be overstated. All of us would like to be praised and appreciated, pay it forward. The number one goal of any manager is finding people doing things well and recognizing it. The best possible trait of a great manager is to advance the career of the people you supervise. When staff leaving have apologized for leaving, I feel rewarded knowing I may have helped them realize their goals.

A motto that would also make a great mission statement that promotes acting better as human beings comes from Ritz-Carlton founder, Horst Schulze (Corporate Board Member, 2019), "We are ladies and gentlemen serving ladies and gentlemen." Your frontline staff are the face of the agency and the most important aspect for achieving success. For a company to have success requires satisfied employees and satisfied consumers. I worked at Merillat Industries, in Adrian Michigan when I was in college unloading semis and selling kitchen and bathroom cabinets on the weekend. The founder, President, and CEO Orville D. Merillat (n.d.) used the principles in Malachi 3:10 "Always a team." The cabinet maker was a major benefactor for two of my employers: Siena Heights University and Adrian College. Wherever your life takes you, this motto "Always a team," will serve you well.

Know Your Limitations

How do you change a client's perspective or introduce a new idea to someone with an unshakable belief? I have had clients that are believed to have a schizotypal personality disorder. This personality disorder is difficult to change as it falls under the category of ego-syntonic disorders. This is a psychological term referring to behaviors, values, feelings that are in harmony with or acceptable to the needs and goals of the ego and their ideal self-image. I will explain the difference between ego-syntonic and ego-dystonic disorders, in later chapters. For now, an ego-syntonic belief is best described as an unshakable belief. A person with this type of personality disorder lacks the awareness that their behavior could be hurting themselves or other people.

Ego-Syntonic Disorders

First let me describe a schizotypal personality disorder briefly with the caveat that the DSM-5 Diagnostic and Statistical Manual of Mental Disorders ((American Psychiatric Association, 2013) will supply a list of criteria and symptoms beyond what I will touch on here. This personality disorder has patterns of poor social interaction with others, often perceived by others as showing odd and bizarre behaviors. People with traits of this personality disorder can believe in odd or magical thinking.

In the book The Unfortunate Gift (Holiday 2014) the author does an excellent job of capturing a character with this disorder that believes that her community has a town witch that can spoil milk or make a horse lame. The author goes on to even discuss that the seeds of the character's belief system are rooted in ghost stories that she heard in front of a fireplace during her childhood and the lack of rational scientific reasoning. The character in the end does not change her beliefs.

People with a Schizotypal Personality Disorder, Narcissistic Personality Disorder or Anorexia are ego-syntonic disorders that may require more time than other types of clients. When you have tried many interventions with little success, sometimes safety planning will be more important than attempting to change a headstrong belief system. A person with an ego-syntonic disorder may not function or act within society's definition of normal behavior. However, the person is acting in line with their own values and belief system. You have to gain a lot of trust to challenge someone's beliefs. You have to hear them non-judgmentally tell their story. Then repeat what they have told you. If they feel you have not dismissed their beliefs, then they may be willing to hear your ideas to provide help.

Power of a Wish List

Innovative ideas can be presented during a brainstorming session. I would like to summarize a story told by the late great radio personality Paul Harvey that was written by his son, Paul Harvey Jr. called The Rest of the Story (paulharveyarchives.com). Paul Harvey tells the story about Lou and how he struggled with depression in the 1960s due to being unemployed and being supported by his wife. As the story unfolds, he was hired to work at South Carolina University at the time, and moved there, yet before going to work he was terminated by a new athletic director that wanted his own crew. Lou said he got into a depression, and his wife gave him a book that supplied a spark. The book encouraged Lou to make a wish list, he wrote things on that wish list, like travel in a submarine, shake hands

with the Pope and become the Notre Dame Football
coach. Lou became Notre Dame's football coach, and
you know him as Lou Holtz. This story is a helpful
illustration because it provides an example of
brainstorming, and generating alternatives, by using a
wish list that set goals for Lou, gave him direction, and
established a starting point. Lou Holtz has had an
extraordinary life; he is a respected coach and sports
analyst. He clearly lives up to one of his famous quotes
(mindzip.net), "I can't believe that God put us on this
earth to be ordinary."

David Carradine, from the television series *Kung
Fu,* played a character raised in a temple run by Shaolin
Masters. Throughout the television series he faces
obstacles as an Asian adult in a prejudiced American old
west. As he confronts one obstacle after another, he has
flashbacks of lessons of wisdom he learned in his
childhood that were rooted in the philosophy of Taoism.
"Turn your wounds into wisdom" by Oprah Winfrey
(n.d.) sounds rooted in Taoism. Carradine's character,
Grasshopper, would recall lessons on how-to live in
harmony with nature, others, and himself, and how to
practice compassion, humility, and moderation.

Carradine, the actor, would go on to write a
book called *Spirit of the Shaolin* (1993) and develop a
list of axioms to live a better life. Carradine wrote that
when you have people that exude negative energy and
have pessimistic opinions, you would benefit by
dropping those individuals from your inner circle. The
wish list is used to fill your life with things you want to
achieve. The removal list can help you to understand
roadblocks and hindrances that keep you from living a
better life. I know that Carradine's removal list does
have some merit, Ben Franklin (1791) points out that
some people remain immovable. The great thinker,

Epictetus's wisdom included understanding externals I cannot control, what is up to us and what is not up to us. Hurling yourself at immovable objects or people would be wasting your time on unwinnable battles.

Adversity is a Catalyst for Growth

The best lessons in the show Kung Fu always happened when the main character Kwai Chang Caine (called Grasshopper as a boy) faced adversity. Adversity is a catalyst for growth, and this gives insight to this quote by Sigmund Freud (n.d.), "One day, in retrospect, the years of struggle will strike you as the most beautiful." With consideration, you may be able to figure out what is immovable from Franklin or Epictetus' view, but do not overlook the benefit of adversity and how it is linked to growth.

I listened to a speech by actor Matthew McConaughey (2015) called "Five Rules for the Rest of your life that echo the principles of Taoism. In this speech he said, "Don't leave crumbs. Crumbs are the choices we make that make us have to look over our shoulder in the future." McConaughey shows growth over his lifetime and gave illustrations of crummy behavior: "If you do not pay that guy, you owe money to, if you have an affair although you are married, or become hung over and forget to take your son to an early morning baseball practice," these are examples of crumbs, and they will have future repercussions. Whether you choose Taoist principles or advice from McConaughey, it is all about being that better person that avoids a future filled with regret, guilt, or remorse.

The Franklin's Three Classes

Venues of change can come from several sources. The wish list is used to fill your life with things you want to achieve. The removal list can help you to understand roadblocks and hindrances that keep you from living a better life. Limiting the time that you spend with abusive people might be on everyone's removal list. Ben Franklin (1791) said, "All mankind is divided into three classes: those that are immovable, those that are movable and those that move." In his other writing it appears that immovable people are people that die at age twenty-five and are not buried until they are seventy-five. My interpretation is that Franklin is talking about the tragedy that exists in people who are not able to entertain a new idea or strategy. A Caucasian colleague at work told me that when he married a woman of color, his best friend terminated their friendship. His tragic friend fails to see the lessons of history, how different cultures, countries, and people join forces to share knowledge and ideas to create a better world, full of greater diversity and unfathomable strides in science and technology.

Positive Thinking

The placebo effect according to Dr. Bruce Lipton (**Gustafson**, 2017), "You didn't get healed by the pill, you got healed by the belief in the pill." He believes that one third of all medical interventions is the placebo effect, healing comes from positive thinking. Lipton does not let negative thinking off the hook, he says that negative thinking is also just as powerful as positive thinking. I believe that superstitions like walking under a ladder or crossing the path of a black cat can have a negative effect, because it can influence you to view your circumstances with a negative perspective. I am not above picking up a lucky penny to improve my circumstances, I know positive thinking can be magical. Marcus Aurelius, the last great and good emperor of Rome I continue to mention, was steeped in his stoic philosophy. He wrote, "Never overhear yourself complaining, not even to yourself ('the biographer' 395 AD). As Aristotle said, "We are what we repeatedly do, excellence is a habit." Aurelias, prepared himself for the coming day, "The people you will meet today will be mean, ungrateful, short sided, frustrating, do not let them implicate you in their ugliness."

Transform Yourself: Buffett, Superman, and the Christmas Carol

Upon hearing Warren Buffett speak, we hear his recipe for transformation. Buffett advised, "Put down the qualities of people you admire and put down qualities of people you cannot stand. Look around at the people you admire. They have certain qualities, they are generous and humorous people, upbeat." Buffett suggested looking at five of your friends and picking the qualities you like and acquire those qualities. Buffett makes a good point (Schwantes, n.d.), "You will move in the direction of the people that you associate with. So, it is important to associate with people that are better than yourself."

In the movie, Man of Steel (Crowe, 2013), Kevin Costner, playing the father of Superman, delivered one of my favorite lines to the young Clark Kent who was dragged out of a car, pushed down, and being egged on by a bully to fight. Clark refuses to fight. Clark's father, who saw the event unfold from a distance, now approaches the bully with his group of teenagers. This causes the group to disperse. Clark's one friend helps him to his feet and leaves. Clark may be viewed as a coward, by onlookers, keeping the secret of his super powers secret. Costner delivers the line, "You just have to decide what kind of man you want to grow up to be..."

There are two types of behavior, effective and ineffective. Listening to your moral compass will fall under effective behavior. For the second time I'm going to use this quote. Socrates said, "A man should not calculate his chances for life or death, he should determine if what he is doing is right or wrong, whether he is a good man or a wicked one." Many times in our life, we would benefit from listening to our inner voice.

The transformation in personality and action is clearly seen in *A Christmas Carol* (1843) by Charles Dickens. In the beginning of the story, Scrooge is a bitter old man with the sole purpose to make money, oblivious to the consideration for his relatives or fellowman that struggles through poverty. After being visited by four ghosts on Christmas Eve, Scrooge, the man with a heart of stone, is transformed into a model of human kindness and decency. Lord Francis Jeffery (1773-1850), an Edinburgh writer and judge, congratulated Dickens for having, "done more good by this little publication, fostered more kind feelings, and prompted more positive acts of beneficence, than can be traced to all pulpits and confessionals in Christendom since Christmas 1842 (Awan, 2017)."

When we are trying to transform ourselves, I can make the argument that two people exist. We are either a king (or queen) or a fool. Great people have two sides to achieve greatness, or they can fall from grace by choosing a foolish path. There is an ancient tale that comes from an Indian called the King and the Ghoul (Chinen, 1993). In this tale the King is asked several difficult riddles from a ghoul. The king must answer the riddles correctly to prevent the ghoul from killing him. In the end the ghoul turns from a tormentor to a teacher. The ghoul helps the king see that enemies can be allies and sometimes an ally can be your most dangerous enemy. The fable is an example for seeing a person's true colors. I strongly believe that we all have a voice we listen to and that is the voice of a King or the voice of a fool.

The Wonder of Nature

The power of nature can also transform a person. Sir David Attenborough, considered a national treasure in the United Kingdom (Clipson, 2020), and Aldo Leopold (2020) are key figures for expressing and sharing the natural world with awe and wonder. Attenborough's television programs are captivating and can be a springboard for building an interest in our world's animal and plant life. Leopold wrote the non-fictional book A Sand County Almanac in 1949 which became a landmark in the American conservation movement. This type of book can be read and re-read for developing an environmentalist's perspective. Leopold, an unexpected, gifted writer, expresses his unique talent to share his experience with those of us who grew up with an untrained eye. Leopold shows a pure knowledge and enthusiasm for the natural world of Sand County that can be intoxicating and transformative. He also outlines the three most important ways people can interact with the land. Leopold masterfully shares his adventures and observations of the land and its animals during a cycle of seasons and the accumulation of years on his wilderness farm in Wisconsin. Leopold penned this quote, "There are some who can live without wild things, and some who cannot..." Leopold the conservationist, naturalist and philosopher was one who could not. The land conservationist inspired this poem to take action (Holiday, 2023. permission granted). For people looking to increase their polymath repertoire this poem is a battle cry for environmental action.

A tribute to *A Sand County Almanac* (Aldo Leopold, 1949)

Aldo's Wild Tomorrow:

A man that hunted and fished this land as a boy
remained disappointed from where he sat.
Warnings from the *Sand County Almanac*
caused a shiver, then a tingle down his back. He
sauntered on a path, in the undulating land and
these words from the prophet bubbled up from a
napping thought, "Some can live…" was the
first part of the memory and all he could muster,
but there was more, much more that he was
taught.

He looked at the remarkably empty sky during
this Indian summer and remembered the
swallow, the harrier, and the hawk. He
remembered reading as a boy Aldo's book by a
campfire, using his knapsack for a pillow and
the prophet's land ethics talk. One thing became
more and more evident, the land was sparsely
inhabited by creatures he held in awe, things that
are wild no longer live here anymore. And gone
was the logger's, the trader's, the trapper's
general store.

The land bore no resemblance to his youthful
days of lost sunshine, wild things no longer live
here and grow and the grizzly saw its seasons
disappear a long, long, time ago.

At one time, he cared little about the matter; yet
this day pressed upon him a melancholy sense of
loss. He could hear a whisper of words on a
gentle breeze, "Some can live without wild
things, and some cannot." The forest was
uprooted, and the river's journey done. Untamed
things were either civilized, torn away, or forced
to run.

He remembered the myth how Aldo once shot a
she-wolf, and watched her green eyes expire and
how this tragedy would inspire a young
conservationist to pledge his work to never stop,
to never tire. "Some can live without wild
things, and some cannot."

Words from Aldo started like a murmur and then
they grew, "Preserve integrity, preserve stability,
preserve the biotic community too."

The man would no longer be an idle pawn, he
would bring back the swallow, the harrier, and
the hawk. He would bring back the trout that
shifted against the current in winter, spring, and
fall.

"Some can live without wild things, and some
cannot."

Habits

Sometimes it is helpful to point out that change is difficult for humans in general. Routines and familiarity do provide a sense of security. It is important that children have routines and consistently scheduled activities. If a child is raised in a chaotic household, it is vitally important to reestablish a routine that is automatic, like bedtimes, mealtimes, and school. This brings a sense of order; it can also lead to decreasing anxiety. When parents divorce, a child's routine can be disrupted. We are pattern forming creatures. Two items that appear universal when given the opportunity of free choice are: parking in the same parking spot or sitting at the same place at the table. I asked several of my friends and co-workers and they agreed with this observation. People in general avoid change or taking a risk. Many of us have heard that great motivational speaker, or pastor that impresses upon us marvelous advice. Yet, come Monday morning we fall back into our routine. As a crisis counselor we must promote the choice to change and grow. Even an adolescent that feels powerless can feel empowerment by making a choice to add a positive habit and develop a treatment plan.

Whether we find useful advice from looking at the works of Dickens, Buffet, or Aurelias, transformation occurs when we have changed our habits. A 'keystone habit' is a term coined by Charles Duhigg (The Power of the Habit 2014). Clients looking for that catalyst for change, may only need to remove one bad habit. When we get rid of a bad habit this can trigger other positive habits, a life can snowball in the right direction. The miracle question (Metcalf 2006) is used by therapists to help their client to envision the future when the problem is gone. Then they describe in detail how the future will be different. The same type of questioning can be used to address your client's unhealthy habits. How will your life be different in the future if you drop a bad habit? Your future can change like McConaughey (2015) said, "It's all about being that better person that avoids a future filled with regret, guilt, or remorse." If you envision a future that looks better than yesterday, it can be a motivator for real change.

Being part of someone else's routine also takes time. When you walk down the street in New York City, people are unfriendly, you are not a part of their routine. You are just a number in the hustle and bustle of a human metropolis. Cape Town, Saint Petersburg, Marseilles, are also described as unfriendly cities. Years ago, I was teaching tennis in North Carolina and joined the local YMCA, everyone in the weight room was unfriendly and cold. My first day was a harsh experience, I felt like an interloper, treading on enemy's territory; however, I kept going. Each day I would gain a small sign of recognition, or a friendly gesture from a fellow weightlifter here or there. In one week, I became a regular. At summer's end, when it was time to go back to college, I had gained four friends. In this situation, I chose to move outside my comfort zone.

Our Emotional Clocks

When survival instincts take over, we may do things without being aware of how it affects our functioning. We could have been in a relationship that ended, and we go through a period of depression. The adage that time heals all wounds has some hints of truth. I believe we can speed up time by instituting positive and rational statements about our situation. The mind and the body still need time to catch each other. You may say all the right things to yourself, "I do not have to put up with a control freak or feel like a hostage anymore because they always threaten to leave the

relationship, and I have less opportunity to grow and
benefit by being in a non-reciprocal relationship."
Regardless, your depression will still be there, it will not
completely and instantly dissolve; it will improve and
usually heal over time. Our clocks vary as individuals.
We have the power to improve the speed of our
timepiece through counseling. An interesting variation
of how our emotional clocks run can be seen in an article
on widows and widowers. The average time for a man to
remarry after the death of his spouse is significantly
sooner than his female counterpart (Olson, 2006).

Brainstorming

If your brainstorming session with a client seems
to fail, it is important at minimum to give their situation
time, explain the possible advantages of waiting a
problem out. Whether we are fully aware, your mind will
work on a problem unconsciously. A simple example
might be we recognize the face of an actor in a movie
but cannot remember his name. A few days later while
walking to work you make the connection even though
you were not consciously thinking about it, the actor's
name is remembered. Large financial investments, like
buying a home or car are choices that most people would
allot a few days to mull over their options. Your client is
likely to find more rational ground when given more
time. The phrase, "cooler heads prevail," is a time-
oriented statement meaning it is good to wait for your
emotions to settle before acting. Several cultures have
similar correlations to time, before acting. In Native
American Indian-Iroquois law (Johansen, 2000) - "In our
every deliberation, we must consider the impact of our
decisions on the next seven generations."

Incubation

When dealing with a person in crisis, we carry out several concepts to reach the problem-solving stage. In 1926 English social psychologist and London School of Economics co-founder Graham Wallas (2018), wrote The Art of Thought. In this book he outlines the four stages of the creative process (Popova, 2015). They are called: preparation, incubation, illumination, and verification. I felt Graham's stage of incubation was the most relevant to *The Crisis Gambit* equation. Getting the mind to brainstorm and into the incubation phase is a critical goal for anyone dealing with a problem. Incubation is a process where the unconscious mind is working on a problem. Getting stuck is not a bad thing, it is not catastrophic, change is always going to happen, incubation is a process we all go through. As a first responder, you cannot always completely resolve a problem. When you identify and frame a problem, the mind will unconsciously deliberate on trying to solve it. This incubation process is an extraordinary gift. When we remember a dream, we can see how our mind is always trying to bring order and logic to our thoughts. If I went to the zoo and thought about an old friend recently, I could have a dream about that friend at the zoo.

The Flying Dutchman

Working on a problem non-stop can be a hellish experience. Think about the story of the ill-fated Flying

Dutchman (ancient-code.com.). In the story the captain swore that he would make it around the Cape of Good Hope in a ferocious storm even if he had to sail to judgment day. The devil heard this oath, and according to legend the ghost ship can never make port and is doomed to sail the oceans forever, the crew never able to rest, or be reunited with loved ones. If you see the Flying Dutchman; it may forecast your own pending doom. Working on a problem nonstop is emotionally and physically draining, an interlude is a pause between acts in a play, giving your problem an interlude on the conscience level may help you get a needed break. Your mind will still be working on the problem unconsciously as the mind goes through incubation.

The unconscious mind is a powerful tool for solving problems. Earlier we talked about the need to identify the primary problem, this is vital prep work for the unconscious mind. We can see this in Conan Doyle's Sherlock Holmes when the detective takes smoke breaks and appears to place his case on the backburner or it can be illustrated below in a story about Archimedes, arguably the greatest mathematician of antiquity.

Volume and Density

Legend tells us that King Hieron II (Trussell-Cullen, 2002) sought Archimedes' wisdom upon receiving a crown from a blacksmith. The king suspected that the blacksmith was dishonest. Rather than making the crown out of solid gold, the blacksmith had slipped silver into the crown and took some gold for himself. Archimedes pondered this mystery. In the beginning, he had no way to test the King's theory without destroying the crown. For days he pondered this question and even put it on the backburner of his mind, he let his unconscious mind slip into incubation and work on the problem. Several days later he was going to take a bath and stuck his foot in the bath water. When his foot hit the water, Archimedes solved the puzzle: submerge the irregular shaped crown into a full bathtub, catch the displaced water, and put the water in a mold for making bricks; mark the waterline and then throw the water away. Then he filled the brick mold with solid gold to the same waterline and compared the weight of the gold brick to the gold crown. If the weight was equal, the blacksmith was an honest man. Archimedes proved the blacksmith guilty by using volume and density in his problem solving. The unconscious mind is a magical apparatus, sometimes just understanding that you have a specific problem can lead to incubation and then resolve.

The Skyscraper

The architect of the world's first skyscraper is also reported to have a similar incubation moment. By watching his wife place a heavy book on a flimsy birdcage, Major William Le Baron Jenney had his eureka moment that led to the construction of the Home Insurance Building in Chicago, erected in 1884-1885. Jenney used steel to create a skeleton structure to surpass the limits of concrete load-bearing walls (Condit,1964). Jenney's incubation and then resolve made him the father of the American skyscraper. He was ranked eighty-nine in the book 1,000 Years: Ranking the Men and Women who Shaped the Millennium (Gottlieb, 2000).

Fishing Reel

The Shakespeare Company has been a leading manufacturer and supplier of fishing equipment since it was founded in Michigan during 1897. At the age of twenty-seven the founder of the company, William Shakespeare, Jr., wanted to solve a problem. Fishing was difficult then for retrieving lures on a reel, it required a fisherman to guide the line back and forth with his thumb. Legend tells us the founder William Shakespeare Jr. was inspired by taking his sock off. If you pull your sock off from the side, it takes more effort than if you pull from the center of the sock. Shakespeare had an incubation moment. What followed was his original patent in 1896 of the level winding fishing reel. This technology, still used today, enables fishing enthusiasts to rewind their line evenly on a spool which aids in line retrieval as well as casting.

Duct Tape

Duct Tape was invented by an Illinois mom named Vesta Stoudt (Steven, E. 2019). She had two sons serving in the U.S. Navy in 1943 at the time of her moment. She noticed that the boxes of ammunition she was packing, and inspecting were seriously flawed. The paper tape and the whole box was then dipped in wax to make it waterproof. When soldiers would try to open the boxes, the tape would break, slowing their access to ammunition. Not a good situation to be in if you are on the frontline in World War II. She had the idea to make cloth waterproof tape, but her supervisors ignored her. Still determined, she wrote a letter to President Franklin D. Roosevelt with her idea. The President sent her letter forward to the War Production Board. Vesta Stoudt's idea was approved, and Industrial Tape Corporation was commissioned to make her idea a reality, saving American soldiers lives in the process. Vesta Stoudt

identified a problem, and her mind went to work helping
to create a product most Americans keep in their homes.

The Assassination of JFK

In my own experience, the assassination of
President John F. Kennedy gave me another example of
the incubation process. If you were raised in my
generation, you have been exposed to the movies,
television specials and conspiracy theories about
whether Lee Harvey Oswald was the lone shooter in the
JFK assassination. Mass Media put this question in my
unconscious mind. To someone like me it looks like the
President was shot from two separate locations. I am not
an expert on high-powered rifles and their effect. My
unconscious mind chose to work on this problem. My
eureka moment came by watching Jim Shockey, a
professional big game outfitter, writer, and television
host to name a few of his accolades. By some, he is
considered the most accomplished big game hunter in
the modern era; he has taken 364 free-range big-game
species, arguably the most taken by any living hunter.
He has shot animals in valleys, on cliffs, on hills, on
mountain tops, and usually has film footage of these
events. He has taken quarry in all types of weather in
forty-five countries and on six continents (Robinson,
2017). I would be satisfied with Jim Shockey's opinion
on the assignation of our beloved thirty-fifth President.
At least a network special on Shockey's view.

Vikings

My next example happened at my brother's
home in Alabama. He wanted to move a large round
wooden planter full of dirt, located in his backyard. The
planter's speculative weight was two hundred pounds

and in the center of the planter was a small ornamental tree. Neither one of us wanted to pick up the planter and risk a back injury. I knew Vikings moved large ships across land using logs. I saw a push broom on his patio. I detached the bush from the handle and placed the handle under the planter. This allowed us to roll the planter to its new location. The incubation of your problems may take days; however, in this illustration the problem was identified, and the solution quickly followed.

Vladimir Putin is Paranoid

Vladimir Putin is the epitome of corruptions; his own advancement and wealth have been achieved with brutal indifference to the rights of his own people and to the rights of the Ukrainian people. Clausewitz, "Civilized nations do not put their prisoners to death." Putin is killing women, children, and non-combatants. The incubation process can be triggered by your knowledge of history or media. Leonard Cohen (1984) wrote the beautiful song, "Hallelujah". The song tells how King David from the Bible saw Bathsheba bathing on a rooftop. "You saw her bathing on the roof. Her beauty and the moonlight overthrew Ya." David killed Bathsheba's husband Uriah by sending him to the front-line of a battle so he could marry Bathsheba (Hebrew Bible 2 Samuel 11; Kings 1, 2). Vladimir Putin, like other corrupt leaders, may send his potential rivals to the frontline. In the book On War (Clausewitz, 1989), the author explains why top commanders must lead from the rear of a battle, because they are the command center. The American Indian war Chief Tecumseh was successful because he also employed this approach. He was one of the first Native American Indians commanders of an army to lead from the rear, not lead from the front into battle. This is war strategy 101. The news reported five of his generals were recently killed (Detsch, 2022). Is Putin purposely killing his own generals to protect his reign and avoid conflict with political rivals? Generals are the type of people that could rally to overthrow this tyrant. Media sources report multiple accounts that the Russian people don't want this war, and face mortal consequences for expressing a view in a communist country. Almost 6,500 people have now been arrested in Russia for participating in anti-war protests (Nicholson, 2022).

Incubation summary

Crisis counseling can work out a plan for immediate action or prepare the unconscious mind to continue to improve a given situation. This is an important concept to explain to your clients, and it also provides hope. Often when a person is in a crisis, it takes time for the body to catch up with the mind. If you tell yourself and believe that a breakup with your significant other will be beneficial in the journey of your life you will still be depressed. So, you conclude, you do not want a relationship with someone who is not loyal, you do not want to be in a relationship with someone who takes you for granted, you do not want to be with someone you cannot count on. Sometimes a person can feel like they are walking on eggshells because the person can leave them at any time. They might allow themselves to be treated like the proverbial doormat. Insight comes from a Civil War General, Lew Wallace (2020), "When people are lonely, they stoop to any companionship,"

In step three of *The Crisis Gambit*, we talked about the three states of the brain, the rational, emotional and survival states. You now tapped into the rational state of your brain, but you still feel depressed. Your unconscious mind will continue to see and think about events that support your rational thinking. Your body might still be severely depressed for a few weeks, moderately depressed for a month and may take you two months to two years to fully get over the event. Each of us has our own clock. When you keep telling yourself rational thoughts the interference from your emotional and survival parts of your brain will subside.

Creativity

All the humans have an innate ability to create or as I like to say, "solve problems." Most people might think that a Kalahari Bushman and a NASA scientist are vastly different. I see them more alike when it comes to problem solving. The one of oldest races of people still living on earth, are the San people of Southern Africa. The San people are also known as the Kalahari Bushmen that are indigenous hunter-gatherers. The San people create and use knowledge to improve their chance of survival (DiCiacca, 2008). They pass information from one generation to the next. According to Canadian Anthropologist, Richard B. Lee (2013), a group of San hunters can track animals by examining footprints. Hunters look at the size, the depth of the impression, the gate of the animal, the deterioration of the print over time, the location and number of animals that have used a route. The expert tracker in the group can tell if an animal is injured, whether the animal is a male, female, young or old, and the time they were at a given location. Desert animals choose routes to stay in the shadows, when possible, as the angle of the sun changes, animals choose a corresponding route. A master San tracker will know where an animal was at ll:00 A.M. or at noon on a given day and what pace it would take to reach the prey. Carl Sagan, the famous American astronomer, once said that meteorite impressions on a planet is how scientists calculate the age of a planet. By examining the size, shape, and deterioration of the planet's creators, a NASA scientist can calculate the age of a planet. This technology is similar to the Kalahari Bushman who examines the impressions of animal tracks.

Plato (1979) wrote in The Republic that "necessity is the mother of invention." If you doubt people's ability to create, all you need to see is a city full of skyscrapers lighting up the night, the Great Pyramid of Giza rising out of the desert or walking the Mackinac bridge on a foggy Labor Day morning. The impact humans have on their environment is unquestionable. My grandma Bryce was born in 1900 and used a horse for transportation for fifty years before the technology of the automobile and television was introduced into her life. Yet, she lived to 1993, giving lifetime a radical viewpoint. In my life, I was delighted with several inventions: the snowmobile boot, the Columbia 3-in-1 jacket, the five-star running shoe, the ultra-light spinning reel, Microsoft Word, the compact car, the microwave, and a yardage laser for golf. It is a fascinating saga in the advancement from primitive cave dweller tools to the heroic achievement of the internet, the world wide web, and the smartphone.

The god Janus

In Christian theology man is believed to be made in the image of the creator and thus given the power to create. In Ancient Roman, the god Janus (Britannica, 2022) is the symbol of new beginnings; some believe January is most likely named after him. Janus is often depicted as having two faces, one looking at the past and one looking forward into the future. If you can imagine a client with Janus' vision, you can only have them look at the past briefly as a crisis counselor. Your focus is geared toward future action and sometimes safety planning. A new beginning starts when your client sees a new perspective. In the prior section on anger, we talked about how one man gained freedom, one man strengthened his faith, and one man gained a friend. In all three situations, the men chose not to be victims and they were looking forward. In a victim situation the act of violation may last two minutes. After the initial crisis, it is up to a person's individual clock how long a person will allow this event to dominate or interfere with their life and how long they will remain a victim. I have seen clients that use the event to springboard themselves to a stronger self and I have seen people choose to remain a victim. Self-pity will not help you live a full life. You must believe that you can oversee your path in life. You are obligated morally to try to be the best version of yourself. Anything less will not keep you content.

Ali

Muhammad Ali was victimized as a child. He was raised in a poor family and on his twelfth birthday his father bought him his first bicycle. His prized gift was stolen, and the young boy was devastated. A police officer hearing the boy's grievances convinced the young Ali to try boxing. This painful event changed the complete trajectory of Ali's life. He would become one of the greatest sporting figures of the 20th century, an Olympic gold medalist and the heavyweight boxing champion of the world (Sharma, 2016).

Malala

Malala Yousafzai is the youngest Nobel Prize laureate, known as a Pakistani activist for female education. She was shot in the face at age fifteen by agents of the Taliban for attending school, and simply being a female. Malala never stayed a victim, her voice for women and girls' right to education became louder and stronger (Anderson, 2019). Her quote sums it up, "We realize the importance of our voices only when we are silenced." Insight on the choices we make come from an important quote from the author, Alice Walker (n.d.)- "The most common way people give up their power is by thinking they don't have any."

Sticks and Stones and Kipling

I want to analyze the phrase, "sticks and stones may break my bones, but names will never hurt me." Of course, words can be hurtful, but let us look at the true meaning of this phrase, Aristotle (n.d.) may agree when he said, "It is the mark of an educated mind to be able to entertain a thought without accepting it." My son told me in third grade that his teacher told him this phrase is false and that words can hurt you. He looks back at that phrase with anger; he said his teacher was willing to teach him how to be a victim and not how to be a stronger individual. Even people raised in horrible, violent, poverty-stricken childhoods can rise out of it. There is always a level of responsibility for what happens to us. It is important to understand this because it will help to guide your steps in the future, rather than thinking there is nothing I can do about it. Rudyard Kipling's poem "If" has two lines that suggest what it takes to be a man, "If neither foes nor loving friends can hurt you." and "If you can bear to hear the truth you've spoken twisted." There are people that speak the truth, talk about growth, beauty, and potential. There are opposite people that speak of failure, look for ugliness, and lack encouragement. You can choose what path you want to follow.

Blueprint Questions: The Butcher, the Baker, the Candlestick Maker

In this brainstorming and generating alternatives section, I came up with a set of blueprint questions. These are major questions and decisions that can influence our journey in life. It appears most people have the following tough adult decisions that include: Should I join the workforce? Should I become a baker, a butcher, or a candlestick maker? Join the military or go to college? What college should I choose? What career should I pursue? Is Science, Technology, Engineering, or Math (S.T.E.M) my calling? Who should I marry? Where should we live? Should we rent or buy a home? Should we have kids? Should we retire? What is my stance on religion? What is my stance on politics? These blueprint questions will chart a course to a particular life. If your client has no direction, looking at these blueprint questions can open dialogue. These questions are stepping stones, and potential goals.

Beware Your Biases

When discussing blueprint questions, be aware of your own biases. Your clients are experts in their own lives. A teacher and basketball coach I respected believed that students leaving high school should work for a few years and then go to college. This plan worked for him; however, this is a narrow-minded view. He felt he needed to grow and mature in the workforce before going to college. His viewpoint had merit for his life circumstances, but he is not you. At age ten I had a paper route, shoveled snow, and raked leaves for money, after that I worked At Vite's Farm picking peas, pumpkins, potatoes, corn, and weeding fields of alfalfa. At age 15 I worked as busboy, from age 16 to age 18 I was a manager at sporting goods store called the Sport Corner. I learned how to sell kayaks, canoes, cross-country skis, tennis shoes, backpacks, take groups up and down the St. Joseph and Dowagiac Rivers, print t-shirts, string tennis rackets, make bank deposits, complete inventory, and run the store when the owner was gone on vacation and business. According to a high school basketball coach, I should work two more years before going to college, his plan did not suit my life. I followed another plan; I worked while going to college.

Age Discrimination

When I graduated from college, I landed a graduate assistantship that would allow me to attend graduate school, earn an income, and afford me free room and board. There were 129 applicants and I felt like I won the lottery when the search committee chose me as one of four candidates. The chair of the graduate program was an elderly Dominican sister still working at age seventy-nine. The one last hurdle to seal the deal was an interview with her. She at once attacked me for being too young to be admitted to the program and said the average graduate student in this program was forty-five. I argued that life should be qualitative not quantitative. My life experience would be enhanced by seeing the world through educated eyes. Fortunately, she was not the only voice on the committee, the Dean of Students, along with two Directors overruled her opinion. This elderly sister brought her own biases with her to my encounter. As a crisis counselor it is important to understand everyone's an expert in their own life, do not allow your biases to limit someone's potential. I cannot attribute this following quote to one person; thousands of people have said this including the novelist Stephen King, "The best lessons we learn in life are our own."

A Lesson from Danny Deckchair

One of the most radical blueprint questions must be where to live. When you move to another town, another state, or another country, everything in your life has the potential to radically change. In Australia, a movie called Danny Deckchair (Balsmeyer, 2003) was released. The movie shows how Danny was stuck and disappointed in his current life struggles. An event happened that gave Danny the opportunity to change. With the magic that is available in movies, friends tied helium balloons to Danny's deckchair while having fun at a barbeque. They lose hold of the deckchair and soon all of Australia is looking for Danny, who floated away. He ends up landing in a small village, miles away from his earlier home. Keeping his identity, a secret, the locals befriend their mysterious visitor. This romantic comedy shows how people can blossom into their full potential. In his new location, Danny becomes politically active and romantically involved. This critic's pick is a delightful example of how people can become more than they once thought possible by making a move.

Henry Box Brown

Moving away from fiction and looking into American history there is an extraordinary account for improving one's life by making a move (Narrative of the Life of Henry Box Brown, 1849). Henry Brown was born a slave on a Virginia

plantation in circa 1815 and spent a life full of unrewarded labor. His joy during those tragic times, according to his autobiography, were tempered by living with his three children and his precious wife. Unfortunately, one day Henry went to work, only to return home to find his pregnant wife and children were sold to another plantation. Henry Brown was unimaginably crushed by this turn of events. Henry Brown, after a few months of depression, devised a plan to escape. Enlisting the help of his friend and a local shoemaker, Henry Brown mailed himself in a crate from Richmond to Philadelphia. In the new location, he was a free man, and he would become a beacon of hope for the abolitionist movement. After that extraordinary mail delivery, he would forever be known as Henry "Box" Brown.

The Jungle Book and Captain Courageous

Crisis counseling is all about looking at problems differently, attacking your own or your client's tunnel vision. Changing your environment is an option that some people never consider. Another example, Rudyard Kipling (1935) wrote in his autobiography that when he lived in Vermont, it was the happiest time of his entire life. It was also the most productive, as he had completed poems, stories and two monumental works of his career: The Jungle Book and Captain Courageous. Kipling attributed his success, and happiness to living in the country, which prevented him from using alcohol or visiting opium dens that were readily available in a city environment.

Gaining Control Over Your Life

In *The Crisis Gambit*, we have a game plan on how to break a crisis down into pieces. As we move through the steps of the equation, we can find the polestar problem. Your client's reaction was heavily influenced by your modus operandi. In an emotional state or survival state, you or clients can lack the ability to problem solve at their best. The fuel to start a crisis comes from love, anger, fear, or hunger. In the problem-solving stage we can brainstorm how to decrease, eliminate or plan how to find a more acceptable fuel source. Just by recognizing the steps in a crisis, you are gaining control and re-establishing logic and reasoning into your arsenal of tools.

Post-traumatic Growth

As we move through life, the traumatic events that a person endures will strengthen or weaken their psyche. Our ability to problem-solve is tested as we move through the continuum of living. Joel Osteen said in a sermon that King David needed the adversity of Goliath to reach his higher destiny. Psychologists call this phenomenon post-traumatic growth, a term coined at the University of North Carolina at Charlotte (Haas, 2016). The belief is that as we become able to fix large and small problems, we gain experience. When we work through a crisis and reach resolve, this situation provides us with significant growth. A light-hearted analogy might be that we are a candidate for Canada's Worst Handyman (2022) television show and as we move through life we become more like the accomplished builders: Bob Vila or Mike Holmes. Again, the quote from Freud appears relevant, "One day, in retrospect, the years of struggle will strike you as the most beautiful."

One of my daughter's passions has always been horseback riding. She watched the remake of the movie *Flicka* around age ten and seemed to fall in love with horses ever since. She, along with her high school equestrian team, would make the cover of *Saddle Up Magazine* and she would go on to compete at the collegiate level. Her post-traumatic growth experience happened at her favorite stomping ground, Stonehaven Farms. Her favorite horse during her early years was Tommy Halfinger. After building a bond with her faithful friend, the school horse was sold to another barn. To most people this sounds like a minor setback, as a crisis counselor I must remind the professional to look at a person's crisis development. This event was a stepping stone for Natalya, and she learned to recover from the experience and develop realistic coping strategies for future relationships, adapting to change is part of our individual crisis development. Unfortunately, years later she would have a friend named Chase DuVall commit suicide at age 20. The young man, just out of high school, was a good-looking, talented and an extremely charismatic performer. In her chorus group, he was often a soloist and dancer in the Bedford Soirée singers. Although these events seem unrelated, they are part and parcel of her crisis development and as a crisis counselor, we must meet our clients where they are in their journey. I personally, remember Chase, his death was extremely upsetting, he was a shining star in my daughter's group performances. I hope I hammer home how critically important crisis counseling can be, and one of you reading this book will feel better equipped to help someone like Chase or understand your own challenges. Natalya's post-traumatic growth is like many of us trying to figure out our next move when life circumstances seem unfair and even catastrophic.

Threshold List

If you want to really know someone and where they are in their crisis development journey, this will open a large talking point. By using the four core motivators identify how you experienced a crisis involving love, a crisis involving anger, a crisis involving fear and a crisis involving hunger. What were the stages of your modus operandi? Then discuss what you learned from these events and the post-traumatic growth.

Adaption Stories: (Ishmael Beach, a British Soldier, and Shakespeare)

In science, the law of evolution states that when the environment changes radically, life must adapt, flee or die. Those are radical words for a crisis counselor, yet they hold some truth. Mother Nature is always throwing curve balls at us like tornados, floods, and Covid-19. Getting your client to accept change is paramount. If a person does not recover from psychological trauma, they could live a tragic life, and not reach their full potential. In another, serious example, Ishmael Beah (2008) was orphaned at age twelve when his parents and two brothers were killed during a civil war in the West African Country, Sierra Leone. Beah also reported that he was forced to become a child soldier, to survive, he developed a hardened facade before being rescued. Beah chose to adapt and then flee when the opportunity finally arrived. His psychological trauma was extensive. He continues to show great promise as an advocate, an author, and a public speaker. He is a significant example of someone willing to accept change. Beah reminds me of the mythical phoenix that is said to die in flames, becomes reborn and rises out of the ashes of his former self.

My own father was forced to make a radical change in his life. My father was in the British Airforce and became a prisoner of war for three and a half years after being shot down over Germany in 1941. He roomed with American soldiers and frequently heard about potential opportunities in the United States, the seeds of change were planted. After World War II, he was released, and he returned home to Scotland and to the family's Ice Cream Store called the Cream Shop. Remember Italy and German combined to form the Axis side of the equation, also known as "Rome-Berlin-Tokyo Axis." Great Britain suffered great civilian casualties when air raids were carried out by Axis forces, my uncle Jim was even born in an Edinburgh bomb shelter in 1940. My father being a second-generation Italian, with a distinctive Italian last name, may have had limited opportunities in his native Scotland. My Uncle Philip told me, once a rock was thrown through the large glass window of the family's ice cream store, possibly an act of prejudice? However, my father carried the seeds for change that became seeds of hope for a better life. His dream to live in America was strengthened by the problems he faced making a living in a war-torn country, maybe this is the catalyst that pushed him to follow that dream. Canada was still a British Commonwealth and they still were flying the British Flag called the Union Jack before the Maple Leaf flag (historymuseum.ca) was adopted in 1965. He and my mother chose to make the trek to America by first going to Canada as part of the process of getting closer to the dream. My father went from Scotland to Canada on the cruise ship the RMS (Royal Mail Steamer: means the ship is an authorized mail carrier) Sylvania and my mother followed him one year later with my older siblings making the transatlantic crossing on the RMS Saxonia. My father chose to adapt to a new location to give himself and his family the greatest chance for success.

According to a murky personal history about William Shakespeare, documents verify he had three children, two daughters and one son (Scheil, 2020). Although little is known about his personal life, his contributions to the English language have never been equaled, and some people say he was the world's greatest writer, and he is believed to have added up to 1,700 words to the English vocabulary. Using crisis counseling detective work, I believe that he was extremely depressed in 1596 after the death of his eleven-year-old son, who died in an outbreak of the Bubonic Plague. Did Shakespeare use the trauma suffered by the death of his son to write his best play in circa 1599? We only know for certain that most experts would say that 'Hamlet" was the Bard of Avon's finest work. According to the article "Three Cheers for Hamlet" by M.J. Franklin (Mashable 2016) 'The Tragedy of Hamlet', better known as just, 'Hamlet' was his best work. A twitter poll selected the winner, and it comes with little to no surprise to Shakespeare enthusiasts around the world. This play shows that Shakespeare was a better writer in c. 1599. It is now worth mentioning, his eleven-year-old son that passed away was named Hamnet, a form of Hamlet. How people deal with devastating grief is an individual matter. The probability appears great that Shakespeare chose to continue to hone and improve his craft and honor his late son's name. Shakespeare genius has had such a profound influence on many parts of life. "We are still walking in the shadows of Shakespeare's dreams."- Neil Gaiman (Sandman creator).

Nampizha

I read a rare book in the 1990's about the Neshnabek Native Americans. "Neshnabek" is an alternate spelling of Anishinabek, which is a name the Ojibway and Potawatomi people use for themselves in their own language. The book was the primary inspiration for my second novel called *Against the Current*. The rare book was written by an anthropologist in 1860's who interviewed surviving Neshnabek elders. The word Neshnabek stood for "The true people" and over time the Neshnabek Indians would become the Potawatomi, a word that means "fire makers." The Neshnabek believed that a spiritual creature named Nampizha lived in all rivers and lakes. Often it was customary to give a food offering to Nampizha before crossing or entering a body of water. This creature was a horned panther that was believed to cause people to drown. The fall into a river is not what kills you, it's your ability to fight against Nampizha. Paulo Coelho said (Spector, 2016), "You drown not by falling into a river, but by staying submerged in it."

A Tree Grows in Brooklyn

My sister, Mari, said one of her favorite books is
A Tree Grows in Brooklyn (Betty Smith, 1943). This
book is clearly an underdog story, about the hardships
that a family must endure. A tree tenaciously grows
through a crack in the pavement, an analogy is drawn
between the family and the tree. Heraclitus (544 B.C.)
said, "No man ever steps in the same river twice, for it's
not the same river and he's not the same man." I like to
interpret this quote to mean that we all can learn and
grow. We can change and grow every day that we
interact with our environment, even a tree surrounded by
pavement can grow against the odds. Getting knocked
down and getting back up is building resilience.
Resilience may be the most important quality that exists
in humanity. As a crisis counselor this quality is a vital
tool for change and adaptation.

Earlier in this book we looked at suicide notes.
The notes were collected from India and Northern
Ireland and even one suicide note was from the inventor
of the FM radio broadband. From these notes we learned
that an overall main element for completed suicides is
shame/guilt/apology. By getting your client to weather
the storm, take the embarrassment, the conversation is
about building and finding resilience. The logic: we only
need to be better than we were yesterday.

Survivor's Guilt

Elie Wiesel (1991) was a Nobel Prize Laureate,
novelist, Holocaust survivor, and keynote speaker at my
graduation. In his book *The Accident*, a fictional survivor
of a Holocaust is struck by a taxicab in New York City.
The book explains that the character is dealing with
Holocaust trauma and survivor's guilt. This character
felt guilty for surviving a Holocaust when so many of his

family, friends and compatriots were not so lucky. The character's irrational thinking and feeling guilty suggest that the character in the book may have unconsciously or consciously stepped in front of a taxicab to end his turmoil with undeserved guilt. Survivor's guilt is a condition that sometimes occurs in people suffering from posttraumatic stress disorder. When children suffer and grow up to be adults, they often feel angry at themselves for not fighting more or reporting the child abuse sooner, they must be reminded they are adults now with significantly more resources and intellectual ability than the child version of themselves. Guilt and shame are key factors to consider in the upcoming chapter on scenario training.

President helps President

When a person in crisis believes they are the lowest form of life on planet Earth or they feel ashamed or shame is placed on them, you must believe in hope and optimism to help them. These are the underdogs. Shame can be paralyzing, being afraid to face people that say hurtful things about you can freeze you in your tracks. If a client is dealing with shame or guilt inspiration can be found in politics. Nelson Mandela, South Africa's President between 1994-1999 was a friend to President Bill Clinton. The President of the United States was charged with articles for impeachment. Mandela (Freedland, 2004) had a piece of advice for Clinton. He said, "A man is not measured by how he falls, he is measured by how he gets up." This statement could give a glimmer of hope if presented the right way to that caller on the edge. "How can you be better than your former self?" is the question that comes up again.

Roosevelt's Man in the Arena

Sometimes a person doing what they believe is right, will also suffer great criticism. Paraphrasing Teddy Roosevelt speech (McCarthy, 2015) at the Sorbonne in Paris on April 23, 1910- "It is not the critic who counts; not the man who points out how the strong man stumbles […] credit belongs to the man who is actually in the arena, whose face is marred by dust and sweat and blood […] who spends himself in a worthy cause […] if he fails, at least he fails while daring greatly, so that his place shall never be with those cold and timid souls who neither know victory nor defeat." Roosevelt sees inaction as a problem, he makes a case that people can be measured by what they do not do. "Our greatest glory is not in never failing, but in rising every time we fall," -Confucius. This paragraph supports exposure therapy (Neudeck, 2012) in an ideological sense to manage fear and anxiety. It is necessary to carefully expose yourself to the situations you fear. In a controlled setting with professionals, exposure therapy is helpful for treating people with obsessive compulsive disorder. Shame and guilt have been identified as some of the leading causes for suicide. When a person feels a great burden of guilt or shame, it may be the most opportune time to point out what they are really saying in a therapeutic approach, "You are saying you recognize you are not the person you want to be. What steps can we take to put you on the right pathway to be that better person?"

The Underdogs: Eva Peron, Betty Zane, Silvester Stallone

Good stories are never written about life without challenges, it is the underdog that is most admired and the best example of resilience. Born in poverty, Eva Peron, brought equality and education to women and the people of Argentina (Fraser, n.d.) At the age of nineteen, Joan of Arc, a peasant girl with her belief in God, led the French to victory over the English (Lanhers, n.d.). In the American Revolutionary War, on September 11th, 1782, Betty Zane made an iconic dangerous run alone to retrieve gunpowder and save Fort Henry and its inhabitants from certain death (Zane, Betty, n.d.). Even in movies we are inspired by the underdog, in the movie Rocky starring Silvester Stallone, can we find a better underdog than the washed-up boxer Rocky Balboa or a better triumph? Stallone said the idea for the movie, "A man who was going to stand up to life, take a shot, and go the distance." Stallone is an amazing underdog story himself. The actor was so broke, he had to sell his dog so it could eat properly (Evon, 2015). Stallone held fast to his dream as a writer, actor, and creative talent. He refused to let the portrayal of his character go to anyone else. Rocky went on to receive nine Oscar nominations and net three coveted wins. By the way, he was able to buy back his dog. The author of Autumn Light (Pico Iyer, 2019) made an insightful statement, "I don't believe what happens to us is as important as what we do with it." The Singer Billy Joel went through a brief depression before his meteoric rise to fame and this is his advice, "You can't fall victim to self-pity, it's one of the most useless emotions you can have."

Hard Workers: Bach and Edison

The Crisis Gambit equation is vital to crisis counseling. It provides the game plan for helping anyone through a crisis. For you to become proficient in any activity it requires practice. Johann Sabastian Bach (1685-1750) was considered a genius, and the first well-known superstar in music. He said, "I have to work; anyone who works just as hard will get just as far." Bach makes a point that he was not born with a natural ability to play multiple instruments, but he put in the hard work. Like a journeyman he learned his craft and trained others to hone theirs. Bach may downplay his extraordinary talent; however, it remains true that practice is essential to success. Edison said, "Opportunity is missed by most people because it is dressed in overalls and looks like work." In your goal to help others through a crisis, practice can make you a crisis virtuoso.

Rules Guide Behavior: The Lieber Code, Driving in Public, Fighting in Hockey

The Lieber Code was a set of rules adopted by U.S. President Abraham Lincoln to govern how a soldier should act during the U.S. Civil War (Gesley, 2018). These rules helped to establish the humane and ethical treatment of populations in occupied areas. It forbade the use of poisons, rape, and torture. The Lieber Code was also adopted in the Hague Conventions in 1899 called together by Nicholas II the last Tsar of Russia (Avalon, n.d.) The Hague was the stage to set the roots for international law that would lead to the League of Nations and then ultimately to the United Nations. A code of conduct is vital to civilized society. Drills and scenario training are even more effective ways for governing human behavior. When you drive your car and have years of practice, you instinctively follow the rules, drive on the right-side of the road and go from point A to point B.

It is interesting how much control humans have with rules in place. Professional hockey is the perfect example of this concept. Fights break out often during games, which is not tolerated in basketball or tennis. But hockey players know they must take off their gloves before throwing punches, they must leave their helmets on, take off their visors, stop once a fighter hits the ice or when the referee blows his whistle.

Drills and Scenario Training

Drills and scenario training are methods of preparation for military personnel, fire fighters, police, and mental health workers. It is better to expect the worst and prepare. In *The Crisis Gambit* Scenario training, it can be like the spare tire in the trunk of your car. In learning, the primary way to learn is practice, you must put in the work. "Increase difficulty, increase struggle during practice actually leads to more learning and greater structural changes in the brain," according to Dr. Lara Boyd (2004), brain researcher at the University of British Columbia. Scenarios were created to test your ability to help others. Not all your situations will be genuine life or death struggles; however, the situation arrives on a regular basis in my field, and it is my hope that you add it to your arsenal of resources to connect with people in crisis. Often a person in crisis has a narrow viewpoint, they can see no other choice, except suicide. Creativity on your part is required to get them to change paths. A serious question is this: Do you have the training to reach into the dark place that lacks the glimmer of hope and pull someone out?

The Kobayashi Maru

In *Star Trek* (creator Gene Rodenberry) the television series, Captain James T. Kirk during his time as a Starfleet Cadet is given a complicated war scenario called the Kobayashi Maru. It was created by Jack Burke Sowards who hilariously named the scenario after his Californian neighbor (Goldberg, 1983). It is a test designed to assess the character of Starfleet Academy cadets in a no-win scenario. In this crisis, another Starfleet ship is in peril and will die without the help from the captain and crew from your ship. If you choose to rescue the ship in jeopardy, you must enter a neutral zone and violate a peace treaty. When you enter the neutral zone, it results in an all-out war for Starfleet with the adversarial Klingons. The Klingons also face your single ship with multiple ships, they are wielding greater firepower, they have also jammed your communication system. Negotiating with the Klingons or escaping their wrath is not an option. Your scenario becomes even more dire when your ship is hit, taking away your ability to fight or flea. And by the way, the Klingons do not take prisoners. A crisis may feel like a tricky situation to some people going through the experience. In the Kobayashi Maru scenario, we want Captain Kurt to think rationally like Sherlock Holmes and less like the emotional Dr. Watson. Crisis counseling, police interactions, requires an understanding of strategy, and you will be faced with situations that appear to be no-win situations. A crisis call from a distraught person, in dire straits, could paint a picture so bleak that they do not feel they have anyway out except suicide. Your ability to stay creative and focused on the present crisis could be paramount to the survival of another person and yourself.

The Sender Thread Scenario:

Scenario I: A caller can be so ingrained in their emotions they are determined to shoot themselves, if you hang up on them, they tell you they will pull the trigger, they called you their "last hope." Your ability to communicate with them is fading as they feel closer and closer to ending their turmoil, if you try to trace the call or send police the caller vows to pull the trigger, the cell phone number is blocked from caller I.D. The caller had some alcohol on board and said he does not deserve to live, he cheated on his wife, she told all our friends and family, I cannot look my daughters in the face. My wife threw my clothes outside for all our neighbors to gawk at.

To be effective in scenario one, you must keep your focus and keep your own emotions in check. You may have to show, "...grace under pressure," (coined by Hemingway 1926) to be effective in helping someone in a crisis. *The Crisis Gambit* is a game plan for crisis intervention. Now that I have covered the factors that create a crisis, it is important to look at factors to get you out of your crisis. In scenario one, we can apply *The Crisis Gambit*.

Step one: Perception of the event, fact finding, asking age-appropriate questions, allowing venting, allowing him to diffuse, building a trustful rapport. In scenario one, if all goes well, you have conveyed to the caller that you are glad they called and they are no longer alone in this crisis. We also want to encourage him to stop any alcohol use if possible. A great question to ask, what chain of events led you to this point?

Step two: Find the Core Motivator (Love, Anger, Fear and Hunger). If all goes well you open their viewpoint, they have been exposed to the world's most powerful motivators it is going to have a clear effect on their mental health. You let them pick what motivator(s) is involved in their situation. Love is an issue because his relationship is in jeopardy. He is angry at himself for his actions. He is afraid of divorce and the unknown. In scenario one they may choose love, anger, and fear. One of these motivators will be slightly more involved. It is better to understand the primary fuel. This will have an impact for devising a treatment direction. Let him identify the primary fuel.

Step three: Identify the modus operandi (states of the brain recipe: Survival, Emotional & Rational). If all goes well here, you can help him understand that not all parts of the brain function at the same time. We want him to begin to realize that when the emotional and survival states of the brain are activated in a crisis our rational state does not fully work.

Step four: Discuss how steps 1-3 effected behavior, emotions, and symptoms. Three possible results can happen: I understand why I feel the way I do; I understand why I act the way I do; I gain insight to understand I might have more control over the situation than I first imagined; I choose a path based on some choices. I have found symptoms that need more treatment.

Step Five: Your strategy is to focus your attention on the polestar problem, where the imbalance is. In this situation our client severely damaged his relationship with his wife and his daughters. He feels embarrassed to be around family, friends, neighbors, but he decided that his relationship with his wife is the first primary problem. If he cannot contract for safety, we work on getting him to a safe location.

Step Six: Problem solving, generating alternatives, brainstorming (conscious) and incubation (unconscious). If all goes well the client that had no control over a crisis, is now changing and has a glimmer of hope to change his situation. He also can be coached that he does not have to make a complete decision today, he can use resources like inpatient and outpatient mental health agencies, or call the helpline, the crisis line, or the Lifeline whenever he needs to, he is no longer alone in his decision. A good question to ask, "You are saying you recognize you are not the person you want to be. What steps can we take to put you on the right pathway to be that better person?"

Step Seven: Goal Setting

He identified improving his relationship with his wife as his polestar problem or his first goal. Because he is a caller, it would be appropriate to make a referral to an outpatient agency for family, marriage, or individual counseling to develop this goal. Vision casting can be used here with questions like these: Now that we have worked the basics, what do you see as your next course of action? Where do you see yourself going from here? After talking, what are your plans moving forward?

Step Eight: Vision Casting

Vision casting is also a safeguard. If you ask your client to visualize what will happen when they leave the agency or end the phone call, this will verify if your client's thinking has progressed into a rational state. It is time to summarize where your client is and how they have made plans to continue. This is clearly a bellwether event. If your client has decided to face life's problems with resiliency, then the session can end. If they are still in the danger zone, then safety planning must occur.

The Vitruvian Principles: Applied to Mental Health

Establishing balance is a key to crisis recovery. Understanding the need for balance in a person's life will help you to generate alternatives with your client in stage six of *The Crisis Gambit*. Balance is such an important subject that I chose to give it its own section. We can apply Vitruvian principles to mental health. Marcus Vitruvius Pollio, commonly known as Vitruvius, was a Roman author, architect, civil engineer, and military engineer during the 1st century BC, known for his multi-volume work entitled De architectura (Gwilt, 2019). Vitruvius asserted in writing that a structure must have three qualities called firmitatis, utilitatis, venustatis – that is, stability, utility, beauty. These are sometimes termed the Vitruvian virtues or the Vitruvian Triad. DaVinci showed us how Vitruvian virtues would look when applied to the human body, in his famous drawing called the *Vitruvian Man*. You may have heard this sometime in your life, when complimenting another person, "He is a well-balanced individual." If you describe someone as well-balanced, you mean that they are sensible and do not have many emotional problems. The synonyms for being well balanced are stable, sensible, rational, level-headed, well-adjusted; etc. The Vitruvian Triad is used to achieve architectural balance, a design without balance will feel off-kilter, inconsistent and even unsettling.

Imbalanced

To understand my concept of balance, first I want to look at the concept of being the opposite or imbalanced. Jim Rohn, author, and motivational speaker, said, "Always be willing to look at both sides of the argument, understanding the other side is the best way to strengthen your own (Rohn, n.d.)." For instance, when the FBI conducts a profile of an imbalanced or unstable individual, they list characteristics that can predict future behavior. With years of analyzing criminal behavior, the FBI's Behavioral Analysis Unit (BAU) can find potential red flags. The BAU was developed to bring in elements of psychology to help develop a criminal profile (Grimminck, 2016). The profile helps to narrow the field of suspects. Recidivistic thieves and murderers have always had signature styles. In the late 1700s Sir John Fielding, founder of the first London police force, used a new media source called the newspaper to list the names and methods of serial criminals in a newspaper called the *Hue and Cry* to help crime fighters (McKay, 2020).

How many times in the news have you heard about a shooter being socially unbalanced? Several headlines will include the phrase: he was a "loner." Consider these headlines: Gunman in Aurora, Illinois, shooting described as 'loner' (*Reuters,* 2022). The accused Walmart shooter was described as a 'loner' with a 'short temper' (*Radar*, 2019). Gilroy Festival killer described as 'kind of a loner,' (Ronayne, 2019). Virginia Tech gunman, described as 'loner' officials confirmed (Kaufman, 2007). Las Vegas Shooting: Attacker described as a wealthy, 'loner' (**Allen,** 2017). The observation is that when people are socially out of balance, they have a greater risk for violence.

The Mad Bomber

The first FBI case to use the term profiling was the George Metesky "Mad Bomber" case. George Peter Metesky, was an American electrician and mechanic who terrorized New York City for sixteen years during the1940s and 1950s with explosives. He believed that he lost his job unfairly, he contracted pneumonia, after being exposed to chemicals, and was sick for a few weeks and was fired by the Edison Company. The hunt for the bomber enlisted the use of a criminologist and psychiatrist named James A. Brussel. During this case, the procedure was called making a portrait of the bomber by Dr. Brussel. The portrait was so brilliantly done that Brussel even predicted with accuracy that the bomber would be wearing a double-breasted suit. When the police arrived at his home, he was wearing pajamas, he went upstairs and put on his double-breasted suit. The police were able to apprehend the mad bomber and after the case the term offender profiling was born (Greenburg, 2011). I make the case that the mad bomber was unbalanced socially, and as Brussel accurately predicted the bomber had no lover, never married, his only friends were biological relatives, "he was a loner" in several areas of his life or lacked balance.

Leopold and Loeb

The Leopold and Loeb murder trial that Chicago newspapers labeled "The Trial of the Century" is worth mentioning. In 1924, the wealthy and privileged Leopold and Loeb kidnapped and murdered a fourteen-year-old Bobby Franks in Chicago (Higdon, 1975). The killing was designed as an intellectual exercise by a twisted mind. Leopold was tested and believed to have an I.Q over 200, in time he would learn to speak twenty-six languages. His attorney, Clarence Darrow successfully represented both defendants against the death penalty. Leopold was described by Darrow as, "An intellectual machine going without balance (Linder, 1995)".

The Cremation of Sam McGee

As we know, art imitates life. The psychological unbalanced behavior can be seen in the poem called "The Cremation of Sam McGee". Often called "the Bard of the Yukon", Robert W. Service (1907) used his life experiences and the stories he had heard while living in the rugged Yukon Territory. He illustrates this in his poem by creating a character named McGee that suffers from a condition called gold fever; "he is always cold, but the land of gold holds him like a spell." His hunger and obsession for gold will lead to his demise and eventual death and then funeral by cremation. Between 1896 and 1899 the Klondike Gold Rush occurred in the Yukon region of Canada (**Wikipedia**). The bitter Arctic temperatures is said to have taken the lives of several ill-prepared and gold obsessed prospectors and their horses.

Moby-Dick

In the classic novel Moby-Dick (1851), Herman Melville's Captain Ahab is another example of instability. The author, using information on mental illness at the time, made Captain Ahab suffer from a condition called a monomaniac, a person having obsessive enthusiasm and preoccupation with one thing, "the white whale." Ahab put everyone around him in peril by following his signal minded quest. In the aftermath, the ship and crew were destroyed, the only survivor was Ishmael (Melville, 2020).

The Shining

In *The Shining*, author Steven King (2008) portrays his main character Jack as becoming unbalanced, writing the same phrase over and over, in Jack's draft novel. "All work and no play makes Jack a dull boy." This line was written thousands of times, when Jack's wife sees what is written in Jack's draft novel, she quivers in fear (Kubrick,1980). The Mad Bomber, George Metesky, mentioned above, also had single obsessive thoughts about causing the Edison Company grief.

Vascular Dementia also known as Multi-Infarct Dementia

Vascular dementia can be described when a person has brain damage caused by multiple strokes. They can become imbalanced. Unfortunately, one symptom can be a cantankerous personality. If a person is weak physically, they can assert strength inappropriately by using verbal strength. A person with a Napoleon complex is someone who has a domineering or aggressive attitude believed to compensate for being small or weak in stature. This opposite phrase is often used in our society, "He is a gentle giant." When people are imbalanced, compensations occur. A person after a stroke may have trouble speaking and to give their few words more strength will choose colorful or shocking language. When a person poorly copes with their physical decline, they may swear more, attempt to dominate others by using disparaging words. When a person is coping well, they may use colorful language to entertain and get others to laugh and become joyful to be around.

Balance

Now, let us look in the opposite direction.
Balance and activity play a significant role in depression.
If you created a pie chart on the daily activities of an
active person vs. an inactive person, the active person
would have less time to think about depression. Robert
Louis Stevenson (n.d.) the author of Treasure Island &
Strange Case of Dr. Jekyll and Mr. Hyde, is quoted,
"Keep busy at something, a busy person never has time
to be unhappy." Take time and think about what a
depressed person looks like and their activity level. Here
is what most people would say," they are hunched over,
looking down, quiet, soft spoken. Think of their activity
level: they are withdrawn from most social activity, they
lack energy, lack enthusiasm, and seek isolation.

Staci Westfall's Father

My daughter introduced me to a championship
horseback riding video by Staci Westfall. Honestly, it is
one of the most beautiful events I have ever seen and
Ellen DeGeneres also featured Ms. Westfall and her
iconic ride on her television show. Westfall dedicates her
ride to her father who went to heaven twenty-four days
before this ride and she also thanks her father for
teaching her to keep trying new things, the ring
announcer's voice cracks when he announces this
message to the idle crowd. When Westfall (2010) begins
to ride without a saddle or bridle on the horse, Whizards
Baby Doll, the music from Tim McGraw's version of
Live Like You Were Dying fills the arena and seems like
the perfect song to commemorate the event. Westfall
does not falter, her love for the horse and her
horsemanship are adored by the cheering crowd. As a
human being, I am privileged to watch this event. As a
crisis counselor I know Westfall's father's advice to "try
new things," is the cornerstone to beating depression.

Edward Sheriff Curtis

I believe what you are doing is one part of the puzzle, it is finding the right niche. Ralph Waldo Emerson said," A man is half himself; expression is the other half," (Emerson, n.d.) The life of Edward Sheriff Curtis may be an example of living a life that fulfilled this need. Curtis devoted his life to compiling the history of the American West through photography and field work, and in the end, he became an advocate, some even say, what he achieved in thirty years was the world's greatest individual effort in an anthropological undertaking. Curtis recorded Native Americans' traditional way of life before that way of life disappeared. Without his work, the customs, images, religions, and myths of over eighty Native American tribes would simply have little to no record (Quintenz, 2018). Curtis is also exposed to his own cultural instincts. The impulses to gain wisdom, discover, and express yourself artistically, this is part of the biological instincts of human behavior.

James Herriot

"I love writing about my job because I loved it, and it was a particularly interesting one when I was a young man. It was like holidays with pay to me." This quote is from Glasgow Veterinary College graduate, James Herriot (n.d.), the author of, "All Creatures Great and Small." Herriot is another individual who found a way to express his love for the animal kingdom, and his intrigue for nature and its miracles. His books cover the day-to-day struggles of a veterinarian, and the goodness and warmth that is achieved by sweat and humor, and how human kindness can outweigh the need for monetary gains.

Personal Expression Summary

Emerson's quote on personal expression can mean several things; however, I believe it to mean being who you want to be is an important concept, whether you spend your time taking photographs, writing poems, improving the health of others, by creating inventions or procedures that improve the environment, or simply helping another person overcome a weakness, trying to a find a place to fit in the world around you, it's important to everyone.

The Four Pillars for Immortality

Balance is a concept that will help you understand the gravity of a crisis. A person who loses their faithful spouse of fifty years is of course going to suffer some depression. The more diversity the widow has in her life the better her coping skills will be. If you are younger and want a full life, or some chance at immortality, four activities could move you to that goal or what I call the four pillars of immortality. If you build a house, plant a tree, have children (or create your social network), and write a book, this could move you in a rewarding direction. This is just one recipe for balance.

Birthdays

As a crisis counselor I have learnt that many suicide attempts happen around the holidays and, in my experience, even more people come into our agency or call our crisis lines around their birthdays. This phenomenon is known as the "birthday blues". Large population-based data studies looking at daily suicide rates were estimated in Switzerland, Japan, England, and Wales found that the suicide risk was 6–40% higher on birthdays than other days (Matsubayashi, 2019).

Physical Health & Movement

Movement is clearly associated with depression; health cannot be separated from your mental health and will add to your balance. I have noticed that healthy runners and weightlifters were rarely treated at my agency for depression. Take an injured runner or injured weightlifter then the potential for depression exists. When we become void of a joyful activity our mental health can suffer. Golfers and pickleball players not only improve their physical health, but they also develop a social network. I always felt that Alcoholics Anonymous has success for many reasons, but one critical reason is that they fill the void. A person in recovery has ample time that was wasted before on acquiring and using alcohol. When a person is no longer drinking, balance is restored by supplying them with positive activity such as attending group meetings.

There are no studies to suggest that exercise is detrimental to the brain. In fact, physical activity may even protect the brain from cognitive decline and enhance memory according to Dr. Sanjay Gupta (2022). According to Jonathan Graff-Radford, M.D. (2021) exercise can prevent memory loss and improve cognitive function. Exercise can increase the size of your hippocampus, which is the part of the brain that is associated with memory formation. I have been a golfer for over thirty years and fortunate to know many golfers of all ages. When twenty to forty golfers show up, teams are drawn. These teams are created by handicap. In short, a team should have an "A player" + "B player" + "C player" + "D player." This system exposes me to many golfers from all walks of life, ages, ability, and vices. Walkers that are in their 70's and 80's appear to have little to no cognitive decline as compared to golfers who ride in golf carts. Smokers appear to age the fastest, followed by drinkers, and drinkers that smoke have the shortest lives.

The Dance

"The Dance" performed by country singer Garth Brooks, is a song (Arata, 1990) that has different meanings. I interpret this song to have a message about risk, about not walking away from life and its hardships, but living in those special moments regardless of the pain, and not missing the dance and pushing yourself to experience more. From a counseling standpoint generating more activity into someone's life is a talking point. I believe all of us walk around with untapped potential. If you can better understand yourself and what makes you tick, it will help you understand your best path for self-development and personal growth. I found that a polymath has less depression than the normal person. Also, when a person has several interests, they are interesting to be around and have an increase in social likability. Don Clark is an example of a polymath that people found interesting to be around.

Asking Why

You must pick up some polymath traits, humans are limitless in their ability to develop, and increase the quality of your chosen life. The title of this article by David Neild says it all, "Your Brain is Still 30 Times

More Powerful Than the Best Supercomputers," Science Alert (Nield, 2015). Most people learn things out of necessity but do not venture beyond what they must do minimally. Performing minimally sounds like a plan for failure, reaching higher out of your comfort zone sounds like a better plan. A child naturally has an abundance of curiosity that would make him or her a natural polymath. Between the ages of two and five, a child will ask the question "why?" over and over trying to understand the world around them.

We should not downplay the ability of humans to learn. An extraordinary example of this is learning to communicate. Being human, we have a genetic desire to learn language. Although chimpanzees are raised in captivity and hear just as many words as a human, they show little desire to learn words (Terrace, 2019). Even a child raised by incompetent parents appears to master the ability to communicate effectively through language. Speech is mankind's greatest evolutionary development. Under normal circumstances, we all have an ability to improve physically, intellectually, socially, and artistically. It appears that with the advancement of age, the wonderment to explore the world goes away for some people, and along with it the imagination and creativity that existed in our youth. Picasso- "Every child is an artist. The problem is how to remain an artist once he grows up."

Interested vs. Intrigued

The difference between two words may explain a key difference in learning styles between normal people and polymaths. The two words are interested and intrigued. To be interested in a subject appears and sounds like exploring the surface and this pertains to the learning style of most people. To be intrigued with a subject has a deeper and compelling aspect for learning that many polymaths own. To a polymath there appears to be a need to peel back the layers of an onion and unravel the mystery.

Civil War General Lew Wallace

Lew Wallace may sound like an obscure example of a polymath to some; however, before this point I have already quoted him twice on early pages. As a child he showed a talent for drawing and later his teachers encouraged his creative writing. He was an inventor that held eight patents, including the traveler's fishing pole. This interesting figure crafted violins, and was a Civil War General (Swansburg, 2013). His name is associated with three U.S. presidents that include Abraham Lincoln, Ulysses S. Grant, and Rutherford B. Hayes. He offered the famous western outlaw, Billy the Kid a pardon. In 1880 he wrote the most popular book in America, Ben-Hur: A Tale of the Christ (Wallace, 1998). He is an example of an individual that journeyed through life improving intellectually, socially, and artistically.

The Butterfly Effect

The butterfly effect is the idea that trivial things can have a non-linear impact on a complex system. The term "butterfly effect" was coined by meteorologist Edward Lorenz in the 1960's (Lorenz, E., n.d.). Minor changes in a person's life can make your life better and more interesting. Recently, I have seen three family members who have increased their polymath repertoire, and because of these changes, they have more enjoyment in their lives and have improved their social likability by sharing their experiences. My wife has become a bird enthusiast and bought oriole and hummingbird feeders and learned a fast-paced card game from my daughter called Dutch Blitz. My son has taught himself to play the guitar, and my daughter has taken on a greater role for an organization called the InterVarsity Christian Fellowship. These activities may not be considered classic examples of the Renaissance man, yet in small ways everyone has enhanced their own lives and the lives of the people around them.

Three Polymaths

Both Leonardo DaVinci and Benjamin Franklin were considered geniuses and polymaths. A polymath is most aptly described as a person with various levels of expertise in a wide range of subjects. DaVinci's reaching into all arenas of life is staggering according to the twelfth Librarian of the United States Congress (Boorstin, 2001). Ben Franklin is no less an achiever with a massive commitment for improving the human struggle. DaVinci was clearly the artistic dreamer, a master of concepts that led to innovation. Ben Franklin the pragmatic, got down to the brass tacks kind of guy, driven to improving the functions of anything that caught his extraordinary wide vision. Davinci appears more futuristic, and Franklin appears concerned about the here and now. Ben Franklin was more concerned with useful knowledge. Don Clark is clearly a Ben Franklin type who is known only to family and friends, but nevertheless his life was extraordinary. Clinical psychologist Jordan B. Peterson said, "liberals start companies and conservatives run them (Shimshock, 2017)."

The Third Polymath

A late family member of mine, Don Clark is a solid example of balance. The tale of Don Clark illustrates the lack of time given to struggle with depression. Logistically a pie chart can illustrate a simple point. If I am doing one thing, I cannot do another. How much time did Don Clark have to struggle with depression? This is an interesting question. Before I explain his back story, let us look at his full life. These are some of his activities: he re-married, kept his physical fitness, enjoyed four-wheeling, waterskiing, bush hogging, gardening, farming, playing the harmonica, building a train from scratch to pull around grandchild and adults alike, fixing electric children's cars, singing alongside his player piano, carpentry, welding, fixing antique clocks, boats, tractors, snow blowers, lawnmowers, making friends at church, collecting antiques, going to breakfast with buddies, building fireplaces, swing sets, basketball hoops, traveling, attending fish fries to raise money, connecting with veterans of the Korean War, enjoying his hot tub, watching nature: cows, hummingbirds and moon flowers.

Don Clark does not sound like a person prone to depression; If the truth be told, Don Clark dealt with severe depression. When he was just thirty years old his first wife died of cancer leaving him with two young daughters. Don once told me that his player piano got him out of his depression. He would load various piano rolls into his player piano singing the lyrics visible off the scrolling rolls. Activity is a critical component to changing a negative habit. As a counselor, the right question to ask is, "What part of your life feels off balance?" Then together you can focus on missing pieces. Don was able to keep busy, but also found something he enjoyed. Depression is present in everyone's life at some point. Two, symptoms of major depression include social isolation and a decrease in activity. If a person addresses these two symptoms the outcome for recovery will improve.

How Balanced Are You?

Look at the natural instincts that humans need to fulfill, where do you need more activity or do you need less (exploringyourmind.com).

Survival instincts. These include the sexual drive, the fight, flight and freeze impulses. This includes obtaining food, clothing, and shelter.

Pleasure instincts. This goes beyond food, clothing, and shelter. This could include a better house, designer jeans, and eating better food. It becomes the refinement of the human survival instincts. For example, you do not just drink water to survive. You may also add flavors to it.

Social instincts. These are the needs for power, prestige, property, and friendship.

Cultural instincts. The impulses to gain wisdom, discover, and express yourself artistically, among others.

Now that you have identified areas to change. What are your polymath characteristics?

The Franklin/DaVinci Traits Identifier:

Franklin: practical and pragmatic, hear and now oriented, focus on essentials, usefulness, task oriented, inventive for improving life now, highly social and extroverted, effort driven.

DaVinci: abstract, theoretical, artistic, future oriented, perfectionistic, self-education, medication, dreamer, explore passions, form and function have equal importance, inventive for improving future concepts, introverted and kept journals.

If we place politicians on the Franklin-DaVinci traits identifier, we can select candidates to serve our needs. If you want someone to protect the future and the environment, a DaVinci type may serve your needs the best. If you want someone to cut through the red tape, streamline the delivery of goods and services to our citizens in need, a Franklin type might serve you the best. If your agency wants a grant writer, the creative DaVinci type may serve your agency best in the planning stage. The Ben Franklin type is orderly, he is best suited to make sure the requirements for the grant award are checked off and submitted. Leonardo DaVinci was a perfectionist and left the world with many unfinished projects, but when he did deliver the product was perfection. Ben Franklin on the other hand, was described as task oriented, hardworking, industrious, conscientious, and was called a walking committee. If you work in management and want your team to function at its optimal performance, knowing your team's polymath traits will enable you to assign the right task to the right person. "Those who dream by day are cognizant of many things that escape those who dream only at night." -Edgar Allen Poe, "Eleanora." Poe may also have realized that the world has two types of people, those that stay closer to the lines of practicality and those that take risks and wander outside the lines of convention. Dreamers look farther and deeper into possibilities.

The Franklin/Davinci Traits Identifier is another tool for opening up conversation. If you were to watch the television show *Parks and Recreation*, the Deputy Parks Director, Leslie Knope, shows more traits of a DaVinci projectionist always arguing with the Parks Director Ron Swanson. Knope, wants everything to be perfect, she likes detailed planning, she uses graphs and notebooks to outline her many dreams and is concerned about the legacy of her parks department. Swanson has pro-Franklin traits, and every agenda item is evaluated on its merit of usefulness. To determine your polymath traits, look at the traits listed next to each character and choose which traits best match your personality and style. Did you choose Franklin or DaVinci? You can choose to be more like your opposite profile to help you grow in new areas or expand in your natural tendencies. *The Crisis Gambit* wants you to discover limitless possibilities. Imagine if you thought like Franklin and needed an auto mobile. And imagine if you were DaVinci and also needed an auto mobile. The Franklin type may want to buy a truck for its usefulness. A DaVinci type may want to buy a sports car for its aesthetic form and beauty.

The Perfect Airport Dog

Humans are limitless in their ability to develop. I believe we are hardwired to adapt to life's struggles, and our DNA wants us to figure out problems. Airport security is concerned about breeding the perfect dog (Markina, 2022). Part of the problem, a domesticated dog does not own the determination that belongs to a wild dog or wolf. According to one experiment, researchers placed a bowl of food on the floor and then put a cage over it. The wolf never stopped trying to get the food. The domesticated dog tried for a few short minutes and then kept looking at the human in the room for help. Sniffer dogs that cannot find drugs or contraband quickly may give up trying, making them less effective. A client that gives up trying will be less effective in finding happiness. Parents that nurture too much don't let their child develop into proper adults. The dog that is nurtured can't survive in the wild like a wolf raised by nature.

The Cuba Trade Embargos

I have found it extremely intriguing, how ingenuity is created by the lack of resources and money. The United States and Cuba have had several trade embargos between them going back to the 1960's. These embargos hindered the Cuban people from obtaining new cars and automobile parts. This forced Cuban vintage car mechanics and parts fabricators to become some of the world's best. The number of classic cars on the road in Cuba is astonishing (anywhere.com).

Real Possibilities

People that go into retirement with the idea to give up working and solving problems are going against what it means to be human. Society's view of retirement appears completely at odds with how the mind works. Sir William Osler was a Canadian physician that has been described as the father of modern Medicine (Barton, 2019) mostly likely for promoting specialized residency programs for new physicians and he wrote the first significant scientific textbook of medicine. In 1905 during his speech at John Hopkins Hospital the incredible Dr. Osler made an age discriminatory comment (Weisman, 1999), "[…] but after age sixty the average worker was useless and should be put out to pasture." Negative thinking wherever it comes from must be eliminated. We no longer use words like mental retardation, addiction, or addiction program, they have been replaced by intellectual disability and substance use disorder or recovery program.

Switching careers and doing what you really love is the better mindset. In 1999 The American Association of Retired Persons dropped "Retired" from its name and created AARP Inc. To mean the American Association of Real Possibilities." Some of the keys to finding happiness, and real possibilities is developing a purpose. When a person has a purpose in life, they can start to choose actions to reach that goal. A counselor can suggest testing to take an inventory of an individual's preferences when they reach their golden years. Older citizens often develop different goals than those goals that were present in their younger self. This is a future oriented task that can bring order to the chaos that exists in most crisis events. The gifted retired person may realize they do not have to be a hamster on a mundane wheel.

Understanding your preferences could lead you to develop in the areas of creative arts, language, travel, sports, cooking, gardening, and community service etc. Although the possibilities are endless, nurturing old and new relationships is a keystone activity. Rage Against the Dying of the Light. The remarkable Don Clark stopped working in the steel mills at age fifty with a pension. I met him when he was beyond the age of sixty. In old age, this effective polymath never stopped working, exploring, taking on new things, he was a man of real possibilities, he never stopped learning and growing. Dylan Thomas (2004) addresses old age in his masterpiece poem, "Do not go gentle into that good night...Rage, rage against the dying of the light."

Flow Theory

Flow Theory (Mihaly Csikszentmihalyi, 1975), states that a person can become fully immersed in a feeling of energized focus. This state is also known as being in 'The Zone' (Biasutti, 2011). The author of Zen and the Art of Motorcycle Maintenance (Pirsig, 1974) also looked at getting your hands greasy as a fully immersed Zen experience. If you look at the Franklin-DaVinci trait identifier you may be struck by the fact, I decided to use two geniuses. I chose them because they are industrious individuals, and they are the type of people that would enter 'The Zone' often. I chose these individuals because of their sheer interest in life, having a willingness to create, and their thirst to learn. Don Clark is also a normal person with genius.

Roman Genius

The idea of a 'genius' originated in ancient Rome. The Romans believed that all people had a guiding spirit that attended them throughout their lives (Collins, 2016). Romans didn't believe an exceptionally gifted person was a genius; they believed that an exceptionally gifted person had a genius (Lambert, 2016). Franklin, DaVinci, and Don Clark had genius. We all possess this spirit or life force; it has to be engaged to become the best possible version of ourselves. Writing is paramount to reaching your genius. If a person was able to recite every state and its capital quickly from pure memory, or every country in the world, you may wonder if they are a genius. However, I could read it off a sheet. I have been writing creatively since sixth grade. I wouldn't waste time writing a paragraph by pure memory. A person has a spirit within them, but they need to initiate it into action. To push your genius, you must possess gumption. From Dictionary.com. Gumption is considered an informal noun, and it's defined as initiative; aggressiveness; resourcefulness, e.g. "With his gumption he'll make a success of himself." The second definition of this word: courage; spunk; guts.

I have painted over forty paintings, written four novels, shot eight under par in my best round of golf, I won a clay court tennis final in North Carolina, I have been in 'The zone.' The first time, I recall being in the zone, was at nine-years-old. I was determined to jump over the benches at an outdoor skating rink. I was often the only one on the ice, jumping over self-made snow boulders until I had enough confidence to try it for real. Time would escape, I barely knew my feet were freezing. To this day, when anybody asks, "What was my favorite all-time Christmas gift?" My reply has always been, "Battery heated socks." My goal is to help change a person's perspectives, find activities that can put them in the zone, and give your brain a rest from the daily trials and tribulations. My wife has been in the zone by scrapbooking or painting a room. My daughter will hit targets with arrows launched from her compound bow; my son will announce he is headed off to Indian Creek Park with his soccer ball to sharpen his skills. I look for the next remodeling project, book, or painting.

When helping others to brainstorm, people clearly can find comfort in writing, reading poetry, keeping a journal or getting involved in theater. The problem with some counseling programs is that sometimes they remain narrow minded in scope, by only fixing a small part of your life. Your natural instincts were listed above to let you see the possibilities for improvement. Another individual may exercise, attend sporting events, build furniture, or take on an auto or home remodel. All of us can have traits of both Franklin and Davinci individuals and will dwell more toward the middle. If you want to break depression, you must get in a zone. You can only get there by engaging your genius by using gumption. "Now, go take on the day," as said by Dr. Laura (Schlessinger, 1996). Or the phrase spoken in the movie (Haft,2021) the Dead Poets Society by Robin Williams, "Carpe diem, seize the day boys. Make your lives extraordinary!"

Neuroplasticity At Any Age

We all can change and acquire more polymaths' traits. According to Dr. Andrew Huberman, Ph.D. is a Professor of Neurobiology and Ophthalmology at Stanford University School of Medicine. He said during his podcast, "Young brains are incredibly plastic, but adults can take actionable steps to improve plasticity by engaging in focused bouts of learning throughout the day (Huberman, 2021)." Every competent coach or therapist believes in this statement, changing behaviors or how we function requires homework or practice. I believe that intelligence is less important than drive and focus. It is clear to me that some of us are better at using our brains to gain happiness and a sense of wellbeing. Some of us utilize our given environment to get the most out of it and others do not.

Macro View of Balance

The fleur-de-lis (mythologian.net) translates to lily flower in English. The three petals of the royal crest stand for: Those that work, those that fight and for those that pray. Bishop Adalberon of Laon, writing around the year 1020, wrote how, "society is threefold and how each group was interdependent upon each other." Those that work, those that fight and those that pray must work together to create a balanced society (medievalists.net.).

Fyodor Dostoevsky, the novelist that wrote Crime and Punishment (1866) put a spotlight on society's sick, poor, and oppressed, as did Charles Dickens when he wrote his second novel Oliver Twist (1838). Flash forward 150 years, the movie *The Joker* received the Academy Award for best actor, and it is a poignant example of the oppressed being overlooked, services and treatment being halted (Phillips, 2018). Part of finding balance is helping others find their ability to contribute. Financial resources are vital to any successful mental health program.

The Information Age

In 1985 I read an article on Alexander Von Humboldt, he was labeled the last universal man upon his death in 1862. The Prussian polymath may have acquired his thirst for knowledge by modeling his older brother who founded the Humboldt University of Berlin (Gardner, 2021). This was a moniker placed on Humboldt as maybe the last human to know all that was known in the knowable world. Today, the amount of information known to humans, a universal man or woman is best described as a mythical person, and the knowable world has exploded on the internet. Today, calling someone a universal man or woman is still a highly dignified compliment. With the explosion of the information age beginning in the1970's with computers, and still going on today with digital information at our fingertips, the tools to surpass the Humboldt brothers are accessible to almost everyone. All of us can use this information to evolve, in so many facets of life.

Zen and the Art of Motorcycle Maintenance

Media is a source to change your perception, the following examples will illustrate this point. In the book *Zen and the Art of Motorcycle Maintenance* (Pirsig, 1974) the author shows two people's view of the world and their problem-solving methods. One character has a romantic viewpoint that focuses on being in the moment, experiencing the emotion, and lacks mechanical skills. The other character's classic experience is heavily involved in the scientific method and rational analysis, who seeks to know details, to understand inner workings, and he is closer to being the master mechanic. The author reveals his theory called the "Metaphysics of Quality." Pirsig postulates that quality is the fundamental force in the universe stimulating everything from atoms to animals to evolve and incorporate ever greater levels of quality.

The Crisis Gambit's use of the idea of quality is quite different from Pirsig's philosophy. *The Crisis Gambit* looks at the need to improve an individual's quality of being a person. It does sound like the title to a book written by psychologist, Carl Rogers, *On Becoming a Person* (2011). My definition of quality looks at natural pleasure instincts that surpasses survival instinct. If drinking water is the survival instinct to survive thirst, flavored water is a luxury item that falls under pleasure instinct. In *The Crisis Gambit*, you can be a person living and breathing, going through the motions, or you can transform to a quality person, challenging him or herself to be that creative, contributing, and exploring, that lives a life that is beyond ordinary.

The Dragon Tattoo and Thin Places

I understand Asperger's syndrome better by reading *The Girl with the Dragon Tattoo* by Swedish Author, Stieg Larsson (2010). In Larsson's novel the character Lisbeth Salander has Asperger Syndrome (now autism spectrum disorder) and struggles to communicate and socialize. *Thin Places: Essays From In Between* book by Jordan Kisner (2020), I have a better understanding of obsessive-compulsive disorder as her main character struggles to fend off intrusive thoughts. I came away understanding the true torment that someone can suffer. On the Moth Radio Hour, I learned how schizophrenia affects secondary consumers. A college professor told a story about the journey he faced with his son who was diagnosed as having schizophrenia. The professor said, "I went from hoping that one day my son could become president to hoping that he would not kill someone." His son's untreated illness made him delusional, and he bought a gun and began thinking he had to protect the famous Alicia Keys, singer/actress he thought lived in a nearby apartment complex. Media is there to strengthen your understanding of clients outside the clinical setting.

The Crisis Gambit in the Land of Oz

One of the greatest American stories ever told from a counseling perspective is *The Wonderful Wizard of Oz,* written by L. Frank Baum (1900). The 1939 movie can be an allegory about humans overcoming adversity. Using *The Crisis Gambit*, we see Dorothy in a crisis as her dog is legally taken away, but fortunately escapes. Dorothy is motivated by love, anger, and fear to protect Toto. She goes into a survival modus operandi and chooses to flee over a fight or freeze response. Professor Marvel points out that Dorothy is trying to run away from her problems. Our lives have wicked witches that place obstacles between us and our goals. The people that encourage us like Glenda the Good Witch of the South or the Munchkins that plant the seeds for building confidence. People that doubt their own ability, like the Tin Man, the Scarecrow, the Lion, only to find through personal journey that they have within themselves the intelligence, courage, and the ability to love. Dorothy will begin to strategize in a rational state and develop a plan to address the problems in her life. When we believe in ourselves, we determine our own destiny, we hold the keys to our own liberation. If we let our minds project failure, that is the world we have chosen to live in. Like his fictional world, L. Frank Baum's personal life promoted the strength of women's and their equality, and he was a supporter of the suffrage movement to win the battle for women's right to vote (Albright, 2020, Torrey, 1918).

The Critical Incident Stress Debriefing: The Thousand-Mile-Stare

Critical Incident Stress debriefing is open to people who are hurt, saw people who were hurt or killed, or are themselves first responders, the goal is to lessen the impact of trauma, help those involved to recover, and to find people who might need extra help. Critical Incident Stress Debriefing (CISD) is one of the most well-known programs and was created back in 1974 by Jeffrey T. Mitchell (1997). When learning about critical incident debriefing, I was introduced to the concept of the thousand-mile-stare. This is a phenomenon, after seeing a tragic event, a person appears to stare off into space. I remember the driver of a pickup truck with this expression on his face, his girlfriend committed suicide by jumping out the truck that he was driving, and I arrived moments after the event. Someone with a thousand-mile-stare is someone dealing with posttraumatic stress, they are trying to handle an event that is a shock to their coping skills. The thousand-mile stare appears to happen when the brain is unable to understand something, like being in disbelief, or a trance of confusion.

Lord Montagne vs. Oscar Wilde

All of us adjust to traumatic events differently, some of us could develop a posttraumatic stress disorder (PTSD). For this reason, critical incident debriefing has the chance of causing harm. A person that wants to forget a traumatic event should not be forced to recount their traumatic event. Michel de Montaigne (1533-1592), Lord of Montaigne was one of the most significant philosophers of the French Renaissance, "If you want something etched in your mind, try forgetting it." Do no harm, resisting the re-traumatization of a person is also one of the four Rs of the Trauma Informed Care approach. Oscar Wilde was arrested and tragically imprisoned, for his sexual orientation. His horrible experience prompted his friend to give him advice: try to forget you were ever in prison. Wilde (2000) takes another choice, he wrote this in De Profundis, "To regret one's own experiences is to arrest one's own development...It's no less than a denial of the soul."

When helping someone in shock, we need to express the opportunity is available if they decide they need to talk. According to Critical Incident Stress

Debriefing, once your client is grounded, you can start the process: The Introductory Phase: Emphasizing Confidentiality. Fact Phase: each member is asked to re-create their role at the scene. Thought Phase: each member is asked to recall their thoughts (no derogatory or offensive thoughts should be directed at others). Reaction Phase: Identify emotions and feelings. Symptom Phase: ask what changes they or others have seen in their behavior since this event. Debriefing should be used cautiously; we do not want someone to relive the experience. I am a fan of using critical incident debriefing for first responders that analyze their delivery of services, the process, and level of efficiency. As I have shown above, Wilde has a different view than Montaigne, I believe both are correct.

Psychological Distancing

Psychological distancing (Nortje, 2021) is a term to help clients understand their separateness from everything around them. During a traumatic event, the mind can choose to distance itself from an event unconsciously. In extreme cases of distancing this may result in a dissociative fugue, a rare psychiatric disorder characterized by reversible amnesia for personal identity. This state can last days, months or longer. Dissociative Identity disorder (multiple personality disorder) appears to use distancing as a coping mechanism for extreme psychological and physical abuse.

Rasputin

Grigori Yefimovich Rasputin (Wikipedia.) was a
Russian mystic and holy man, he was revered by the
family of Nicholas II, the last Tsar of Russia. Rasputin is
said to use his healing power and soothing voice to
improve the health of the Tsar's son Alexei, who
suffered from hemophilia, an inherited bleeding
disorder. This is a medical condition in which the ability
for the blood to clot is severely reduced, a person with
this condition can bleed severely from only a slight
injury. It is believed that the mysterious mystic
employed hypnosis, meditation and breathing evenly and
smoothly to put Alexei at ease, helping to control the
bleeding. Diaphragmatic breathing (Nestor, 2021) is a
term used to describe breathing slowing, calmly, and
fully from the diaphragm.

Breathe

When treating a client in shock after a traumatic
event, it is helpful to get them to concentrate on
breathing evenly, use distancing, and assure them they
are in a safe place at this moment. A mother might do
this naturally, after her daughter runs home crying after
an encounter with a bully, her mother reaches out and
hugs her young daughter, "Don't worry, you're home
now, I got you." The mother softly strokes the top of her
daughter's head, you can imagine the frantic daughter,
calming, and her breathing slowing down and becoming
under control. James Nestor (2021) the author of
Breath: The New Science of a Lost Art, explains the
many proven physiological and psychological benefits of
breathing properly.

The Big Two Hearted River

Critical Incident Stress Debriefing (Mitchell, 1997) came under fire because it could do harm. Making someone relive a traumatic experience may not be helpful. Some people refuse to dwell on the past and want to move forward. If past trauma is not interfering with their functioning a counselor does not have the right to open that door for their client. The short story: "The Big Two Hearted River," written by Hemingway (1996) would be great reading for any soldier suffering from posttraumatic stress. In the story, a young soldier numbed by his war experience is re-connecting with nature by hiking, camping, cooking outdoors, fishing, and watching wildlife. I interpret this short story to mean that beauty still exists in the world. Some psychologists call exposing yourself to the world around you as grounding. This technique works by concentrating on at least your basic five senses, it will help you stay in the present moment. By focusing on your sense of smell, seeing colors, counting objects, or feeling textures, you are staying in the present moment. Grounding does have elements of meditation such as training attention, awareness, and reaching emotional calm. This is a valuable activity that can purify your innermost spirit.

Do not Open that Door

Here is an example of why you do not open doors until a person is ready. Years ago, I was at a wedding and a couple that I know was enjoying the festivities, laughing, dancing, and singing. They were friends of ours and over ten years ago their daughter was murdered in her apartment while enrolled at Bowling Green State University. The local news often brought up that this unsolved murder was being investigated by new advancements in DNA technology. Another guest at the wedding mentioned to the father that he had seen his daughter's murder case on television. The smiles ran away from the father's face, like a true trooper, he never shared that conversation with his wife allowing her to enjoy the night.

Outside the Box: Iacocca

At the beginning of this document, I shared my goal to apply as many disciplines as possible to a crisis that I have found useful. By reading the autobiography of Lee Iacocca (2011), a mechanical engineer by training, we learn the former CEO of Chrysler Corporation attributed much of his success to psychology classes. Lee Iacocca practiced the art of persuasion (Levin, 2019), Iacocca was willing to think outside the box and outside the realm of engineering.

Cosmology

The field of Astronomy looks beyond the limits of this world, a branch of Astronomy called Cosmology studies the origin and evolution of the universe. From a cosmologist's scientific view, there is no escaping change in the cosmos. To most of us a crisis will feel like a radical change and outside our comfort zone. Changing perspectives is the foundation of *The Crisis Gambit*. If we look at technology, there is no escaping change.

Step Seven: Goal Setting (evolution of quality)

Goethe & Carl Rogers

Goal setting can be a small step that can have far reaching benefits. *The Crisis Gambit* wants you to reach your highest potential. Consider applying this advice from Johann Wolfgang von Goethe (1749-1832), "Every day we should hear at least one little song, read one good poem, see one exquisite picture, and, if possible, speak a few sensible words (BrainyQuote.com). We are taking control and we are now on the road to self-improvement. Goethe was a poet, playwright, novelist, scientist, statesman, theater director, critic. This polymath is listed consistently in the top five geniuses of all time (Goethe, 2018). Self-improvement is becoming a person of quality. Carl Rogers, the founder of the humanistic approach to psychology, believed humans can reach self-actualization when they are put in the right environment. Rogers believed humans are primarily driven by the motivation to self-actualize or achieve their full potential.

Les Brown: The Ghost of Your Ideas

Les Brown (2016), the motivational speaker, used this analogy to point out failure. Imagine you are on your deathbed, and you are confronted by the ghosts of your ideas that you never acted on. They would be angry, disappointed that you are now going to die without bringing them to life. *The Crisis Gambit* is about developing a new perspective and a new coping strategy. The principal element for success is self-improvement. Ultimately, the equation is asking that you reach your potential and become a polymath in your own life.

Step Eight: Vision Casting

This step occurs at the end of *The Crisis Gambit* and can be used as an added safeguard. If you ask your client to visualize what will happen when they leave the agency or end the phone call, this will verify if your client's thinking has progressed into a rational state. It is time to summarize where your client is and how they have made plans to continue. This is clearly a bellwether event. If your client has decided to face life's problems with resiliency, then the session can end. If they are still in the danger zone, then safety planning must occur.

Lie To Me

A Health Officer is a person trained and qualified to identify risk; those risks include danger to self and others. A health officer's evaluation will generally have two extreme results at opposite ends of the spectrum. One, the evaluated person goes home with a safety plan, or two, the person is placed on a pink slip and admitted to the hospital. There are, of course, more options that include interviewing multiple family members, friends, co-workers, fellow students, etc., that can corroborate a story. The area between those two extremes could include calling the police, getting a second opinion from a colleague, or admitting a client for twenty-four hours of observation, etc. Much of your decision can come down to whether a person is telling the truth or lying.

WARNING

Warning: It takes a lot of training to spot a liar, this is not part of this training program. A person that is interested in exploring this area is encouraged to seek expert training. The information below is only a small window into a unique field. For someone wanting to increase their educational and professional growth, this may be an area of interest. Behaviors that are often associated with lying are observable. Psychopaths and a majority of sociopaths may be able to mask some of these symptoms. You will not know the baseline behavior of people you just met; however, there are common behaviors that can give you signs that people use when potentially lying. NO ONE CAN KNOW IF SOMEONE is lying unless they know the truth. Here we have deceptive behaviors associated with lying.

1.) Look at the body language of a guilty dog and its avoidant behavior, they look away, walk away, close their eyes, put their head down (Seriously Science, 2017). Humans are more subtle; they point their feet away from the interviewer, sometimes toward the exit. They can also put obstacles between them and the interviewer (attempting to hide), they may choose to sit behind a desk, rather than a closer chair, holding a book or papers above their toro. Humans also use evasiveness to lie, by not giving you an answer or a denial (Khalmetski, 2017). Saying, "I wouldn't do that," is not the same as saying, "no." A person acting somewhat withdrawn, not engaging in the conversation, looking down or lowering one's voice, is also evasive behavior.

2.) A liar can laugh their way out of a question and avoid the actual question (Wiseman, 2017).

3.) Perception qualifiers are used to dress up the lie with qualifying language: "... to tell you the truth, in all candor, honestly, frankly, etc." Making a great exaggeration of one's honesty, like promising and swearing about their word. Invoking religion, "I swear to God on a stack of Bibles" (Houston, 2012).

4.) Telling a lie takes more time than telling the truth, maybe 30 % longer (Britt, 2009). Excessive talking and giving unwanted details are common in liars. They can also use stalling, filler words like uh, I'm, like, etc. Answering questions with a question is a way to avoid the question and actually buying time to come up with excuses. This is also done by freezing, giving long pauses, thinking up ways to tell a story. Occam's razor is the problem-solving principle that the simplest explanation is usually correct (Duignan, 2022), it may also be the most truthful.

5.) During interrogations, CIA agents put suspects in swivel chairs to accentuate movements. Under stress an accused person will attempt to seek greater comfort by moving and adjusting their position. Being caught in a lie is uncomfortable, "Blood draws away from our nose, ears, and hands, which makes them colder. Therefore, a liar might be more likely to scratch or touch these body parts (Wu, 2019).

 6.) Compulsive lying usually involves embellishing the truth that they swear is true. This sometimes is caused by a low self-esteem, lack of impulse control, or simply trying to avoid getting in trouble for telling a previous lie (MantraCare Author, 2022).

7.) It takes about five seconds for your mind to form a lie. Look for discrepancies between words and facial expressions. Unconscious facial expressions cannot be hidden in those first five seconds. A video presentation by former CIA officer Susan Carnicero, who spent more than 20 years interrogating suspects, shows that a person who is "not being candid will show deceptive behavior within five seconds. (Conner, 2018)

8.) A liar can use exclusionary qualifying statements like: "for the most part "or "… to the best of my knowledge…" or "... fundamentally" "… as far as I know…" (Imke, 2019).

9.) Slang words and contractions are used by people that know each other well or belong to a similar social group or have a closeness to each other. Using formal language is another deception tactic. A liar may have reasons to appear not associated with another person and use formal language to appear distant. Distancing language: e.g., "I did not have sex with that woman." They could even try to blame the situation on you, removing themselves farther from the lie. Distancing language avoids using the words: we and us. They may say, "that man," instead of using his name. (Coffman, 2018).

10.) A liar may use what is called a Dominique Strauss-Kahn or freeze their upper body (Houston, 2012). This condition is attributed to the controversial figure Dominique Gaston André Strauss-Kahn (n.d.). He is a French politician, former managing director of the International Monetary Fund (IMF). Strauss-Kahn was involved in several financial and sexual scandals that put him on the witness stand. He showed this unique physical response while testifying.

11.) A liar may ask questions like: "Do you know what I mean?" or "Are you with me?" They want to see if you are going along with the lie. They can then smile at the delight of someone believing in the lie. It is called a duping delight (Ekman, 2012). According to body language expert **Dr. Paul Ekman,** a psychopath will smile due to, "the pleasure they get over having someone else in their control and being able to manipulate them".

12.) Liars will shift their blinking rate, most people do not blink when lying or blink very slowly, but 8 x faster after the lie (Leal, 2008).

Risk Factors

Male vs. Female

The anterior cingulate cortex (ACC) governs thinking and emotion (neurosurgery. directory, 2019). It is also the rational decision-making center of the brain. This region of the brain is larger in women than in men. The ACC governs risk. Ask any teacher about adolescent girls vs. adolescent boys in terms of managing behaviors. My daughter is a teacher, and she will tell you that the maturity and organizational level is significantly higher in females in her classes than males, at least during early adolescents. In an article called "Strong Evidence for Gender Differences in Risk Taking" (Charness, 2020), the finding concluded that there was an extremely robust result that women are more risk averse than men. In *The Crisis Gambit* equation, my argument is when the brain is in a more rational state it is less likely to commit suicide or engage in homicidal activity. If you were to see a mob full of guys or a mob full of women, you may conclude that one group is more likely to get into trouble than the other. Males have a much higher rate of completed suicides (Värnik, 2012).

Jealousy vs. Gain Homicides

Belinda Parker is a senior research assistant in criminology at Queensland University of Technology, her research is worth a highlighted mention. Men are responsible for 85% of murders committed, for multiple reasons. Women tend to commit "gain homicides" for personal benefit, such as money, business, and personal advantage. Women carry out homicides mostly for insurance payouts, assets, or due to being removed from a will, like after a divorce. "Jealousy homicides" tend to involve only male offenders. Men have a propensity to be more motivated by jealousy of their partner's perceived infidelities than by monetary envy (Parker, 2018).

Ego-Syntonic vs. Ego-Dystonic

In psychology, ego is a concept that simply describes an aspect of yourself. Your ego is to differentiate yourself from others. Ego-syntonic is a psychological term referring to behaviors, values, feelings that are in harmony with the needs of the ego. Ego-syntonic disorders include narcissistic personality disorder, anorexia nervosa, and schizophrenia. Ego-syntonic thoughts are acceptable to a person's belief system. Ego-dystonic (or ego alien) is the opposite of ego-syntonic and refers to thoughts and behaviors (e.g., dreams, impulses, compulsions, desires, etc.) that are in conflict, with the needs and goals of the ego, or, further, in conflict with a person's ideal self-image. Obsessive compulsive disorder and homicidal ideations are examples of Ego-dystonic thinking. Ego-dystonic thoughts are considered unreasonable thoughts, unacceptable or repugnant and alien to a person's beliefs. The terms ego-syntonic and ego-dystonic were coined by Freud (Burgemeester, n.d.).

Ego-syntonic case:

Suzie's mother died a year ago, but Suzie just cannot seem to move on. Suzie is still having a challenging time sleeping at night and concentrating in school. Last week, she was even caught crying in the school washroom. Other students have seen her take some pills. She wrote a vague social media post: telling her close friends goodbye. The school counselor called law enforcement. Suzie tells police she just misses her mother and claims she not suicidal. Love is a major motivator for action as we have seen in *The Crisis Gambit*. Suzie believes that to be a faithful daughter she must find a way to reach her mother, this is a false belief or delusion. Delusions can happen when a person develops major depression with psychotic features. The ego is your concept of yourself, and her recent delusional thinking is aligned with her self-concept of wanting to be a faithful daughter, this an example of ego-syntonic thoughts.

Ego- dystonic case:

Chris is constantly worried about catching colds. In fact, Chris washes his hands about twenty times a day. When asked, Chris says that he cannot afford to be sick, and then goes into a lecture about how many germs thrive in our immediate environment. Sometimes Chris washes his hands so much that they bleed. His landlord called the police because he saw Chris throw out his good butter and stakes knives. The landlord states that his tenant has been acting "bizarre." Chris has an obsessive-compulsive disorder (OCD) with symptoms that include negative intrusive and unwanted thoughts. OCD is an ego-dystonic disorder that puts Chris at a lower risk. Chris took precautions by throwing away things that are dangerous to avoid harming himself or others, his negative thoughts to harm himself or other people are considered alien thoughts and not consistent with his ego beliefs.

Ego-syntonic case:

Bridget is a middle-aged widow and mother who had lived with psychotic symptoms for nearly thirty years, she has been experiencing an increase in psychotic symptoms following the death of her husband who had helped manage therapy appointments and take medications. Her children reported they are worried, and they have a laundry list of concerns. They report she hears the voice of her husband and sometimes God accuses her of not being religious and tells her to go to church and pray. She is not sleeping; her grooming skills are barely adequate. Bridget has strong religious beliefs. Recently she became extremely distressed because the voices are telling her to seduce her priest. Gradually she gained some control of her hallucinations through medication and what she termed 'the love of my family and my God.' She has been having command auditory hallucinations from her husband since his death. She washed the car in the middle of the night because she had an auditory hallucination that her deceased husband told her, "Cleanliness is close to godliness." Her ego-syntonic thoughts are aligned with her concept. Command hallucinations that are identifiable are also a risk factor, especially if it is from people you trust like a dead uncle, deceased husband, or God. Her behavior is influenced by a delusional thought system she believes. Bridget command hallucinations from two people she trusts, her deceased husband and God. If Bridget were hearing voices of people in general or unrecognizable shadows, she would be less likely to have an impulse to act. However, Bridget is having ego-syntonic thoughts and needs immediate treatment.

Three Types of Rhetoric

Rhetoric is the art of persuasion used to convince an audience. According to Aristotle, the pillars are Ethos, Pathos, and Logos (Kennedy, 1991). Plenty of situations arise when you literally must persuade someone not to kill themselves. Letting somcone know you are there for them and you are available goes a long way.

Ethos

The first pillar is called Ethos. This pillar is used to convince an audience of the counselor's credibility. Adjectives that capture credibility are trustworthiness, ability, authority, reputation, and similarity. Two leaders from history used similar tactics to gain the trust of their followers. They include Juan Peron (Evita, n.d.), the former president of Argentina who took off his tie and rolled up his sleeves when addressing the working class. The Ugandan president, and military leader, Idi Amin also gained the trust of his men at the beginning of his quest by action. According to his biographer (Leopold, 2021), Idi Amin would never take his dinner until his men were served first. Peron and Amin were searching to gain credibility from their followers.

A nurse recently told me a story of three surgeons. She revealed that each doctor drove a different vehicle, an Italian sports car, a German sports car, and a Ford truck. Can you identify her favorite doctor? The surgeon that drives a Ford truck to work has conveyed his approach ability. A nurse admired his ability to appear to be like "one of us." This simple action goes a long way in keeping a critical connection with his staff. A crisis counselor gains credibility or Ethos by showing genuine concern for a person in need; a willingness to share in the struggle to overcome a problem. This is achieved by welcoming statements, open questions, and assurances that a client has called or came to the right place. Like Peron, Amin, or the surgeon that drives a Ford truck, your physical gestures, and non-verbal cues will be seen by your consumers.

Pathos

Pathos is an appeal to the audience to gain an emotional reaction. A counselor will achieve an emotional connection through engagement with body language, speech inflections, the attention he/she gives to a client or simply put the energy and effort that is given to a unique event. When Bennett Cerf died a friend at his funeral described the television personality from *What's My Line?* author, and founder of Random House, as a life enhancer, (Raymont, 1971) someone who loved life. Cerf said, "he hoped to make the sun shine brighter," by publishing worthwhile authors and making their work available to the public. If you show passion in your work, your clients will respond in kind. Cerf was an excellent example of someone bringing passion to their vocation. When you make eye contact with your clients, give them your best effort, it projects your interest in them.

The way we use words is important to stir emotions or pathos. Inspiring words influence our thinking, move us into action or strengthen our heart and soul. NFL coach, Vince Lombardi, is an excellent choice for the name on the Super Bowl trophy. To stir emotion in my son, there is a picture of Lombardi on my son's bedroom wall with this quote (BrainyQuote.com), "The difference between a successful person and others is not the lack of strength, not a lack of knowledge, but a lack of will." Recently, I heard the name of a fishing line called Unicorn Hair. The name of the line is an excellent way to make the product sound extra special and even magical. If you have a student athlete your treatment plan might sound more appealing if it is called a game plan. If we navigate, build a blueprint, design a strategy, lay the foundation, or challenge the wind, we are saying you are unique, and your situation requires special attention. A word can trigger a creative partnership.

Logos

Logos is the art of persuasion by demonstrating logical proof, whether it is real or apparent. Part of being an effective crisis counselor is being persuasive. Sometimes, a person might tell you they cannot survive without their significant other after a breakup. Letting a person know that feeling this way is a natural response and if you had no feelings that would be unnatural. Sometimes, it is appropriate to point out that they lived a life before their love interest ever entered their life. Statistically speaking, marriages before age twenty-five have a poor survival rate according to the CDC in 2011 (WISQARS). If a person wastes time in a non-reciprocal relationship, pointing out pros and cons will at least logically suggest the right course of action. Getting your client from an emotional or survival state into a rational state is paramount.

Political Speeches Using Rhetoric

Few speeches can match and inspire action to reach a lofty goal than a particular speech given by President Kennedy on the race to the moon. JFK spoke on November 1963: "Frank O'Connor, the Irish writer, tells in one of his books how, as a boy, he and his friends would make their way across the countryside, and when they came to a wall that belonged to an orchard that seemed too high and too doubtful to try and too difficult to permit their voyage to continue, they took off their hats and tossed them over the wall-and then they had no choice but to follow them." When JFK announced, "This nation has tossed its cap over the wall of space," the crowd cheered. Kennedy told the crowd the time for procrastinating is over, and a strong commitment has been made; his voice full of pathos stirred the crowd (jfklibrary.org). When a politician plays music, this will evoke a powerful emotion. Our leaders understand pathos when they play patriotic songs to exploit our emotions. President Reagan also stirred emotions and strengthened our soul during a mournful event (reaganlibrary.gov). After the explosion of the space shuttle Challenger, America mourned the loss of the crew and Reagan introduced the nation to words from the Aviator's poem (John Gillespie Magee,1941), During his speech he spoke these unforgettable words about the brave souls that died exploring space: "they... slipped the surly bonds of earth to touch the face of God."

The Suicides of Famous People

Sometimes we hear about famous or wealthy people that appear to have everything that most people would consider a clear life advantage. The son of Maria

Osmond (Blosil, 2011), the grandson of Elvis Presley (Silverman, 2020), fashion designer Kate Spade (Levenson, 2018) are people that appear to have unique advantages; however, they still have ended their lives. If you delve deep into a person's life and they have a history of substance abuse, I have noticed a proclivity for developing a physical type of depression. There is also a connection that exists through genetics. Depression, bipolar disorders, and schizophrenia run in the family. Before science showed biological connections for developing schizophrenia, family case studies in Ireland, Sweden, Denmark were used to illustrate these disorders and their re-occurrence in family trees. The mobile people in America, tending to be nuclear families, were lacking the traceable large extended families we can see in Europe. Americans tend to be unaware of their family trees or lineage (Murherjee, 2016).

When trying to persuade a person to stop their plan for suicide. It is also important to advocate the use of psychotropic medications under the supervision of a licensed Psychiatrist. Psychotropic medications often have a clear and beneficial effect for recovery. Biological psychiatry is an advancement in science that aims to understand mental disorders in terms of the biological functions of the nervous system. We have a chemical called serotonin in our brains that makes us feel good. Sometimes, people can deplete this chemical by substance use, and other people naturally lack this chemical. According to Foundations Recovery Network (2015), "All drugs interact with the brain in some way, and most affect how it communicates with other parts of the body." Researchers have discovered that the following substances influence serotonin in one way or another: Cannabinoids, Ethanol, Opioids, Psychostimulants. Fluctuations in serotonin may explain why so many people experience depression, anxiety, and other symptoms of lowered mood. Kevin Risher, an intellectual resource, close friend, and R.N. stated, "By using drugs you lower your full potential. You have a choice to function at your highest level, say ten out of ten versus nine out of ten or even a lower number."

13 Reason Why

The television series 13 Reasons Why is a worthwhile conversation. In this series a main character, named Hanna, commits suicide, and sends a box of video tapes to a friend. The video tapes have messages from Hanna to people she left behind (Asher, 2013). The Sandy Hook shooter also had difficulty communicating to make his needs known and experts believe his social isolation was part and parcel of his autism spectrum disorder (Rozsa, 2018). If violence toward yourself or others has a common thread it could be the inability to communicate. Although, subjects in this paragraph are both fictional and real, they can also be linked with people who have written detailed suicide notes. I have read several suicide notes in my career by making programs that give people a voice to communicate their thoughts could prevent violence and suicide.

Isaac Asimov (n.d.) said, "Violence is the last refuge of the incompetent to allow a dispute to come by to the point of violence, means someone wasn't smart enough to settle the matter before then." School shootings and suicides are problems that faces school program throughout the country. Programs that have a sounding board, a listening post, could provide an alternative to the suicide note. A suicide note is a form of communication. Understanding and using your brain to a fuller extent can give confidence and competence to navigate problems in your life. Asimov was asked why there is so much violence in the world and the answer is "incompetence." Suicide is violence against yourself and your loved ones, *The Crisis Gambit* will allow you to make competent and rational choices, and provide you with a bellwether, to self-regulate your modus operandi.

13 Reasons Why Not

I have thirteen reasons why you should not commit suicide in high school. Reason one, look at your problems as an opportunity, "It is through the pain of confronting and resolving problems that we learn." - M. Scott Peck (n.d.). Reason two, the world changes, it is the law of nature: "The situation we hoped to change because it was intolerable becomes unimportant" - Marcel Proust (n.d.). It is not a bad question to ask yourself, "In four years will this really matter?" The next four reasons involve love, in time four types of love can bless your life: Eros or romantic love, Philia or friendship, Storge or parent-child love, Agape means self-sacrificial love or helping others. Reason seven, you will miss the journey and will never experience life's blueprint questions: Should I join the workforce? Should I travel overseas? Join the military or go to college? What college should I choose? What career should I pursue? Who should I marry? Where should we live? Should we rent or buy a home? Should I live off the grid? Should we have kids? Should we retire? Reason eight, your suicide will never equal the pillars of immortality: to build a house, have children (or create a family of your own choosing), plant a tree, and write a book. Nine, high school is only a small window of time in a life full of stepping stones (Jackson, 2003). Ten, the world celebrates the underdog. Eleven, you have not likely even created a bucket list or began the journey.

Twelve, the friends you have today or do not have, does not predict your future friends. Thirteen, your skillset has not yet developed. In your future you could build many things: furniture, a house, a sport's program, a blog, a political movement, a business, or a haven for animals. Few people have an extensive reading list under their belt until after high school, learning the thoughts and ideas of other people will reward you with expediential growth. I like hearing that Jeopardy champion Matt Amodeo was upset looking back at his high school quiz bowl performance and he remembers missing an "easy question." He had thirty-eight consecutive wins on the game show, his expediential growth is in the record books (McCleary, 2021). Like most people, you have only scratched the surface of the miracles and natural beauty of nature, what have you yet to touch, hear, see, feel, or taste. Death will find you eventually, before that happens find and fulfill your mission.

Knowledge from the Past is Vital

In art, perspective is used to create the illusion of depth and distance. Basically, a painting or drawing must have a vanishing point to make it look real and three dimensional. The Greeks and the Romans used the vanishing point in their art and well as knowing the golden ratio, called Phi. When the fall of the Roman Empire occurred in the 5th century Gibbon, E. (2019), the world of art suffered a tragic blow, the vanishing point, or the ability to paint with a true three-dimensional perceptive was lost. Most paintings that come from the Middle Ages, also known as the "Dark Ages" appear one dimensional, flat, and even basic in ability. In the 15th century at the onset of the Italian Renaissance, the mathematical laws of perspective were rediscovered by the architect Filippo Brunelleschi (Famous Architects website), who worked out some of the basic principles, including the concept of the vanishing point, bringing back that which had been known to the Greeks and Romans a thousand years earlier. It took centuries to create building material for *The Crisis Gambit*, and I hope I have shown my genuine appreciation for those trailblazers and enhancers of life.

Conclusion

The transistor created in 1947 transformed the world of electronics. Its small size, durability, low power consumption, made possible the home computer, cell phone, and digital camera to name just a few inventions. In the field of crisis counseling, it is important to use *The Crisis Gambit* to move crisis counseling forward. I want this equation to be viewed like a transistor, a building block in the scientific process. We should never start at square one, like painters in the "Dark Ages." The strategies and techniques presented in *The Crisis Gambit* with practice can arm a crisis counselor, teacher, police officer for greater success. First responders will see there is more behind the curtain and use some of the teaching in this guide to improve their fieldwork. To the lay person or young student, it is my hope that you are inspired to reach the full extent of your life and career.

Crisis counseling is an art in its purest form, full of challenges and wonderment. I am forever grateful for all the hundreds of co-workers and thousands of consumers that have contributed to my journey, for I was fortunate to be a long-distance runner in my chosen vocation and at my chosen agency. Every crisis, every school shooting, every police encounter gone awry can be analyzed and understood by four components from *The Crisis Gambit*: the chain of events + core motivators +

modus operandi thermostat = unbalance. Restoring balance into someone's life, increasing their polymath traits is the key to living a life of unlocked potential.

The Crisis Gambit Equation

Step one:

Address medical emergencies and safety protocols

The philosophy: "Nothing within the bounds of human nature is beyond the wit of man, or woman, to solve," author of the Scotland Yard Puzzle Book (McKay, 2020)

The Chain of Events (United Nations & Sidney Poitier movie)

a.) Safety vs. Freedom (**Ohio Rev. Code, Olmstead decision, Tarasoff**)

b.) Rapport & dynamics of numbers (**Battle of Pease River in 1836**) Build a relationship: A sentence does two things: convey a message and continue to negotiate a relationship (from The Stuff of Thought by Steven Pinker).

 c.) Paraverbal Language, take notice of the tone, volume, and cadence of your speech (Fabius Quintilianus, book Institutio Oratoria circa 95 A.D.)

Step two: Four Core Motivators & The Motivational Triad (**ethology & behaviorism**) Lorenz & Watson a.) Love-5 types, Eros, Philia, Storge, Agape, love of expression

b.) Anger: anger (the emotion), rage (targeted & propaganda), resentment (long-term) Rabbi Twerski

c.) Fear: socialized & memorized

d.) Hunger: physical and psychological. Motivational Triad: seek pleasure, avoid pain, extend the least amount of energy. Drive Reduction Theory to maintain balance or homeostasis (Hull & Spence)

Step Three: Modus Operandi Thermostat (Yale neuroscientist: Dr. Paul MacLean), crisis threshold, agents of socialization

a.) Rational State

b.) Emotional State

c.) Survival State (crowded hour syndrome)

Step four: The Reaction (imbalance) & The Bellwether Monitor

Step Five: Polestar Strategy & Occam's Razor (Franciscan friar c. 1287-1347)

Step Six: Problem Solving: generating alternatives, better than your former self

a.) Life instincts: pleasure, social & cultural

b.) Find your polymath: Franklin/Davinci traits: pragmatic conservative vs. idealistic liberal, activate your Genius life force, develop gumption.

c.) Balance (Vitruvius circa 27 B.C. stability, usefulness, beauty), blueprint questions, 4 pillars of balance and the construction of hope. Identify areas of imbalance.

d.) Brainstorming (conscious) and incubation (unconscious). (**London School of Economics co-founder Graham Wallas**)

Step Seven: Goal Setting (the evolution of quality), patterns and routines. Realistic: negative forces are always present.

Step Eight: Vision Casting (construct and conceptualize your own evolution)

End of The Crisis Gambit Equation

Section II: The Bellwether Policing Model

INTRODUCTION TO BELLWETHER POLICING:

This is a joint venture between mental health, crisis counseling and law enforcement. MARCUS TULLIUS CICERO in 63 B.C. said, "Let the welfare of the people be the ultimate law." In the U.S., officers must be educated with constitutional laws including the 1st, 4th, 5th & 6th amendments during engagements with citizens. A thumbnail sketch of these amendments: The 1st grants you the freedom of speech and the right to protest peacefully. It also allows you to record interactions with the police. The 4th prohibits unreasonable searches and seizures. The 5th provides freedom from self-incrimination or right to remain silent. The 6th provides the right to be informed of pending charges. Officers' other concerns include knowledge of laws, ordinances, rules, regulations, and their own policing policies. "During a stop people care how they are treated, is the officer legitimate and lawful as possible." -Tracey Meares.

This Model Considers Other Models

The President's Task Force on 21st Century Policing was created by an executive order signed by United States President Barack Obama on December 18, 2014. It advocated the removal of policies that reward police who produce more arrests and convictions. The Warrior and Guardian Models are two distinct approaches to policing. The task force recommended developing programs that advocate the **Guardian Model** (Hudson, 2014).

According to James Q. Wilson there are three types of policing (Wilson, 1982).

1.) **The Watchman Style** is highlighting peace without aggression.

2.) **Legalistic Style** is aggressively enforced crime fighting by following the letter of the law.

3.) **Service Style** focuses mainly on service to the community and its citizens.

The Crisis Intervention Team (CIT) model was developed in 1988 in Memphis after police shot an individual having a mental health crisis. CIT programs are geared at getting mental health care to those in need.

The Bellwether Model: strives to serve the community and citizens, build officer trust, officer value, officer loyalty, and officer legacy (This a new program presented by this book *The Crisis Gambit*). The motto or mission statements of a few North American law enforcement agencies gives us insight into the passion felt in this field:

The Lucas Co. Sheriff's Office Mission is to provide: "A safe place to live, work and raise families"

The Royal Canadian Mounted Police use: "Maintiens Le droit" in French translated to "Uphold the right" New York Police use: Fidelis Ad Mortem in Latin translates to "Faithful unto Death"

San Francisco Police, "Oro en Paz, Fierro en Guerra" in Spanish translated to "Gold in Peace, Iron in War"

Atlanta Police: "Resurgens" (Latin for "Rising Again") is linked to rebuilding after the Civil War.

Toledo Police: "To Protect and Serve"

"HERE ARE EIGHT POLICIES THAT CAN PREVENT POLICE KILLINGS" by Alice Speri Sept. 21, 2016, Theintercept.com. Speri makes many good points that require officers to de-escalate, limit the kinds of force used, restrict chokeholds, use verbal warnings before force, no shooting at moving vehicles, exhaust all alternatives before using deadly force, require comprehensive reporting, and stop colleagues from exercising excessive force. The Bellwether Model agrees with these points, and creates a system that specifically shows in detail how a colleague can prevent a fellow officer from losing control as well as several verbal engagement tactics.

Police Officer's Creed (Laredo Independent School District): As a law enforcement officer, my fundamental duty is to serve mankind; to safeguard lives and property, to protect the innocent against deception, the weak against oppression or intimidation, and the peaceful against violence or disorder; and to respect..." Bellwether Policing agrees with the Police Officer's Creed.

Police Officer's Survival Creed (written by Mike Williams, Chattanooga Tenn. Circa early 1990's): this creed has merit; however, in modern policing it falls short. The creed cannot be printed here, so I encourage you to read it. I agree with some points; however, here are my criticisms:

Both parties surviving is the objective to strive for, being deceptive can cause mistrust and can escalate the event and pre-planned options will serve both parties better, trained skills and pre-planning is a must for effective policing and letting an assailant go is also a possible option. All reactions require a level of restraint, an officer should have the defender mindset and not the aggressor mind set. I agree an officer in peril has the right to defend him/herself and must remain on guard for this possibility.

The OODA LOOP

During a mass shooting tenets of the officer's survival creed must be considered. The mindset should be closer to the OODA Loop. United States (Ford, 2010) to help pilots survive and succeed in life and death situations. The OODA loop is the cycle **observe–orient–decide–act**, The OODA loop has become an important concept in enforcement (Papenfuhs, 2022).

Five principles of verbal Judo (Thompson, 2013)

Treating everyone with dignity and respect, asking instead of telling, explain why you are asking questions. Give citizens options, rather than threatening them. Explain a positive scenario + negative scenario and repeat the positive scenario again in that order. Remember everyone wants a second chance.

GOALS OF PROGRAM:

Law enforcement officials must employ Art and Science to avoid violence. All spheres of human activity have a margin for uncertainty. Planned reactions are rehearsed to elicit the best possible result. Policing at a high level is a calculated endeavor. By employing *The Crisis Gambit* equation, a partnership between crisis counseling and policing will be achieved. This program will increase the chances for allowing law enforcement officials to safely arrest offenders in a suitable and safe method. This program will increase diversion over arrest by employing mental health treatment teams to assess and evaluate citizens that suffer from mental health conditions that are overlooked in many policing programs. The officer will be trained to have an acute eye for discrepancies.

SERVICE AREA: Law Enforcement agencies and counties to be determined

TARGET POPULATION: male and female adults and adolescents, veterans, homeless, severe mental illness (SMI) and co-occurring disorders (COD) (1) schizophrenia; (2) bipolar disorder; (3) Schizoaffective (3) posttraumatic stress disorder (PTSD); (4) major depressive disorder;(5) delusional disorders; (6) substance use disorders (SUD); (7) an individual with a breakdown in coping skills. (8) Arresting individuals that are a risk to the community at large.

HOURS OF OPERATIONS AND AVAILABILITY: This program will exceed regular clinic hours (V.A. shortcoming) and offers real time intervention 24/7. This is a frontline intervention.

COST BENEFITS:

This program will reduce the prolonged reliance on emergency service providers such as police, sheriff, 911 operators, ambulance and EMT personnel, hospital and emergency room staffing. This program's cost benefits will far exceed the multi-pronged mandates to house, feed, punish, rehabilitate, and educate inmates & court costs. Financially this is a more effective chronic-disease management program.

MISSION STATEMENT:

This program will re-establish the officer as a guardian and protector of the people and no longer facilitate the warrior mentality. This Law Enforcement partnership will include quality mental health care as a key contributor to any successful program. A continuum of mental health care begins with acute crisis and mental health care.

BELLWETHER POLICE TRAINING

Macro View of Balance

The fleur-de-lis (mythologian.net) translates to lily flower in English. The three petals of the royal crest stand for: Those that work, those that fight and for those that pray. Bishop Adalberon of Laon, writing around the year 1020, wrote how, "society is threefold and how each group was interdependent upon each other." Those that work, those that fight and those that pray must work together to create a balanced society (medievalists.net.). Bellwether Policing is interdependent on the three folds of society. **In what fold of society do you categorize your police department?**

Social Disorganization Theory or Chicago Theory of Crime

From a macro standpoint, a person that lives in a healthy balanced society, also has a better chance at being happy. If your neighborhood has crime, homelessness, unemployment, poor community government and leadership, it will have some effect on your mental health. Shaw and McKay's core principle of social disorganization theory states that environment matters, and it has an explanation for criminal activity. These theories hold that people are not simply born good or bad, they are influenced by the people, social situations, and other external forces that surround them (Bond, 2015). **How can your police department become a positive influence in the community it serves?**

Broken Window Theory

James Q. Wilson wrote an article with criminologist George Kelling (1982) that stated that crime and disorder in a community are usually linked. If a window in a building is broken and it is left unrepaired, all the rest of the windows will soon be broken. To these authors it was important to fix the window as soon as possible, keeping order in a community. The broken windows theory states that visible signs of disorder and misbehavior in an environment encourage further disorder and misbehavior, leading to serious crimes. The principle was developed to explain the decay of neighborhoods, but it is often applied to schools and areas of business. You should never punish employees from speaking up, they are the one that will reveal the broken window. Humans develop patterns, if we accept our behavior that is less than honorable or we don't strive to improve or fix our shortcomings, we let broken windows creep into our life. **If a police officer sees his co-worker fail and turns a blind eye, does the officer perpetuate future failure?**

To be a Bellwether Trained Officer you must follow the following program:

1). **The mindset must be correct:** An officer cannot enter a situation with instinctive hostility and hostile intention (Clausewitz). An officer of the law must have strength in body and in mind to reach for high character. Ritz-Carlton founder, Horst Schulze, "We are ladies and gentlemen serving ladies and gentlemen." Calm awareness will keep you alive.

2.) Prepare for the belligerent and uncooperative citizen. The emperor of Rome, Marcus Aurelias prepared himself for the coming day, "The people you will meet today will be mean, ungrateful, short sided, frustrating, do not let them implicate you in their ugliness." ('the biographer' 395 AD).

A critical training step in Bellwether policing is how to react to belligerent people. Unfortunately, angry, disgruntled people are cruel. As an officer you are going to be exposed to a filthy mouth. **You are going to be called every name under the book,** your appearance is going to be attacked, your gender, your skin color are all going to be attacked, how you dress and how you walk will be attacked. Citizens will even criticize your family or even threaten your family.

3.) You must remember to leave your ego at the door. This is a ploy to turn attention away from them. Don't fall under this tactic. When you prepare for this, it will not throw you a curveball. The response is, "We are here to talk about you and what you are doing."

4.) Delay judgment against first impressions: What is the chain of events that led a citizen in question here? Ask open and probing questions. Never promise an outcome. Remember the **dynamic of numbers** one officer talking projects more equality, it does not feel like two against one. When you convey equality, you also convey respect. "We should not aim at being possible to understand but be impossible to misunderstand," Marcus Fabius Quintillius. When dealing with a group or mod, ask to speak to a leader or representative in private.

5.) An officer must remain aware of propaganda anger; therefore, we continue to call belligerent citizen's "Sir" and "Madame." Using words "Sir" and "Madame" can set a tone. You are making a person feel important, you must also remember their name. The motivation of anger is often used to gain a result. This happens all the time in war. The adversary is demonized by being called negative words: barbarian, cannibal, heathen, Nazi, and other derogatory or racial terms. Police fall into **"Us" and "Them" propaganda.** Humans have an evolutionary need to form a group, but this leads to irrational thinking. Both citizen and police officer are members of the same community.

The game plan configuration for one or two officers:

1.) Environmental safety through careful observation is the first step before any action.

If there is **only one officer** available, the officer must have a vibrating minute app that warns him to monitor his own presence of mind and to use grounding. When working alone the primary objective is self-monitoring: In summary, step three of *The Crisis Gambit* is called modus operandi. Your brain is triggered by the perception of an event and fueled by motivators. This results in your brain operating from a command center in various degrees called: rational state, emotional state, and survival state. The modus operandi is like a thermostat for gauging intensity.

With Two Officers: one officer will be the **negotiator** and one officer will be the **bellwether**. The negotiator is the team leader and the primary communicator with the citizen being questioned. The bellwether is the supportive and monitoring staff.

2.) **The negotiator will employ paraverbal language and non- threatening body language.** (Marcus Fabius Quintilianus, book Institutio Oratoria (circa 95 A.D.) I.E., take notice of the tone, volume, and cadence of the officer's speech. Your behavior will have a considerable influence on the citizen you are interacting with. If you walk up to the car looking like you want a battle, your work is off on the wrong foot. Look for commonality? Direct eye contact also shows that you are confident in what you are saying, and nodding will also assure your confidence and persuade an agreement. You must maintain eye contact to continue to project your interest in them.

3.) **The negotiator should employ active listening by summarizing the citizen's story, using paraphrasing.** Once they are heard, they will be more receptive to the officer's viewpoint. If you ask a question, allow them an opportunity to respond. If a client has a real problem, you will not have to look for it, give them an opportunity to talk and they will hit you over the head with it." (Brady, 1985).

4.) **A defiant citizen must be able to see the advantages for complying with an officer's request.** He must see that non-compliance has greater disadvantages. The negotiator must hinder the citizen from fleeing the scene verbally. "We have your license plate, we have your face, and your vehicle is being recorded on my body camera and on my squad car dash cam. (This unconsciously influences the citizen to think that fleeing may not be wise). An officer can also tell the citizen, that even law supports cooperation case examples: and lawmakers also need to tailor the law to uphold this principle.

5.) **The officer negotiator must strive to give the citizen three options** I.E., A.) Are you ready to hear why we pulled you over? B.) How do you think we can safely handle this situation? C.) Do you want me to explain your best options currently? Giving options **prevents the citizen from feeling threatened or backed into a corner**. Give the positive option first to gain their attention, then follow with the negative alternative option. If the citizen is impaired or intoxicated, you may have to slowly paint a detailed picture of their options.

6.) **If a standstill occurs. The officer must remain flexible and able to adjust to the situation encountered. Sometimes, the officer must wait for a more favorable moment for action** (Clausewitz). In an argument, the question, "Is this the hill I want to die on?" A retreat must be considered as an option. If an altercation is to be expected, then it can only be favorable to one side. If a better condition to act is possible, then the officer has sufficient grounds for putting off the time of action. This **prevents the officer from being threatened or backed into a corner.** A citizen feeling fear or wanting to avoid a penalty has the potential to run.

7.) **The bellwether officer must increase his knowledge of the circumstances.** a.) Estimate the power of a citizen's resistance & degree of tension b.) Can the balance of cooperation be restored? What level of polarity exists between law enforcement and civilian parties. c.) Where is the negotiator's command center: rational, emotional, or survival state. If he is emotionally compromised, the bellwether officer must intervene. When the bellwether orders the negotiator to stand down to regain control, he must disengage, and step back; they are the law. Often when humans face a survival threat, it triggers an emotional and instinctual reflex, it happens naturally and so quickly we might not even realize it is happening. The survival state is mostly reactive.

8.) **The bellwether must gauge the polarity between citizen and negotiating officer:** Trust vs. Mistrust (Erikson), Motivational Triage: Both officer and citizen want to seek pleasure, avoid pain, and extend the least amount of energy. Mistrust will lead to suspicion and communication problems.

9.) **When a citizen tries to pull you into an argument**, remain professional, remember the agency's creed. Using the power of speech to eloquently persuade others is in your toolbox. Plato's three types of rhetoric: **Ethos:** You have credibility, you are acting like a responsible officer, you walk, talk, and look like a professional. **Logos**: You give a logical reason why you are involved, and your information is clearly understood (all cell phones can translate). You will have to present logical reasons for working together, the pros and cons of choices. **Pathos:** We do not want to use pathos; we want to avoid making the situation emotional. Pathos is the persuasive technique used to stir emotions, making your enemy sound like a monster is an example. Instead, become like the Hemingway character that must shoot the hammerhead shark to prevent a boy in water from being ripped apart. An officer must show "grace under pressure."

10.) **Awareness of three types of anger** (Rabbi Twerski, Abraham, 2017), **targeted anger** (rage) will cause your modus operandi to move from rational to emotional, thus hindering your decision process. The feeling of anger has three phases according to Hasidic Rabbi Abraham Twerski: anger, rage, and resentment (Twerski, 2017). Simple anger is just the emotion. If you stub your toe, it makes you angry, and from that initial emotion, most people will let that feeling dissipate. Rage is an act of choosing to do something with anger. Anger is now at a higher level and the anger is directed toward a target. Refer to your citizen as Sir or Madame. Never use police slang and do not think about it. Words like: Perpetrator, offender, culprit, thug, gangster, idiot, bitch, asshole, etc.

11.) Pre-planning: no choke holds, no shooting into cars, never shoot someone retreating (scenario training and critical incident debriefing).

12.) To protect yourself and partner, to protect other citizens in jeopardy, exceptions exist. Beware the clear and lucid citizen, they could be near the edge. Beware "The Crowded Hour Syndrome" covered on page 80. When a person has decided to end their life, they can, in rare cases, have complete focus.

How to Respond to Five Personality Types
Preparing for personality types is empowering. An officer must prepare for the lie by expecting it.

Anger is often caused by unforeseen behavior. A citizen may not only choose between truth-telling and (explicit) lying but may also engage in evasive lying by credibly pretending not to know. (This is a pilot program and problematic personality types will continue to develop, friendly or cooperative citizens are excluded).

How to Respond to Each Personality Type
You're looking for dialog that reaches peace and discusses options in a productive way. The negotiator officer should always remember Ethos (credibility), Pathos (emotion) and logos (logic) into every conversation. If the officer is asked a question that also contains an insult, the citizen is attempting to incite pathos. The office could ask the citizen to rephrase the question without the attached insult. If the officer is told he is in a group e.g., "You police always…" Anytime you are categorized you can't respond as a speaker for a group, this has no logos. The officer must use your language to tell he/she is an individual. Thinking how dialog is constructed will also keep the officer using his prefrontal cortex or the rational state of his brain. An officer can also use a basis for transactional analysis that people can exist in three ego states: the adult (the healthy interaction), parent (critical talk), and child (victim language), always strive to remain in the adult state. Transactional Analysis is psychoanalytic theory used to understand behavior developed by Eric Berrne (Harris, 2012).

Personalities:

Type one: The Clueless Mouse who does not know how, why, or where.
Type two: The Imagination Dragon will tell you a long fairytale.
Type three: The Uncooperative Constitutionalist quotes the law and knows a lawyer.
Type four: The Emotional Hamlet is a bad dramatic actor.
Type five: The Combatant is full of aggression and ready for conflict.

***Personality type one*: **The Clueless Mouse who does not know how, why, or where**
The negotiator officer will ask the citizen, "What chain of events led them here? The officer must avoid being sarcastic and stick to the rehearsed script. The officer cannot have an ego. You will have to educate them on the law and the rationale of police involvement. You must avoid showing frustrations and irritation. Acknowledge that being stopped or involved with the police can be scary for some people. Give them time to collect their thoughts. Say, "I will explain your options, not to worry I'll do the work for you. Summary: Chain of events phrase + I'll do the work phrase will work.

***Personality type two:* The Imagination Dragon will tell you a long fairytale or sell you snake oil.**
To get them to stop talking, you must gain control by paraphrasing, I.E, "So, you are saying..., "I understand you to say (…)," "I'm hearing that you feel (…)" "I want to see if I understand you correctly?" "So, you're telling me (…) When you

summarize an event, the citizen will be compelled
to move on. The word "now" can be used. Keep the
Dragon in the box, don't let them wander too far off
course. "This is what I said," phrase will work.
"Now, we are going to this," "Now is the time to
move on, it's time to wrap it up." Summary: use
summary phrases + a now phrase will work.
Personality type three: **The Inflexible
Constitutionalist quotes the law and knows a
lawyer.** The Constitutionalists will use big words
to confuse and obscure what is really being said.
They will use legal terms or quote the laws in an
attempt to intimate or confuse an officer attempting
to perform his/her duty. "I said this," phrase will
bring them back on course.

You are likely to feel disrespected and angry in this
situation. "Reign in ego because it is an impediment
to leadership" Lee Scott former CEO of Walmart.
If you have no reasonable suspicion, no probable
cause, no plain view, no extenuating circumstances,
and no grounds for a Terry stop, or an investigatory
stop or investigatory detention, from the legal case
Terry v. Ohio, 392 U.S. 1 (1968). In a Terry Stop,
the Supreme Court held that police may briefly
detain an individual who they reasonably suspect is
involved in criminal activity. You cannot act on a
"hunch" You should let the Inflexible
Constitutionalist go.

They are looking for a fight, do not give them one.
Your time is valuable. When police have a
checkpoint, and pull over a law quoting a citizen,

refusing to give his name, and quoting amendments, officers cannot waste time: The officers should have a written decree of what they are doing and stick to the script. Example, we are trying to devise a plan that will protect you, your family, and your neighbor from intoxicated drivers. Our county had # of crash, # fatalities due to intoxicated drivers. The following authority decided by decree that this is the best method of handling this problem. Because phrases also work. You are having a police checkpoint because it is important. Summary: If they try to put words in your mouth, use: I said this phrase + A because phrase will work to explain your logic + Ask them to ask the same question without the insult attached.

The checkpoint: must pre-plan for uncooperative citizens. If they refuse to give information and move into action, your time is valuable. A.) Let them go. B.) Write a citation for obstruction of legal business. In 1990 the U.S. Supreme Court ruled in favor of constitutionality of sobriety checkpoints, some states have deemed sobriety checkpoints illegal as they violate the fourth Amendment as police typically lack probable cause.

Personality type four: **The Emotional Hamlet is a bad dramatic actor.**

This person could have histrionic personality features. They have a lot of absolute thinking. Their emotions are at a higher level than that of the circumstances. They use a lot of extreme ways of looking at their problem. They use the words: always and never. "I will never find another job, I'm always going to fail," "The whole world is a mess." Your job is to break their view into manageable parts. There is no need to change their "whole life." You cannot answer the questions: I am, I was, I were, you can only look at behavior that is effective or ineffective. No situation is extremely one way, a situation is not black or white, there is always the gray middle ground. Summary: Let us work on one thing at a time phrase + a now phrase will work.

Personality type five: **The Combatant is full of aggression and an officer must be ready for conflict.**
a.) Build a rapport and employ active listening and paraphrasing, if The Combatant is not talking or yelling due to anger, find a way to comment on this condition. "I just want to talk to you, I'm here to help. I'm here to help." "I can see you're angry. I'm not here to fight you, I don't want to get injured, I have a softball game next week." You are honestly trying to understand their point of view. "It seems like we live in an angry world, and there are a lot of things to be angry about, can you tell me what's bothering you?" When you mentioned you play softball, The Combatant hears you as a person not just a cop. Tell him he is right, in some way, this will lower his resistance.

b.) Your acknowledgement of them and their anger is a show of respect. Remember your calm paraverbal language to have The Combatant

shadows you. The tone, volume and cadence of the officer's speech is paramount, behavior begets behavior. The Combatant is in a crisis state, what is heard is more important than what you say, their comprehension of your words will likely be poor.
c.) Remember the dynamic of numbers, only one talker, the negotiator.

d.) When an officer that is feeling threatened his or her own modus operandi is also moving. If The Combatant calls you a name, they are looking for targeted anger. You will try to avoid being a target by remaining informed, friendly, and professional, do not react to the insult.

e.) The balance of language is key, if their language is quick, loud, and abrupt, your language cannot shadow theirs. If you nod and call them their name, if you do not have a name, use respectful language like Sir, Madame, or Miss, young man, etc.
f.) Give The Combatant options, he or she will feel less cornered and more in control. You can always talk about your diversion program, when a person is showing a breakdown in coping skills or signs of mental illness. "We have counselors and social workers standing by, I can take you to them, if you are interested?" Complete what the client is willing to do, before taking compulsory action.
Summary: I just want to talk to you + I'm here to help + tell him you are not here to fight or get injured phrase + tell them you can see how angry he is phrase + Tell him you want to hear his story phrase + Tell him he is right about somethings

phrase + Tell him you would like to work on options together and you are willing to do most the work phrases (coming up with options). If you find a way to make the client laugh, his anger will disengage a little, he/she will become more comfortable and they will become more rational.

How to determine a diversion over arrest:

THE SIX LEVEL SYSTEM: (level 1-3, appropriate for diversion center, level 4-5 open to consideration)

LEVEL 1: Client is cooperative and willing to seek treatment but has a breakdown in coping skills.

LEVEL 2: Client is cooperative, has a breakdown in coping skills, suicidal & homicidal thoughts-no plan.

LEVEL 3: Severe Mental illness including (1) Schizophrenia; (2) Bipolar Disorder; (3) Schizoaffective (3) Posttraumatic Stress Disorder (PTSD); (4) Major Depressive Disorder;(5) Delusional Disorders (6) Substance Use Disorders (SUD) (consider ego-syntonic vs. ego-dystonic disorders).

LEVEL 4: Client has mental illness and homicidal or suicidal ideations. (Pink-slipped for treatment).

LEVEL 5: Client not agreeable to treatment, having homicidal and suicidal plans. (Pink-slipped for treatment) Client not agreeable to treatment, having homicidal and suicidal plans. (Pink-slipped for treatment)

LEVEL 6: Client clearly at risk to the community at large, violent, requires higher level medical treatment (physical restraints required)

CAVEAT LEVEL: It is important to realize that sometimes a person meeting the criteria for psychopath and sociopath or with the definition of antisocial personality traits, may feign symptoms, employ the falsification of or exaggeration of illness to gain an external benefit, and use malingering tactics.

Contact a diversion specialist:

A.) Law Enforcement will call the diversion Intake line and ask for the **Diversion Specialist**. This will alert staff to route the call to the program area. The **Diversion Specialist** will complete the **Diversion Intake Sheet.** Calls of this nature are almost exclusively from dispatch. At this point staff will take the name, birthdate, estimated time of arrival, and any situational information to cross check alerts and medical information. The specialist can offer Outreach if police transport is less desirable. A collaborative partnership between law enforcement and the diversion center will create a mobile team consisting of one officer + one diversion team member (also known as the bellwether).

Engage Stage II: Our action team (the meet and greet), health assessment, mental health assessment, cognitive behavioral therapy (CBT), side-effect monitoring, frequency, Opiate-substitution maintenance therapy, patient capacity, hours of operation, provider workloads: monitoring symptom levels (create rounds board, symptom monitor).

THE ACTION TEAM:

1. LAW ENFORCEMENT OFFICERS

2. DIVERSIONS INTAKE SPECIALISTS,

3. NURSE PRACTITIONERS, REGISTERED NURSE, PSYCHIATRIC NURSES,

4. SOCIALWORKERS COUNSELORS,

5. CLINICAL SUPERVISORS

6. MENTAL HEALTH TECHNICIANS

7. HEATH OFFICERS

8. CRITICAL INCIDENT DEBRIEFERS

9. BELLWETHER TRAINERS

PROGRAMS: THE CONTINUUM OF MENTAL HEALTH CARE BEINGS WITH ACUTE CRISIS.

10. DIVERSION INTAKE PHONE LINE

11. DIVERSION MOBILE RESPONSE TEAM

12. ACUTE DIVERSION PROGRAM

13. DIVERSION Center 24-hour observation room

14. OUTREACH 24/7 (3 Vans, 1 Car, 1 Bus)

15. EMERGENCY SERVICES

16. RECOVERY HELPLINE

17. LIFELINE

18. CRISIS LINE

19. CSU 16 ADULT BEDS

20. CACSU 8 ADOLESCENT BEDS

How the program runs:

Law Enforcement /Dispatch identified an individual that requires diversion.

1.) Law Enforcement or Dispatch will contact an on-board mental health agency by calling the INTAKE LINE: 999-999-9999 and request a Diversion Specialist. This will alert staff to route the call to the program area. The Diversion Specialist will complete the Diversion Intake Sheet. Calls of this nature are almost exclusively from dispatch. At this point staff will take the name, birthdate, estimated time of arrival, and any situational information to cross check alerts and medical information by records. The Diversion Specialist will expect the client to hand off as law enforcement transports directly to an on-board mental health agency or they will organize a Mobile Crisis Team. A Mobile Crisis Team Member can be dispatched 24 hours a day to provide assessment, de-escalation, safety planning or scene support when an individual with behavioral health concerns may be experiencing a crisis. This is a real time intervention program.

2). The location of the event and the one or two assigned mobile staff will be placed on the Intake board along with their cell phone number(s).

3.)   A standby in-house nurse will be alerted that a mobile team is taking to the field and their name will be placed on the Intake Board. The nurse will review the client's chart if a prior chart exists. The Mobile team will call the contact agency's standby nurse for medical advice when needed (the nurse must be available to answer the call without delay and greet new arrivals).

4.) Law enforcement will update the Diversion Specialist with available information. The goal is to have a mental professional evaluate the situation first hand whenever possible.

5.) The Mobile team (must have at least one MHP and preferred health officer when available) will greet officer (s) at the requested location. (In pure transportation situations mental health technicians MHTs may be employed with supervisory approval) They will go to the site and receive a handoff from police. Police may assist getting the client in the van. (The MHTs can call base for consultation.)

6.) The MHP will employ crisis training to defuse the situation and engage clients (or family). A.) Assess Safety (B.) Build a Rapport (C) Give options to the consumer other than jail

7.) The officers and MHP will use the Level scale to determine treatment options.

8.) Law Enforcement will aid in getting clients into the outreach van. If only one mobile staff is available, Law Enforcement will transport to a diversion agency unless there is a gender match, and the client is considered cooperative.

9.) Uncooperative clients that require involuntary status will be placed on a pink (emergency application) by a Health Officer (if qualified) or the field police officer. The client will be transported back to the mental health diversion location.

10.) A continuum of mental health care begins.

11.) A future training for mental health clients is also geared at training them how to interact with law enforcement to avoid unnecessary violence by police or client, I.E., keep your hand visible, follow police commands, announce that you went through police interaction training, explain you want to cooperate although your mental illness does not help you communicate, etc.

Enable: STAGE III linkage, social-skills training, supported employment with individual assistance, mental health intensive case management (MHICM), family education. Briefly, *patient outcomes* (e.g., symptom severity, patient satisfaction, quality of life, functional status) are influenced by both the structure of care (e.g., type/level of staffing, how many patients can be served, hours of operation, provider workloads, availability of evidence-based practices) and the process of care.

Evaluate: STAGE IV:

Quality: Deliver high-quality care to its beneficiaries and to find and rectify problem areas, support quality measurement—review electronic medical records, telephone surveys, this is acute care and new quality measurement will be created, patient satisfaction, quality of life, functional outcomes.

Outcomes: We evaluated strength of the process-outcome link according to the three-tiered grading system developed by the U.S. Public Health System Task Force (USPHSTF).

Patient outcomes (e.g., symptom severity, patient satisfaction, quality of life, functional status)

Standards the program will adhere: Our agency adhere to policies or standards created by Ohio Department of Alcohol and Drug Abuse Services (ODADAS), SAMHSA's Best Practices, Joint Commission on Accreditation of HealthCare Organizations (JCAHO), the Ohio Department of Mental Health (ODMH), HIPAA: The Health Insurance Portability and Accountability Act of 1996, Ohio Counselor, Social Worker & Marriage and Family Therapist Board, the Ohio Board of Nursing. Also, our employees are Bargaining Union employees, and we adhere to that SEIU contract. The Mental Health & Recovery Services Board of XXXX County provides funding with money that requires detailed reports that measure program quality and utilization, peer, and consumer review. If we want to be paid, we must follow Medicaid, Medicare, and private insurance policies for billing. Staff must be trained yearly in CPI (The Crisis Prevention Institute is an international training organization that specializes in the safe management of disruptive and assaultive behavior) and 1st Aid, CPR.

PROGRAMS:

OUTREACH 24/7 (3 Vans, 1 Car, 1 Bus)

EMERGENCY SERVICES (SERVICE AREA COUNTIES TO BE DETERMINED)

RECOVERY HELPLINE

LIFELINE

CRISIS LINE

CSU 16 ADULT BEDS

CACSU 8 ADOLESCENT BEDS

URGENT CARE

HEALTH OFFICER TRAINING

Until recently, a health officer required five years in the mental health field, a master's degree, a recommendation from your agency's CEO, a letter of recommendation from a qualified professional in your agency and a recommendation from a professional outside of your agency. The nominated health officer would have to have an active license by the State of Ohio, attend health officer training, pass an FBI background check, be nominated by a Health Officer Committee composed of local agency leaders and then get the final approval from the governing mental health board. It may also require participating staff to be trained in First Aid, CPI (The Crisis Prevention Institute), and CPR & AED.

The Game Plan Proposal (stop mass shootings)

1. Utilize the Bellwether Policing & Diversion over arrest models in conjunction with this proposal program. Crisis intervention will be based on The Crisis Gambit equation.
2. Teach how the mind works during a crisis starting in 6th grade using *the Crisis Gambit* equation. Each student will develop their own crisis plan within the acceptable framework. Just like fire drills, lockdown drills, tornado drills, the crisis plan will be reviewed quarterly with scenario drill training. When a student starts falling into a crisis, they have a plan to return to rational thinking.
3. The course curriculum will teach *The Crisis Gambit* equation, review agents of socialization, the danger of following a herd mentality, review how the mind falls into targeted anger, propaganda anger, "us" vs. "them" mentality, The Werther Effect, The Columbine Effect, crisis threshold development, and three key stages to address from Erikson: Industry vs. Inferiority, Identity vs. Role Confusion, Intimacy vs. Isolation,
4. The completely anonymous crisis hotline
5. Billboard and ad campaigns that identify social media influencers that are in jail or lose their lives due to targeted or random violence.
6. Address road rage, target anger and propaganda anger in driver's education courses.

7. In 1840's France 237 people died by suicide due to Ennui (boredom). In this century, it remains a current problem. To attack Ennui a person must always grow in some way.

8. The baby lab at Yale university clinical proves children know the difference between right and wrong, the age of criminal responsibility must be lowered, power of the unconscious mind.

9. The agents of socialization and the herd mentality will be discussed in scenario training & the power of incubation.

The pride of Toledo:

The rich history of the city of Toledo and its surrounding area has always included its strategic Lake Erie location, a location that has fostered the development of businesses run by mobsters to legitimate businesses like the twenty-three In & Out Marts named by my mother-in-law, or Tiedtke's Department store, Champion Spark Plug, and the Waldorf and Commodore Perry Hotels to name just a few. The legacy of businesses like Tony Packo's, Barry Bagels, Marco's Pizza, the Anderson's, Jeep, and Owens Corning still leave an imprint. Toledo also attracted a stellar list of movie stars and political celebrities that included: Muhammad Ali, Eleanor Roosevelt, Winston Churchill, nine United States Presidents, and natives like Jamie Farr, Gloria Steinem, Anita Baker, Danny Thomas, and rapper Hunter/Prey to name just a few. Our Zoo and Art Museum are world renowned. Simply put we have much to be proud of. Rescue, Inc. is another notable agency worth mentioning, and it happens to be my home agency.

Bob Latta's Question:

On January 23rd, 2020, Ohio Congressional Representative Bob Latta along with the Federal Communications Commissioner Ajit Pia, visited Rescue, Inc. They were promoting the use of Lifeline and the three-digit national hotline, 9-8-8. This was an exceptional show of support and recognition for our agency. Congressman Bob Latta asked a simple question; "What do you say to someone in crisis?" Our team asked me to field this question. To me this was an infinite question, almost like asking, "What is the meaning of life?" I had just provided a fifty-five-minute PowerPoint training program for counselors answering the crisis line. I was expected to give a short and quick response. Although there remain millions of responses to that not-so-simple question, this book fundamentally supports one possible theoretical construct. It is my hope that this literary project can be transferred into a six-week course of instruction. And subsequently, when Congressman Bob Latta reads this book he will gain an understanding of the science, the art, and the fuller complexity of tools first responders use to get the real answer to his question.

Author's Note: The inspiration

Two events merged to plant the seeds for *The Crisis Gambit.* The first event began in 1994 when I was reading the Journal of Lewis and Clark and I became astounded by the clarity in which Merriweather Lewis described plants, animals, and birds in which he

247

witnessed for the first time between 1804 and 1806. It was no wonder that Thomas Jefferson chose Lewis to lead an expedition across the continent and report firsthand about the land acquired in the Louisiana Purchase that would eventually provide the United States with fifteen additional states. The second event occurred by having parents living in southern Tennessee. To reach my parents, my wife, children, and I would sometimes take a scenic drive on the Natchez Trace Parkway, a historic travel corridor used by American Indians and early settlers. The Parkway stretches 444 miles; it is maintained by our National Park Service. Visitors can simply drive through the miles of forest, take walking trails, stop for views of wildlife, waterfalls, overlooks, camping areas, rest stops or visit historical markers. Around the year 2000, I stopped at historical marker mile post 385.9 that had a monument dedicated to Merriweather Lewis and this is also the location where he met his death by suicide.

I read the journals of the Lewis and Clark's expedition and I was saddened to learn a man with such an extraordinary mind might have committed suicide at the age of thirty-five. How did Merriweather Lewis categorize plants or animals completely unknown to non-native Americans? What were his potential motives for suicide?   I left these two questions on the table for over twenty years.

To understand question one; I looked at Merriweather's use of taxonomy, the branch of biology that classifies all living things. It was developed by the Swedish botanist, Carl Nilsson Linnaeus who lived during the 18th Century (1707-1778). He also used a classification system some of you may recognize called the taxonomic hierarchy, which ranks from general to specific: kingdom, phylum, class, order, family, genus, and species. Linnaeus was the first to use a uniformed system to define and name plants and animals. This classification system was available to Merriweather Lewis during the Corps of Discovery Expedition that took place between 1804 and 1806. So, I gained an understanding of my first question, but what about question two? What was his motive for suicide? The Eureka moment happened, I decided I would develop my own systematic approach; I would classify and categorize the crisis that can lead to suicide.

Author's Note: biases against rating scales.

I chose not to categorize a crisis by using numbers. The Diagnostic and Statistical Manual of Mental Disorders, published by the American Psychiatric Association, was moving away from numbers to qualify circumstances in a person's life. This could be seen with the removal of the Global Assessment of Functioning Scale and Psychosocial Stressors Scale on Axis IV of multiaxial versions in the DSM-III-R and DSM-IV. The reliability and validity of using numeric rating scales were evaluated by professionals with mixed results. I read in the DSM III that the death of a child and the death of a spouse had different numbers in terms of psychological stress. I saw this as a significant flaw, everyone will determine their own magnitude of grief and an individual experiencing a personal tragedy of this proportion could be offended by giving their personal level of grief a number. Therefore, *The Crisis Gambit* looks at motivations in a crisis as a key to understanding its magnitude.

14,400 Psychiatric Evaluations, 74,000 Cases

As line staff, then a working supervisor, then director, I completed 1 to 7 psychiatric evaluations daily using the Diagnostic and Statistical Manual (DSM), this is the standard classification of mental disorders used by mental health professionals in the United States. Depending on the clinician, the average time needed to complete a psychiatric evaluation takes 1-3 hours, and time differences between completing an update assessment and a full assessment. Unofficially, if I worked only 48 business weeks a year and completed 3 psychiatric evaluations per day that would equal a low estimate of 720 evaluations per year. If I worked 20 years that would equal 14,400 completed psychiatric evaluations. However, I worked for Rescue, Inc. for 34 years. This also includes fielding 2-6 crisis calls daily, assisting with triage, completing health officer evaluations at area hospitals or in the community, authoring admissions to our adult and adolescent crisis units, or for private hospitalization or state hospitalization diversions. I also would take report or listen to report from Intake, CSU and CACSU daily. I may consult and concur on the diagnosis or disposition of a client, respond to code "violet" that could result in a client being placed in restraints or seclusion. Now, if I worked for 34 years, was involved in 10 cases per day from multiple sources and again only worked 48 weeks (a business week of 5 days) or 240 days per year, not including being on-call for the agency, I would have been exposed or involved with 81,600 people in some form of a crisis or mental health condition. This is a conservative number, and the actual cases could be significantly higher.

My Mentors:

Mrs. Couchman: 2nd grade teacher. Robert Storm: high school teacher and basketball coach. Tom Seagar high school tennis coach. Richard Proud: County Commissioner, Principal, President & Owner of the Sport Corner, Inc. Sister Beth Butler: Siena Heights University (SHU) Professor. Sister Eileen Rice: Professor SHU. Fredrick Dobens: Dean of Students SHU. David Barnes: Student Activities Director SHU. Dr. Steven Weintrob: Director of Adrian College Counseling Center. Psychiatrists: Dr. Kul Gupta, MD & Dr. Agha Shahid, MD. John DeBruyne, President and CEO of Rescue Mental Health and Addictions Services.

Grants:

First Responder's Training: crisis counselors, police, airport security

Criminal Justice Diversion

Law Enforcement Scenario Training

Health Officers training

Road Rage and Driver's Education

A bellwether program for NBA and College Basketball, the Academy Awards

School shootings

Airport Security

Restraining Orders and their Failure

Endnotes

A shadow of your former self. Cambridge Dictionary, cambridge.org Retrieved 2 Feb 2022

Acheson, D. (1987). *Present at the creation: My years in the State Department.* New York: Norton.

Adams D. (2007). Why do they kill: men who murder their intimate partners (1st ed.). Vanderbilt University Press.

Aerial View (Apr 24, 2019) The Most Important
Moment in Jordan Peterson-Zizek Debate
https://www.youtube.com/watch?v=foUATcfD9rg.
Retrieved February 4, 2022

Aesop. (2007). The Horse and Goats. In D.L.
Aeschliman (Ed.), Aesop's Fables (pp. 102-116). New
York: Penguin Group

Alan Jackson (Apr 12, 2013) "Remember When" —
Live.
https://www.youtube.com/watch?v=xM3_dtGyspQ.
Retrieved February 03, 2022.

Albright, Jane (March 1, 2020)
https://www.ozclub.org/2020-suffrage-and-oz/.
Retrieved 2 Feb 2022.

Alexander, S., Pollack, S., Silliphant, S., Poitier, S.,
Bancroft, A., Savalas, T., Hill, S., ... Olive Films.
(1965). The Slender Thread.

Allen;Whitcomb, Dan (Oct. 03, 2017). Las Vegas
shooting: Stephen Paddock described as wealthy,
gambler, loner. Retrieved February 7, 2022,
LiveMint.com Website:
https://www.livemint.com/Politics/pE4ookW3sXYQcB
wVPWbsrI/Las-Vegas-shooting-Stephen-Paddock-
described-as-wealthy-gam.htm.

American Psychiatric Association (2017). Diagnostic
and Statistical Manual of Mental Disorders : Dsm-5. 5th
ed. Arlington VA: American Psychiatric Association;
20172013.

American Rhetoric Top 100 Speeches. "A Plea for
Mercy delivered September 1924. Retrieved January 5,

2023:
https://www.americanrhetoric.com/speeches/cdarrowple
aformercy.htm Clarence Darrow.

Ammer, C. (2003), "The American Dictionary Heritage
of Idioms". The Christine Ammer 1992 Trust,
dioms.thefreedictionary.com/between+a+rock+and+a+h
ard+place retrieved 2 Feb 2022

Ancient Code Website (n.d.) The Bone Chilling Story
Behind the Flying Dutchman Legend. Retrieved
February 17,2022: https://www.ancient-
code.com/flying-dutchman/.

Anderson, W. (Schoolworkhelper Editorial Team),
"Malala Yousafzai: Activist and Female Education," in
SchoolWorkHelper, 2019,
https://schoolworkhelper.net/malala-yousafzai-activist-
and-female-education/. Retrieved February 5, 2022.

Arata, Tony (1990) "The Dance".
https://www.lyrics.com/lyric/3449872/Garth+Brooks/Th
e+Dance

Aristotle (384 BC - 322 BC) It is the mark of an
educated mind to be able to entertain a thought without
accepting it. https://philosiblog.com/2012/03/07
Retrieved February 03, 2022.

Armstrong, K., O'Callahan, W., & Marmar, C. (1991).
"Debriefing Red Cross disaster personnel: The multiple
stressor debriefing model." Journal of Traumatic Stress,
4(4), 581–593.

Asher, J. (2013). Thirteen Reasons Why. London:
Penguin.

Aurelius, M. & Long, G. (2021). Meditations of Marcus Aurelius. White Plains, NY: Peter Pauper Press, Inc.

Author: EAM5611 (August 30, 2015) Eureka! Sites.psu.edu/solvingproblems/2015/08/30/eureka/Retrieved 4 February 2022.

Avalon.law.yale.edu. "The Hague peace conferences of 1899 and 1907; a series of lectures delivered before the Johns Hopkins University in the year 1908".

Avvo Staff (Apr 12, 2010) Marriage and divorce statistics LEGAL GUIDE. Retrieved February 10, 2022, from AVVO website: https://www.avvo.com/legal-guides/ugc/marriage-divorce-statistics.

Awan, S. (December 23, 2017). "Why Dickens' A CHRISTMAS CAROL is Still So Relevant For Today…" Retrieved July 1, 2022, https://burningblogger.com.

Bale, R. "Why Killing a Bull Elephant with Big Tusks Hurts the Herd," National Geographic, Published October 17, 2015

Ballou, G. (2015). Handbook for Sound Engineers. Burlington, MA: Focal Press.

Balsmeyer, Jeff, dir. "Danny's Deckchair", Release date: 16 May 2003 (Cannes), 11 August 2004 (US) https://www.moviefone.com/movie/danny-deckchair/17724/where-to-watch/. Retrieved February 5, 2022.

Barba, John (February 12, 2020) "Callaway Releases its Financial: 1.7 Billion". https://mygolfspy.com/callaway-

releases-its-2019-financials-1-7-billion/ Retrieved
February 4, 2022.

Bartholomew, Abigail. (2013). Behaviorism's Impact on
Advertising: Then and Now.
DigitalCommons@University of Nebraska - Lincoln.

Barton, Marc (Oct 14, 2019) William Osler – The Father
of Modern Medicine
https://www.pastmedicalhistory.co.uk/william-osler-the-
father-of-modern-medicine.

Bauer, Patricia, Rocky film by Avildsen [1976]
https://www.britannica.com/topic/Rocky-film-by-
Avildsen. Retrieved 6 February 2022

Bates, T., & Petouhoff, N. L. (2021). Empathy in action:
How to deliver great customer experiences at scale.
Washington, DC: Ideapress Publishing.

Baum, L. Frank (2020) *The Wonderful Wizard of Oz*.
Place of publication not identified: MINT EDITIONS.

Baumeister R. F., Masicampo E. J., Vohs K. D. (2011).
Do conscious thoughts cause behavior? Annu. Rev.
Psychol. 62, 331–361
10.1146/annurev.psych.093008.131126 - DOI -
PubMed

Beacham, G. (January 27, 2020) "Los Angeles Lakers
legend Kobe Bryant dies at 41 in helicopter crash". The
Associated Press, https://www.nba.com/news/kobe-
bryant-dies-helicopter-crash.

Beah, I. (2008). *A Long Way Gone: Memoirs of a Boy
Soldier*. New York: Large Print Press.

Benjamin Keough: "Coroner says Elvis's grandson took his own life" (Published 15 July 2020). BBC News website: https://www.bbc.com/news/entertainment-arts-53415154. Retrieved February 11, 2022.

Bernstein, D. (October 18, 2020) Revisiting the Myles Garrett-Mason Rudolph helmet incident on 'Thursday Night Football'.
https://www.sportingnews.com/us/nfl/news/myles-garrett-mason-rudolph-helmet.

Biasutti, M. (2011) Flow and Optimal Experience, in Encyclopedia of Creativity (Second Edition), Publisher: Academic Press; 2nd edition, ISBN: 0123750393, 978-0123750396.

Birley, A. (2016). *Marcus Aurelius: A Biography*. London: Routledge, Taylor & Francis Group.

Bond, Mark (March 1, 2015) Criminology: Social Disorganization Theory Explained, Retrieve February 8, 2022w from Linkedin website:
https://www.linkedin.com/pulse/criminology-social-disorganization-theory-explained-mark-bond.

Bonfiglio, M. (Jan 22, 2012). Directed by Michael Bonfiglio with Oprah Winfrey, Morgan Freeman on the lessons he learned throughout his rise to success. Retrieved February 13, 2022 from IMDB website: https://www.imdb.com/title/tt2183549/.

Boorstin, D. J. (2001). The Creators. London: Phoenix.

Boorstin, D. J. (2001). The Discoverers. London: Phoenix.

Boyd, L. (November 4, 2020) Neuroplasticity Gives You the Power to Shape the Brain You Want: Dr. Lara Boyd. https://www.newworldai.com/neuroplasticity-gives-you-the-power-to-shape-the-brain-you-want-dr-lara-boyd/ Retrieved February 6, 2022.

Braams, Barbara, "Adolescents in Love: What makes a first love special?" September 11, 2013leidenpsychologyblog Retrieved 2021-01-31.

Brady, B. (1985). Author's firsthand account from a SHU professor during graduate school.

Bright, Celeste (February 1, 2017) "Madness in Moby-Dick". Retrieved February 7, 2022, Study.com Website: https://study.com/academy/lesson/madness-in-moby-dick.html.

Britt, R. (January 25, 2009) "Lies Take Longer Than Truths". livescience.com/7654-lies-longer-truths. Retrieved May 10, 2022.

Brown, Henry Box (1849) Narrative Life of Henry Box Brown. https://publicdomainreview.org/collection/the-narrative-of-henry-box-brown-1849. Retrieved February 5, 2022.

Brown, L. (May 29, 2016) "Ghosts" Speech retrieved February 19, 2022. https://motivationalwisdomblog.wordpress.com/2016/05/29/les-brown-ghosts-speech/

Brown, Les (July 30, 2020), "On the Meaning and the Purpose of Life", Excellence Reporter. Retrieved February 10, 2022, from Excellence Reporter website: https://excellencereporter.com/2020/07/30/les-brown-on-the-meaning-and-the-purpose-of-life/

Burgemeester, A. (n.d.) "What is the Difference Between Ego Syntonic and Ego Dystonic?" Retrieved February 10, 2022 from Psychologized Website: https://www.psychologized.org/what-is-the-difference-between-ego-syntonic-and-ego-dystonic/.

Burkhardt, R. W. (2005). Patterns of Behavior: Konrad Lorenz, Niko Tinbergen, and the founding of ethology. Chicago: University of Chicago Press.

Burns, R., & Dougall, C. S. (1927). *Robert Burns: The Poems, Epistles, Songs, Epigrams & Epitaphs*. London: A. & C. Black.

Calautti, Thomas (April 27, 2017) "13 Reasons Why' is a haunting and worthwhile show" Retrieved February 11, 2022, from Amherst Wire website: https://amherstwire.com/20481/entertainment/13-reasons-why-is-a-haunting-and-worthwhile-show/.

Calhoun, L. G., & Tedeschi, R. G. (Eds.) (2006). *The Handbook of Posttraumatic Growth: Research and Practice*. Mahwah, NJ: Lawrence Erlbaum Associates Publishers.

Calou, Y., Zeavin, H. (April 01, 2022) "Who's Listening When You Call a Crisis Hotline? *State Of Mind. slate.com/technology/2022/04/crisis-lifelines-surveillance-geolocation-algorithms.html*. Retrieved February 11, 2023.

Canada's Worst Handyman. https://en.wikipedia.org/wiki/Canada%27s_Worst_Handyman. Retrieved 5 February 2022.

Cannell, M. T. (2018). Incendiary: The Psychiatrist, The Mad Bomber, and The Invention of Criminal Profiling. New York: Minotaur Books.

Cari Miller (Jul 20, 2019) Book Review: 'The World According to Mister Rogers" by Fred Rogers. Anythinklibraries.org. Retrieved February 03, 2022.

Carnegie, Dale (2006). How to Win Friends & Influence People. UK: Vermilion.

Carradine, D. (1993). Spirit of Shaolin. Boston, Mass: Charles E. Tuttle.

Catel, Amanda, (February 7, 2019) "I Wish I knew About the Cost of Mental Health Care before being Hospitalized". www.bustle.com. Retrieved February 1, 2022.

CBSNewYork/AP. (September 9, 2019) "Rutgers Student Reportedly Left Suicide Note", https://newyork.cbslocal.com/2010/09/29/prison-time-may-await-pair-of-rutgers-students/.

CDC. Web-based Injury Statistics Query and Reporting System (WISQARS). Atlanta, GA: US Department of Health and Human Services, CDC; 2021. Retrieved April 5, 2022. https://www.cdc.gov/injury/wisqars/index.html

Challenger: Speech File - Ronald Reagan Presidential Library and Museum. Retrieved February 10, 2022, from https://www.reaganlibrary.gov/public/documents/challenger-workbook.pdf.

Chandler, S.F. (July 20, 2018) JFK & Hemingway: Beyond "Grace Under Pressure, The JFK Library

Archives: https://jfk.blogs.archives.gov/2018/07/20/jfk-hemingway

Chapman, M. (1999). *Constructive Evolution: Origins and Development of Piaget's Thought.* Cambridge: Cambridge University Press.

Charness, Gary; et al. (June 1,2020) "Strong Evidence for Gender Differences in Risk Taking" (Journal of Economic Behavior & Organization Volume 83, Issue 1, June 2012, Pages 50-58.) Retrieved February 10, 2022, from Science Direct website: https://www.sciencedirect.com/science/article/abs/pii/S0 167268111 001570.

Chawla, Dalmeet Singh (July 24, 2018) "To Remember, the Brain Must Actively Forget". www.quantamagazine.org Retrieved 2 Feb 2022.

Cherry, Kendra, (April 17, 2021). "What Motivation Theory Can Tell Us About Human Behavior." Medically reviewed by Amy Morin, LCSW. Retrieved April 5, 2022: https://www.verywellmind.com/theories-of-motivation.

Cherry, Kendra (July 18, 2021) "Erik Erikson's Stages of Psychosocial Development". Retrieved on May 13, 2022: https://www.verywellmind.com/erik-eriksons-stages-of-psychosocial-development.

Chinen, Allan B. (1993), Beyond the Hero. New York: G.P. Putnam's Sons.

City of Whittier (1/24/2015) Video Historic Whittier - John Greenleaf Whittier. https://www.bing.com/videos/search?q=historic+john+g reenleaf+whittier Retrieved February 04, 2022.

Clark, Mike (August 29, 2002). "Jerry Lewis Tells It Like It Is – And Was". USA Today. Retrieved January 31, 2022.

Classic Cars and the Cubans That Keep Them Running https://www.anywhere.com/cuba/travel-guide/classic-cars

Clausewitz, C., Howard, M., & Paret, P. (1989). On War. Princeton, N.J: Princeton University Press.

Clipson, E., Bugler, D. (19 March 2020) "Why David Attenborough is a National Treasure". https://www.gq-magazine.co.uk/article/david-attenborough. Retrieved April 8, 2022.

Coffman, S. (May 2018). E18 – Distancing Language – Deception Tips Podcast. Retrieved: May 10, 2022: spencercoffman.com/deception-tip-18.

Collins. (July 14, 2016) We take a look at the etymology behind the word 'genius'. Retrieved January 6, 2023: https://blog.collinsdictionary.com/.

Condit, C. W. (1964). The Chicago School of Architecture: A history of commercial and public building in the Chicago area. Chicago: University of Chicago Press.

Confucius & Sheba, B. (2020). Analects of Confucius. La Vergne: Sheba Blake Publishing Corp.

Conner, C. (February, 10, 2018) "How To Spot A Lie In 5 Seconds (And The Biggest Lie I Ever Told In PR)" www.forbes.com/sites/cherylsnappconner/2018/02/10/how-to-spot-a-lie-in-5-seconds. Retrieved May 29, 2022.

Coppola, F.F. (1987) Cruise, T., Dillion, M., Hinton, S.E.O. Howell, C.T., & Macchio, R. (1987). "The Outsiders." Burbank, CA, Warner Home Video.

Corporate Board Member (Apr 04, 2019) Member Ritz-Carlton Founder Horst Schulze on the Secret to Customer Service. https://boardmember.com/ritz-carlton-founder-horst-schulze/2/ Retrieved February 4, 2022.

Covington, Taylor (August 9, 2021) Road Rage Statistics in 2021, thezebra.com. Retrieved 2021-01-31.

Crisis Prevention Institute. (2011). *Nonviolent Crisis Intervention: Participant Workbook.* Brantford, Ont: W. Ross MacDonald School, Resource Services Library.

Crowe, R., Costner, K., Lane, D., Fishburne, L., Adams, A., Shannon, M., & Cavill, H. (2013). "Man of Steel." United States: Warner Bros.

Cummins, I. (2015). "The Link Between Unemployment and Suicide, World Economic Forum: https://www.weforum.org/agenda/2015/02/the-link-between-unemployment-and-suicide/

Currier & Ives. (ca. 1876) "Give me liberty or give me death!" Patrick Henry delivered his great speech on the rights of the colonies, before the Virginia Assembly, convened at Richmond, March 23rd, concluding with the above sentiment, which became the war cry of the revolution. United States Williamsburg Virginia, ca. 1876. New York: Published by Currier & Ives. [Photograph] Retrieved from the Library of Congress, https://www.loc.gov/item/2001700209/

Danny Thomas Story (2002) Internet Archive Website: http://www.stjude.tv/danny_thomas_story.cfm

Davis, J. (1950). *Character Assassination.* New York: Philosophical Library.

DeCandido, Keith R. A. (May 23, 2017). "Star Trek the Original Series Rewatch: Star Trek II: The Wrath of Khan". Tor.com. Retrieved February 6, 2022

Detsch, J. (March 21, 2022) 'Winging it', Russian is Getting Its General Killed on the Front Lines. https://foreignpolicy.com/2022/03/21/russia-generals-dead-ukraine.

DiCiacca, D (2008) *Give or Take a Thousand Miles,* Publisher: PublishAmerica.

Dickens, C. (1912). *The Cricket On The Hearth,* etc. London: George G. Harrap & Co

Dickens, C. (2021). *Christmas Carol.* Left of Brain Books.

Dickens, C., & Doss, L. (2008). *Oliver Twist.* Harlow: Pearson Education.

Dickinson, E. (1927). *The complete Poems of Emily Dickinson:* With an Introduction by her Niece Martha Dickinson Bianchi. Boston: Little, Brown, and Co.

Ditton, J. (1980). *The View from Goffman.* New York: St. Martin's Press.

Dolan, B. (2000). *Malthus, medicine & morality: Malthusianism after 1798.* Amsterdam: Rodopi.

Dopico, Alex (December 5, 2020) What makes a speech persuasive according to Aristotle? Retrieved February 10, 2022 from https://janetpanic.com/what-makes-a-speech-persuasive-according-to-aristotle/#What_are_the_2_types_of_persuasion.

Dopico, Alex (December 5, 2020) What makes a speech persuasive according to Aristotle? Retrieved February 10, 2022 from https://janetpanic.com/what-makes-a-speech-persuasive-according-to-aristotle/#What_are_the_2_types_of_persuasion.

Dostoyevsky, F., Garnett, C., & Simmons, E. J. (1950). *Crime and Punishment*. New York: Modern Library.

Duhigg, C. (2014). *The Power of Habit*. New York: Random House Trade Paperbacks.

Duignan, Brian. "Occam's Razor". Encyclopedia Britannica. Retrieved 2 Feb 2022 https://www.britannica.com/topic/Occams-razor.

Dyzenhaus, David (October 25, 2016) The Safety of the People Is the Supreme Law. The New Rambler website. Retrieved February 10, 2022, from https://newramblerreview.com/book-reviews/classics/the-safety-of-the-people-is-the-supreme-law.

Eckstein, A. M. (2006). "The Searchers: Essays and reflections on John Ford's Classic Western." Detroit, Mich: Wayne State Univ. Press.

Editors of Encyclopaedia Britannica, Janus, Roman God. https://www.britannica.com/topic/Janus-Roman-god. Retrieved February 5, 2022.

Ehrmann, M., & Tauss, M. (2003). "Desiderata: Words for life." New York: Scholastic Press.

Ekman, P. (2012). *Emotions revealed: Understanding faces and feelings*.

Ellis, A. (1994). *Reason and Emotion in Psychotherapy*. Secaucus, NJ: Carol Pub. Group.

Ellis, A. (2004). *The Road to Tolerance*: The philosophy of rational emotive behavior therapy. Amherst, N.Y: Prometheus Books.

Emerson, R. W. (n.d.) Quotes.net. A man is only half himself; expression is the other half. Retrieved February 7, 2022, from Quotes.com Website: https://www.quotes.net/quote/603

Emerson, R. W., Ferguson, A. R., Carr, J. F., & Emerson, R. W. (1987). *The Essays of Ralph Waldo Emerson*. Cambridge, Mass: Belknap Press.

Emerson, Ralph Waldo (1844) Essays: Second Series is a series of essays (The Poet) Public Domain.

Encyclopedia of Greek Mythology: "Sisyphus." www.mythweb.com. Retrieved 2 Feb 2022.

Epictetus, ..., & Oldfather, W. A. (2018). The Complete Works of Epictetus. Hastings, East Sussex, United Kingdom: Delphi Classics. Epstein, Julius; Epstein, Philip G.; Koch, Howard (released 1942) "Casablanca". Based on the play Everybody Goes to Rick's by Murray Burnett, Joan Alison.

Erikson, E. H. (1974). Identity: Youth and Crisis. London: Faber & Faber.

Ernest Hemingway Quotes. (n.d.). BrainyQuote.com.
Retrieved February 7, 2022, from BrainyQuote.com
Website:
https://www.brainyquote.com/quotes/ernest_hemingway
_152913.

Ethics Reminder Offered About 'Goldwater Rule' on
Talking to Media". Psychiatric News. May 18, 2007.

Evans, R. I. (1975). *Konrad Lorenz: The Man and His
Ideas*. New York, N.Y: Harcourt Brace Jovanovich.

Evita (n.d.). Scripts.com. Retrieved February 10, 2022,
from https://www.scripts.com/script/evita_7824

Evon, Dan (22 July 2015), "Did a Struggling Sylvester
Stallone Sell His Dog for $25?"
https://www.snopes.com/fact-check/stallone-sold-his-
dog/. Retrieved 6 February 2022

Farnam Street Blog (n.d.) "Warren Buffett: The Three
Things I Look for in a Person" fs.blog/warren-buffett-
the-three-things-i-look-for-in-a-person. Retrieved 31
May 2022.

Fender, J. (2019). Hunger Marketing. Retrieved
February 15, 2022, from toolshero:
https://www.toolshero.com/marketing/hunger-
marketing/.

Fensch, T. (2014). The Man Who Was Dr Seuss: The
Life and Work of Theodor Geisel. Cork: BookBaby.

Filippo Brunelleschi" Retrieved February 11, 2022, from
Famous Architects website: https://www.famous-
architects.org/filippo-brunelleschi/

Flaubert, G., & Aveling, E. M. (2021). Madame Bovary. Vancouver: Engage Classics.

Flaubert, Gustave (1886), Madame Bovary: Provincial Manners. Vizetelly & Co., London

Foundations Recovery Network (September 23, 2015). Posted in: Drug Abuse, Mental Health

"The Effect of Drugs on Serotonin." Retrieved May 11, 2022: foundationsrecoverynetwork.com/the-effect-of-drugs-on-serotonin.

Ford, D. (2010). A vision so noble: John Boyd, the OODA Loop, and America's War on Terror. Durham, New Hampshire: Warbird Books.

Francois, Claude, Gilles Thibaut, Jacques Revaux, Paul Anka (1967) "My Way" Lyrics © CONSALAD CO., Ltd., BMG Rights Management, SUISA, Concord Music Publishing LLC, Warner Chappell Music France, Jeune Musique Editions. https//www.lyrics.com/lyric/29135945/Paul+Anka/My+Way. Retrieved February 03, 2022.

Franklin, Benjamin (1791)"The Autobiography of Benjamin Franklin". standardebooks.org. Retrieved 3 February 2022.

Franklin, MJ (April 23, 2016). "Three Cheers for 'Hamlet,' the greatest Shakespeare Play of All Time." Credit: Bob Al-Greene/ *Mashable* ... https://mashable.com/article/this-be-madness-hamlet-winner. Retrieved 5 February 2022.

Fraser, N., & Navarro, M. (2008). *Evita*. United States: Paw Prints.

Freedland, Jonathan (Mon 21 Jun 2004) "How Mandela Helped Clinton Survive Scandal". https://www.theguardian.com/world/2004/jun/21/usa.int erviews. Retrieved 6 February 2022

Freud, S., & Berasaluce, A. J. (2019). *The Ego and the Id*. New York, N: Clydesdale Press,

Freud, S. (n.d.) https://www.quora.com/What-did-Sigmund-Freud-mean-when-he-said-%E2%80%9COne-day-in-retrospect-the-years-of-struggle-will-strike-you-as-the-most-beautiful%E2%80%9D. Retrieved 5 February 2022.

Frost, R., & Lankes, J. J. (2019). New Hampshire: A poem with notes and grace notes. New York: Vintage Books, a division of Penguin Random House LLC, 2019.

Frost, R., Rogers, B., & Pforzheimer Bruce Rogers Collection (Library of Congress). (1949). Complete poems of Robert Frost, 1949.

Furqan, Zainab, Sinyor Mark, Schaffer Ayal, Kurdyak, Paul, Zaheer Juveria, (July 16, 2018) "I Can't Crack the Code": What Suicide Notes Teach Us about Experiences with Mental Illness and Mental Health Care. The Canadian Journal of Psychiatry, vol. 64, 2: pp. 98-106.

Gagnon, Danny (n.d.) "Understanding Tony Robbins 6 Needs That are Core to Humans". https://www.montrealcbtpsychologist.com Retrieved February 3, 2022.

Gaiman, N., Keith, S., Dringenberg, M., Jones, M., & hoopla digital. (2020). *The Sandman*: Volume 1.

Gaiman, N., (n.d.) Wikipedia. Retrieved October 24, 2022, from website: https://en.wikipedia.org/wiki/Neil_Gaiman

Gardner, Howard (October 17, 2021) "The Remarkable von Humboldt Brothers". Retrieve February 8, 2022, from The Real World of College website: https://www.therealworldofcollege.com/blog/the-remarkable-von-humboldt-brothers

Gaudin Sharon (December 12, 2007) "The Transistor: The Most Important Invention of the 20th Century." Retrieved February 11, 2022, from Computerworld website: https://www.computerworld.com/article/2538123/the-transistor--the-most-important-invention-of-the-20th-century-.html.

Gavaler, Chris (September 15, 2007) "The Patron Saint of Super Heroes". Retrieved February 7, 2022, WordPress.com Website: https://thepatronsaintofsuperheroes.wordpress.com/2015/09/07/superman-on-trial/

Geromeap, John (2007-12-13). "Trace Adkins' life is an open book with 'A Personal Stand'". NevadaAppeal.com. Retrieved February 1, 2022

Gesley, J. (April 24, 2018) The "Lieber Code" – the First Modern Codification of the Laws of War. https://blogs.loc.gov/law/2018/04/the-lieber-code-the-first-modern-codification-of-the-laws-of-war/ Retrieved February 6, 2022

Ghost/shadow of one's former self. Merriam-Webster.com Dictionary, Merriam-Webster, https://www.merriam.webster.com/dictionary/ghost%2F

shadow%20of%20one%27s%20former%20self.
Retrieved February 22, 2022.

Gibbon, E. (2019). *Decline and Fall of the Roman Empire*. Forgotten Books.

Goethe, L. (2018). "Why is Goethe Consistently Ranked Among the Top Five Greatest Geniuses of All Time." https://www.quora.com/Why-is-Goethe-consistently-ranked-among-top-five-greatest-geniuses-of-all-time. Retrieved April 18, 2022.

Goldberg, E. (2002). The Executive Brain: Frontal Lobes and The Civilized Mind. Oxford: Oxford University Press.

Goldberg, Lee (February 1983). "Jack Sowards: The Man Who Killed Mr. Spock". Starlog (67): 22–25 – via Internet Archive. Retrieved February 6, 2022.

Gottlieb, A. H. (1998). 1,000 years, 1,000 people: Ranking The Men and Women Who Shaped The Millennium. New York: Kodansha International.

Goffman, E. (2022) Presentation of Self In Everyday Life. S.I.: Penguin Books.

Graff-Radford, J. (May 12, 2021). "Can exercise prevent memory loss and improve cognitive function?" Retrieved July, 19, 2022 from https://www.mayoclinic.org/diseases-conditions/alzheimers-disease/expert-answers.

Graham, W. (October 30, 2018). "Faith and Forgiveness: Louis Zamperini." www.faithgateway.com Retrieved February 1, 2022.

Green, P. (2013). Alexander of Macedon, 356-323 B.C: A historical biography. Berkeley: University of California Press.

Greenburg, Michael M. (2011). The Mad Bomber of New York: The Extraordinary True Story of The Manhunt That Paralyzed A City. Union Square Press. ISBN 1-4027-7434-6.

Greenleaf Whittier (1837) Our Countrymen in Chains. https://en.wikisource.org/wiki Retrieved February 03, 2022.

Griffin, J. (2008). Homer, the Odyssey: [a student guide]. Cambridge: Cambridge Univ. Press.

Grigori Rasputin (n.d.) Wikipedia. Retrieved February 10, 2022, from website: https://en.wikipedia.org/wiki/Grigori_Rasputin#CITERE FWilson1964.

Grimminck, Robert (November 21, 2016) "10 Cases That Shaped the FBI's Behavioral Analysis Unit". Retrieved February 7, 2022, from TopTenz.com Website: https://www.toptenz.net/10-cases-shaped-fbis-behavioral-analysis-unit.php.

Gupta, S., & Loberg, K. (2022). Keep sharp. New York: Simon & Schuster Paperbacks,

Gustafson, Craig (2017) Bruce Lipton, PhD: The Jump from Cell Culture to Consciousness.

Gwilt, J. (2019). Architecture of Marcus Vitruvius Pollio: In Ten Books. Forgotten Books.

Haas, M. (2016). Bouncing forward: Transforming bad breaks into breakthroughs. Place of publication not identified: Enliven. Haft, S., Weir, P., Witt, P. J., Thomas, T., Schulman, T., Williams, R., Leonard, R. S., ... Swank Motion Pictures, Inc., (2021). "Dead Poets Society."

Haley, A. (1976). Roots. Garden City, N.Y.: Doubleday.

Haley, A., & Olusoga, D. (2018). Roots. London: Vintage Classics.

Halloran, Liz (January 17, 2008). "Lloyd Bentsen To Dan Quayle: "Senator, You Are No Jack Kennedy"; Texas Sen. Lloyd Bentsen delivered one of the most devastating slights ever". U.S. News & World Report.

Haltiwanger, John (December 10, 2014) "Love and Money: Why the Man behind Victoria's Secret killed himself". Elitedaily.com. Retrieved February 1, 2022

Hannaford, A. (September 12, 2018). "We asked 12 mass killers: 'What would have stopped you?' gq-magazine.co.uk. Retrieved 11 February 2023.

Harris, T. A., & Harris, T. A. (2012). *I'm Ok, You're Ok.* London: Arrow.

Harrison, R. (August 8, 2016) Urban Dictionary. Retrieved February 13, 2022 from website: https://www.urbandictionary.com/define.php?term=Rick%20Harrison

Hedstrom-Page, D., & Martinez, S. (2007). *From Ranch to Railhead with Charles Goodnight.* Nashville, Tenn.: B & H Publishing Group.

Heller, Joseph (June 1961) *Catch-22*. New York: Simon & Schuster.

Hemingway, E. (1996). *The Nick Adams Stories*. New York: Charles Scribner's Sons.

Hemingway, E. (2003). *In Our Time*. Simon and Schuster.

Hemingway, E., & Hemingway, P. (2004). *True at First Light*. London: Arrow Books.

Henry Raymont (Sept. 1, 1971), Cerf Rites Draw Friends of 2 'Worlds', New York Times. https://www.nytimes.com/1971/09/01/archives/cerf-rites-draw-friends-of-2-worlds.html

Herculano-, Houzel Suzana. (2020, February 14). Count Your Neuron When You Count Your Blessings. Madras Courier https://madrascourier.com/opinion/count-your-neurons-when-you-count-your-blessings/.

Herriot, J. (n.d.). Quotes. BrainyQuote.com. Retrieved February 7, 2022, from BrainyQuote.com Web site: https://www.brainyquote.com/quotes/james_herriot_362612.

Heyen, Billy (01-02-2021) Why did Myles Garrett hit Mason Rudolph with his helmet? Sportingnews.com. Retrieved January 31, 2022.

Heyen, Billy (01-02-2021) Why did Myles Garrett hit Mason Rudolph with his helmet? Sportingnews.com. Retrieved January 31, 2022.

Higdon, H. (1975). The crime of the century: The Leopold and Loeb case. New York: Putnam.

Hinton, S. E. (1967). The Outsiders Viking Press, Dell Publishing.

Historymuseum.ca/blog/the-maple-leaf-flag-is-adopted Retrieved 5 February 2022.

Hoberman, J. (2019-08-21). "Why 'Gaslight' Hasn't Lost Its Glow". The New York Times. ISSN 0362-4331. Retrieved February 1, 2022.

Holiday, Dean O. (2014) The Unfortunate Gift. America Star Books.

Holiday, Dean O. (2023) "Aldo's Wild Tomorrow". Author's nom de plume.

Homer, Lattimore, R., & Martin, R. P. (2011). The Iliad of Homer. Chicago: University of Chicago Press.

Hosted by Jonathan Bastian (Apr. 25, 2020) Spiritual writer Pico Iyer says now is the time confront who we really are. https://www.kcrw.com/culture/shows/life-examined/contemplation-in-isolation/pico-iyer-interview-quarantine-coronavirus-tips. Retrieved 6 February 2022

Houston, P., Tennant, D., Carnicero, S., Floyd, M., Berman, F., & Macmillan Audio (Firm). (2012). Spy the lie: Former CIA officers teach you how to detect deception. New York: Macmillan Audio.

Howell, James (1659). Primagraphia. Proverbs, or old Sayed Sawes & Adages in English (or the Saxon Tongue). Tetraglotton (1660). Retrieved February 7, 2022, Wikipedia Website: https://en.wikipedia.org/wiki/All_work_and_no_play_makes_Jack_a_dull_boy.

https://en.wikipedia.org/wiki/William_Le_Baron_Jenney
#cite_note-4 Retrieved 4 February 2022.
https://www.goodreads.com/quotes/68707. Retrieved
February 5, 2022.

https://www.shakespeare.org.uk/explore-
shakespeare/shakespedia/william-shakespeare/william-
shakespeare-biography/ Retrieved 5 February 2022.

Huberman, A. (January 29, 2021) *Huberman Lab.*
"Episode 1: How Your Brain Works & Changes".

Huberman, A. (May 26, 2022) *Huberman Lab.* "Episode
73: Dr. Wendy Suzuki – Boost Attention & Memory
with Science-Based Tools".

Hudson, D. (December 18, 2014) President Obama
Creates the Task Force on 21st Century Policing.
https://obamawhitehouse.archives.gov.

Hull, C. L. (1943). Principles of behavior. New York:
Appleton-Century-Crofts.

Iacocca, L. A. (2011). Iacocca: An Autobiography. S.l.:
Random House Publishing Group.

Inflection." Merriam-Webster.com Dictionary, Merriam-
Webster, https://www.merriam-
webster.com/dictionary/inflection. Accessed 9 Feb.
2022.

Instinct Theory Explains Motivation July 14, 2021/in
Psychology /by admin/Facts checked by Eisle Wedd
Opena. Retrieved from
https://zerotoeternity.com/psychology/instinct-theory-of-
motivation/

Integr Med (Encinitas). 2017 Dec; 16(6): 44–50.
https://www.ncbi.nlm.nih.gov/pmc/articles/PMC643808
8/. Retrieved February 2022.

International Enneagram Association. (1997). Mountain
View, Calif.: International Enneagram Association.

Imke, S. (Last updated: 31 July 2019) How to Tell if
Someone is Lying Using Questioning Techniques.
Retrieved May 10th, 2022:
business2community.com/communications.

Isaac Asimov quote (n.d.) Retrieved February 11, 2022,
from Everything2 Website:
https://everything2.com/title/Violence+is+the+last+refug
e+of+the+incompetent#:

Jackson. Alan (2006). "Like Red on a Rose," Album:
Like Red on a Rose.www.elyrics.net: Retrieved 2
February 2022.

Jackson. Alan (2003) "Remember When", Album:
Greatest Hits Volume II. En.m.wikipedia.org: Retrieved
19 June 2022.

Johann Sabastian Bach (1685-1750), "I have to work;
anyone who works just as hard will get just as far."

Johann Wolfgang von Goethe (n.d.), BrainyQuote.com.
Retrieved February 10, 2022, from BrainyQuote.com
Web site: https://www.brainyquote.com/authors/johann-
wolfgang-von-goeth-quotes.

Johansen, B. E., & Mann, B. A. (2000). Encyclopedia of
the Haudenosaunee (Iroquois Confederacy). Westport,
Conn: Greenwood Press.

John Kennedy (November 21, 1963) Remarks at the Dedication of the Aerospace Medical Health Center, San Antonio, Texas, November 21, 1963. Retrieved February 10, 2022, from JFK Library and Museum website: https://www.jfklibrary.org/archives/other-resources/john-f-kennedy-speeches/san-antonio-tx-19631121

Jones, Meghan , 12 Stan Lee Quotes That Are Downright Heroic Updated: Oct. 08, 2021, RD.COM Arts & Entertainment Quotes

Justin McCurry (12 Oct 2004) theguardian.com/technology/2004/oct/13/japan.internationalnews Nine Japanese die in suicide pacts. Retrieved February 03, 2022.

Kanel, K. (2019). A guide to crisis intervention. Boston, MA: Cengage Konnikova, M. (2014). Mastermind: How to think like Sherlock Holmes. Edinburgh: Canongate.

Kaufman. Gil (Apr 17, 2007) Cho Seung-Hui, Virginia Tech Gunman, Described As 'Loner' Retrieved February 7, 2022, MTV.com Website: https://www.mtv.com/news/1557332/cho-seung-hui-virginia-tech-gunman-described-as-loner/.

Kaus, R. J. (November 1992) Psyche (Stuttg) [Archaeology of childhood. Psychoanalytic conditions for realizing childhood daydreams exemplified by Heinrich Schliemann] [Article in German] https://pubmed.ncbi.nlm.nih.gov/1438887.

Kemp, Martin (February 9, 2016) Why Leonardo da Vinci was a genius

Kennedy, G. A. (1991). Aristotle on rhetoric: A theory of civic discourse. New York: Oxford University Press.

Khalid, R. (April 7, 2015) | Three Unforgettable Cyberbullying cases. WordPress website: retrieved February 16, 2022:
 https://roshanykhalid.wordpress.com/2015/04/07/three-unforgettable-cyberbullying-cases/

Khalmetski K., Rockenbach B., Werner P. "Evasive Lying in Strategic Communication" (2017) Journal of Public Economics, 156, pp. 59-72.

King, S. (2008). The Shining. London: Hodder and Stoughton.

Kipling, Rudyard (1935). "Something of Myself". https://web.archive.org/web/20140223004314/http://ghostwolf.dyndns.org/words/authors/K/KiplingRudyard/prose/SomethingOfMyself/index.html. Retrieved 5 February 2022.

Kisner, J. (2020) Thin Places: Essays from In Between. Publisher: Farrar, Straus, and Giroux.

Kobayashi Maru (n.d)
https://en.wikipedia.org/wiki/Kobayashi_Maru#cite_note-:0-3. Retrieved February 6, 2022

Krupp, Marshall(October 8, 2015) Benjamin Franklin Said… "Lost Time Is Never Found Again" https://www/pulse/benjamin-franklin-said-lost-time-never-found-again-krupp- Retrieved February 03, 2022.

Kubrick, S. (1980). The Shining. Estados Unidos: Warner.

Lanhers,Yvonne, Vale, Malcolm G.A. St. Joan of Arc, French heroine. https://www.britannica.com/biography/Saint-Joan-of-Arc Retrieved 6 February 2022.

Lambert, M. (April 12, 2016) "The True Meaning of the Word Genius How Our Modern Definition is Hurting Us".Retrieved January 6, 2023: The True Meaning Of The Word Genius (theodysseyonline.com).

Lardner, Ring (n.d.) The Chicago Literary Hall of Fame, Retrieved February 15, 2022: https://chicagoliteraryhof.org/inductees/profile/ring-lardner.

Larsson, S., Keeland, R., Larsson, S., Larsson, S., & Larsson, S. (2010). Stieg Larsson's the girl with the dragon tattoo trilogy. New York: Vintage Books.

Leal, S., Vrij, A, (January 2008) "Blinking During and After Lying. Journal of Nonverbal Behavior 32(4):187-194.

https://voidnetwork.gr/wp-content/uploads/2016/08/The-Dobe-Ju-hoansi-by-Richard-B.-Lee.pdf Retrieved February 5, 2022.

Leopold, A., Schwartz, C. W., & Kingsolver, B. (2020). A Sand County almanac: And sketches here and there. New York, NY: Oxford University Press.

Leopold, M. (2021). Idi Amin: The story of Africa's icon of evil. New Haven: Yale University Press.

Lessing, L. (1969). *Man of high fidelity: Edwin Howard Armstrong;* a biography. New York, NY: Bantam.

Levenson, Eric; Gingras, Brynn, (June 6, 2018), "Kate Spade, fashion designer, found dead in apparent suicide". Retrieved February 11, 2022, from CNN News website: https://www.cnn.com/2018/06/05/us/kate-spade-dead/index.html

Levin, Doron (July 3, 2019) Lee Iacocca Practiced Persuasion at a World-Class Level, Lacking Only Twitter In His Arsenal. In Forbes.com Retrieved February 9, 2022, from: https://www.forbes.com/sites/doronlevin/2019/07/03/lee-iacocca-practiced-persuasion-at-a-world-class-level-lacking-only-twitter-in-his-arsenal/.

Levine, Daniel (December 27, 2021). "Tom Selleck Was Confronted About His NRA Support Live on TV, Relive the Tense Showdown." Retrieved July 31, 2022, from: popculture.com/tv-shows/news/tom-selleck-rosie-odonnell-nra-interview-video.

Lewinsky, Monica (March 21, 2015) monica-lewinsky-on-shame-and-cyber-bullying-ted-video. Socialnewsdaily.com Retrieved 2022-02-02

Lewis, CS (1942)   goodreads.com/quotes/6657734. Retrieved 2 Feb 2022

Liam Quinn (22 Jun 2017, updated 08:56 22 Jun 2017) https://www.dailymail.co.uk/news/article-4627818/amp/Town-declares-emergency-suicide-pact-death.html. Retrieved February 03, 2022.

Liddell, H. G., & Scott, R. (1996). An intermediate Greek- English lexicon. Oxford: Clarendon Press.

Lightfoot, G. (1976). The wreck of the Edmund Fitzgerald: Race among the ruins. Burbank, Calif: Reprise Records.

Linder, D.O. (1995). "Nathan F. Leopold, Jr. (1904 - 1971)" Retrieved February 16, 2022: https://famous-trials.com/leopoldandloeb/1668-leopold#.

Lindvall, Helienne (30 July 2010). "Behind the Music: Beyond Bertrand lies a history of plastic performances". The Guardian. ISSN 0261-3077. Retrieved 20 January 2019

Lockie, A. (June 8, 2018). "Anthony Bourdain has died in an apparent suicide at 61". Business Insider. Retrieved January 31, 2022.

Lorenz, Edward (n.d.) When Lorenz Discovered the Butterfly Effect Retrieved February 7, 2022, from OpenMind.com Website: https://www.bbvaopenmind.com/en/science/leading-figures/when-lorenz-discovered-the-butterfly-effect/.

Lorenz, K., & Leyhausen, P. (1973). Motivation of human and animal behavior: An ethological view. New York: Van Nostrand Reinhold.

Lou Holtz (Down and out achiever) http://www.paulharveyarchives.com/trots/l/ Retrieved February 4, 2022.

Lou Holtz https://mindzip.net/fl/@LouHoltz/quotes/ Retrieved February 4, 2022.

MacLean, Paul D. (1990) The Triune Brain in Evolution: Role in Paleo Cerebral Functions New York, New York, U.S.A.: Springer.

MacPhee, Nancy (7 October 2011). "Red Green's wisdom and duct tape coming our way". Retrieved 17 January 2014.

Maj. Edwin Armstrong, Father of FM, Other Radio Inventions, Dead at 63", Broadcasting-Telecasting, February 8, 1954, pages 67-68.

Malkin, C. (2016). Rethinking narcissism: The secret to recognizing and coping with narcissists. New York: Harper Perennial.

Manning, A. (April 01, 1977). Father of ethology. Nature, 266, 5605, 782-783.

MantraCare Author (20220). "Compulsive Lying: The Sad Truth About It." mantracare.org/therapy/what-is/compulsive-lying. Retrieved: May 10th, 2022.

Marcel Proust (n.d.) Lib Quotes. Retrieved February 11, 2022, from Lib Quotes website: https://libquotes.com/marcel-proust/quote/.

Marcus Tullius Cicero (n.d.) BrainyQuote.com. Retrieved February 10, 2022, from BrainyQuote.com Web site: https://www.brainyquote.com/authors/marcus-tullius-cicero-quotes.

Marcus, A., & Long, G. (2021). Meditations of Marcus Aurelius. White Plains, NY: Peter Pauper Press, Inc.

Markina, Nadejda, media contact (August 5, 2022) Dog and jackal hybrids are perfect dogs. Retrieved February 8, 2022, from Innovations Report Website: sniffer https://www.innovations-report.com/interdisciplinary-research/report-9792/.

Marks, John E (Jun 22, 2019) No Man Ever Steps in the Same River Twice. Heraclitus (544 B.C.) https://medium.com/swlh/no-man-ever-steps-in-the-same-river-twice-867ec5afc857 Retrieved 6 February 2022.

Marlowe, Lara (Jun 5, 2021) Strauss-Kahn scandal: 'Never again, he promised. I am naive. I believed him.' www.irishtimes.com, Retrieved February 1, 2022

Marshall, Colin (February 4, 2016). "The Wisdom & Advice of Maurice Ashley, the Jamaican Chess Grandmaster". Open Culture. Retrieved February 02, 2021.

Masicampo,E.J., Baumeister, R. F. (July 26, 2013). "Conscious thought does not guide moment-to-moment actions-it serves social and cultural functions". Front Psychol. 2013 Jul 26;4:478. doi: 10.3389/fpsyg.2013.00478. PMID: 23898318; PMCID: PMC3724120.

Matsubayashi, Tetsuya, Lee, Myoung-jae, Ueda, Michiko (2019)."Higher Risk of Suicide on Milestone Birthdays: evidence from Japan". Scientific Reports. www.nature.com/scienticreports.Retrieved 2 January 2023.

McCarthy, Erin (APRIL 23, 2015) Roosevelt's "The Man in the Arena" https://www. mentalfloss.com/article/63389/roosevelts-man-arena. Retrieved 6 February 2022.

McCleary, K. (Oct 12, 2021) Matt Amodio's 'Jeopardy' winning streak ends after 38 consecutive victories. CNNhttps://www.cnn.com/2021/10/12/entertainment/jeopardy-matt-amodio-winning-streak-ends/index.html.

McClure, B.(May 21, 2019). Polaris is the North Star. https://earthsky.org/brightest-stars/polaris-the-present-day-north-star/

McConaughey, Matthew (May 17, 2015) Always Play Like an Underdog https://time.com/collection-post/3881954/matthew-mcconaughey-graduation-speech-university-of-houston/. Retrieved February 4, 2022.

McKay, S. (2020). The Scotland Yard puzzle book: Test your inner detective by solving some of the world's most difficult cases. New York: Black Dog & Leventhal Publishers.

MDA History. MDA website: https://www.mda.org/about-mda/history. Retrieved February 13, 2022.

Means, H. (2014). Johnny Appleseed: The Man, the Myth, the American Story. New York: Simon & Schuster.

Meares, T. (November 3, 2010). "Don't Jump the Shark: Understanding Deterrence and Legitimacy in the Architecture of Law Enforcement." https://nij.ojp.gov/media/video/23771. Retrieved June 2, 2022.

Medievalists.ne: https://www.medievalists.net/2016/01/those-who-pray-those-who-work-those-who-fight/.

Meeropol, Abel (1937) "Strange Fruit" recorded by Billie Holiday in 1939. https://www.bravowaukegan.org/billie-holiday-strange-fruit-live-1959/. Retrieved February 4, 2022.

Mehrabian, A. and Wiener, M. (1967). "Decoding of inconsistent communications," Journal of Personality and Social Psychology, 6, 109-114

Mélon, Jean (1996), Notes on the History of the Szondi Movement (French original). Text for the Szondi Congress of Cracow, August 1996. Retrieved February 15, 2021: https://en.wikipedia.org/wiki/Drive_theory

Melville, H., & Melville, H. (2020). Moby Dick. London: Penguin Books.

Mental Health Professionals' Duty to Warn" (October 12, 2018) National Conference of State Legislatures. from https://www.ncsl.org/research/health/mental-health-professionals-duty-to-warn.aspx#: Retrieved February 10, 2022.

Merillat. Orville D. (n.d.)
 https://en.wikipedia.org/wiki/Orville_D._Merillat. Retrieved 4 February 2022.

Mero Pen, (August 13, 2020) Nelson Mandela's forgiveness to his abusive jailer meropen.com Retrieved February 1, 2022.

Merriam-Webster. (n.d.). Cosmology. In Merriam-Webster.com dictionary. Retrieved February 9, 2022, from https://www.merriam-webster.com/dictionary/cosmology.

Merriam-Webster. (n.d.). Wicked. In Merriam-Webster.com dictionary. Retrieved February 9, 2022, from https://www.merriam-webster.com/dictionary/wicked.

Metcalf, L. (2006). The miracle question: Answer it and change your life. Carmarthen: Crown House Publishing Ltd.

Meyer, C. (2012). Where the broken heart still beats: The story of Cynthia Ann Parker. Boston: Graphia.

Meyers, J. (1999). Hemingway: A biography. New York: Da Capo Press.

Michael Blosil Suicide: Marie Osmond's Son Dies, Leaves Suicide Note04/29/2010 05:12am EDT | Updated May 25, 2011, Retrieved February 10, 2022, from HuffPost website: https://www.huffpost.com/entry/michael-blosil-suicide-ma_n_479483.

Michael S. Rozeff (05/06/2020) Death and Unemployment, Mises Institute, mises.org. Retrieved February 1, 2022

Michel de Montaigne (1533-1592),

Miller, Daniel (May 16, 2015) Alan Mulally: The Savior of Ford www.fool.com 2 Feb 2022.

Mitchell, J. T., & Everly, G. S. (1997). Critical Incident Stress Debriefing: CISN: An operation manual for the prevention of traumatic stress among emergency service and disaster workers. Ellicott City, Md: Chevron Publishing Corporation.

Moore, W. (1975). Confessions of a Mooseheart Den Mother. Personal interview, Dean O. Holiday, unpublished, the author's mother.

Morri, M., Shore, C. (2013) Natural Environment In Development and Well-Being. Published by Natural Environment and Climate Issues on behalf of World Vision International.

Murherjee, Siddhartha (March 21, 2016) "Runs in the Family" The New Yorker. Retrieved February 11, 2022, from The New Yorker website: https://www.newyorker.com/magazine /2016/03/28/the-genetics-of-schizophrenia.

Murtinho, V. Leonardo's Vitruvian Man Drawing: A New Interpretation Looking at Leonardo's Geometric Constructions. Nexus Netw J 17, 507–524 (2015). https://doi.org/10.1007/s00004-015-0247-7

Muschert, G. W. (2014). Responding to school violence: Confronting the Columbine effect. Boulder, Colorado; London [England]: Lynne Rienner Publishers.

Mythologian.Net. Fleur De Lis Symbol, Its Meaning, History and Origins. Retrieved February 8, 2022: https://mythologian.net/fleur-de-lis-symbol-its-meaning-history-origins/.

Naisbitt, J. (1982). Megatrends: Ten New Directions Transforming Our Lives, Warner Books.

Namie, G., & Namie, R. F. (2009). The bully at work: What you can do to stop the hurt and reclaim your dignity on the job. Naperville, Ill: Sourcebooks.

Nampizha

Namratha, P. (2015) & M Kishor, T S Sathyanarayana Rao, Rajesh Raman Mysore Study: A study of suicide notes Indian J Psychiatry. Oct-Dec 2015; 57(4):379-82. doi: 10.4103/0019-5545.171831.

Nathan Hale Quotes. (n.d.). Quotes.net. Retrieved February 10, 2022, from https://www.quotes.net/authors/Nathan+Hale+Quotes.

National Center for Health Statistics (U.S., 2018). Suicide rates in the United States continue to increase.

National Center for Injury Prevention and Control (NCICP)

Neshnabek, http://www.native-languages.org/definitions/neshnabek.htm. Retrieved 6 February 2022.

Nestor, J. (2021). Breath: The New Science of a Lost Art. S.l.: PENGUIN LIFE.

Neudeck, P., & Wittchen, H.-U. (2012). Exposure therapy: Rethinking the model: refining the method. New York: Springer.

Neurosurgery.directory (2019) "Anterior cingulate cortex functions". Retrieved April 19, 2022: https://neurosurgery.directory/2019/03/05/anterior-cingulate-cortex-functions.

New York Times. "Armstrong, FM Inventor, Dies in Leap from East Side Suite". The New York Times. February 2, 1954. p. 1. ISSN 0362-4331.

Nicholson, K. (Updated March 3, 2022) , "Do Ordinary Russian People Really Want War? Here Are The Citizens Fighting Back Against Putin". Huffpost.

Retrieved December 31, 2023 from
huffingtonpost.co.uk.

Nickerson, C. (January 11, 2022). "Activities Routine
Theory" *Simple Psychology*. Retrieved August 9, 2022:
simplypsychology.org/routine-activities-theory.

Niederkrotenthaler T, Voracek M, Herberth A, et al.
Role of media reports in completed and prevented
suicide–Werther v. Papageno effects. British Journal of
Psychiatry. 2010; 197:234–243.

Nield, David (August 28, 2015). Your Brain Is Still 30
Times More Powerful Than the Best Supercomputers.
Retrieved February 7, 2022, from ScienceAlert.com
Web site: https://www.sciencealert.com/your-brain-is-
still-30-times-more-powerful-than-the-best-
supercomputers.

Nimoy, L., & hoopla digital. (2015). The way I feel.
United States: Geffen.

Nortje, Alicia (September 12, 2021) What Is
Psychological Distancing? 4 Helpful Techniques.
Retrieved February 10, 2022, from Positive
Psychology.com website:
https://positivepsychology.com/psychological-
distancing/#

Norton, Justin M. (February 21, 2007). "States Pushing
for Laws to Curb Cyberbullying". Fox News. Retrieved
February 16, 2022.

O'Connor, Anahad (February 19, 2006). "He Takes the
Shout Out of Talk Radio". The New York Times.
https://www.nytimes.com

Odyssey Book 12, lines 108-11, Translated by Ian
Johnston, Vancouver Island University, Revised Edition
2019 johnstoniatexts.x10host.com, retrieved

Oelze, P. (Updated December 16, 2021). "Who Is John
B. Watson?"
https://www.betterhelp.com/advice/editorial_team/patric
ia-oelze. Retrieved March 2, 2022.

Olson, ELIZABETH (June 1, 2006). Widowers Are
Eager for Another Whirl.
https://www.nytimes.com/2006/06/01/fashion/thursdayst
yles/01marry.html. Retrieved February 2022.

On the Moth Radio Hour

O'Neill, S. (February 19, 2002)
 https://www.telegraph.co.uk/news/uknews/1385318/Re
venge-of-the-cheated-women.html.

Papenfuhs, S. "The OODA loop, reaction time, and
decision making". PoliceOne.com. Retrieved June 2022.

Parker, B. (Posted 4 Feb 20184 Feb 2018, updated 5 Feb
2018). "Female Murder Have Motives Different from
Men Who Kill." Retrieved May 5, 2022:
abc.net.au/news/2018-02-05/female-murderers-more-
likely-motivated-by-love-financial-gain.

Parker, Ian (February 6, 2012). "The Story of a Suicide".
The New Yorker. Archived from the original on
February 1, 2012.newyorker.com Retrieved February 1,
2022.

Parsons, Alan; Woolfson, Eric (1977) Breakdown by
The Alan Parsons Project. Album: I Robot.

Paterniti, Michael (August 15, 2010) The Suicide Catcher. https://www.gq.com/story/suicide-catchers-nanjing-bridge-yangtze-river-mr-chen

Paul Kedrosky (November 29, 2009) What is it About Golfers, Spouses, Cars, and Clubs, carfnz.blogspot.com. Retrieved February 1, 2022.

Perry, Richard; Schreifels, Jeff (Jun 21, 2019) Don't Use the Word Retirement. Retrieved February 8, 2022, from Veritus Group Website: https://veritusgroup.com/dont-use-the-word-retirement/.

Peterson, Dave (1 January 2020) Haruki Murakami's Top 10 Popular and Famous Quotes, Australia Unwrapped, Fair Dinkum Entertainment.

Phillips, T, (December 1,2018), Silver, S. JOKER An Origin. Final Shooting Script. Retrieve February 8, 2022:
 https://d2bu9v0mnky9ur.cloudfront.net/academy2019/screenplay/joker/joker_new_final.pdf

Picaro,Chris (August 10, 2020) Woody Hayes Punched a Player and Never Coached Again. Fanbuzz.com. Retrieved January 31, 2022.

Pink Floyd. (2002). Wish you were here. https://nbn-resolving.org/urn:nbn:de:101:1-201402256529.

Pinker S. *The Stuff of Thought : Language As a Window into Human Nature*. London: Allen Lane; 2007.

Pirsig, R. M. (2014). Zen and the art of motorcycle maintenance: An inquiry into values. London: Vintage Books,

Plato,., & Adam, J. (1979). The Republic of Plato: 1. Cambridge, Cambridge Univ. Pr. 1979.

Plato,., Tredennick, H., & Tarrant, H. (2003). The last days of Socrates: Euthyphro, the apology, Crito, Phaedo. London: Penguin Books.

Popova, Maria (Jun 08, 2015) The Art of Thought: Graham Wallas on the Four Stages of Creativity, 1926. https://main.vma.bz/design/the-art-of-thought-graham-wallas-on-the-four-stages-of-creativity-1926. Retrieved February 4, 2022.

Powers R. (2011) Basic Training for Dummies. Hoboken NJ: John Wiley & Sons.

Post Wire Report November (15, 2012) 'Dog Whisperer' Cesar Millan attempted suicide. https://nypost.com/2012/11/15/dog-whisperer-cesar-millan-attempted-suicide.

Presidential Debate 1984. CNN. Archived from the original on March 8, 2007. Retrieved 2 Feb 2022.

Proverbical.com. Swedish proverb, "Guld blindar manga, karleken blindar alla," retrieved January 31, 2022.

Quin, L. (July 1, 2013). Dailymail.com 06:45 22 Jun 2017, updated 08:56 22 Jun 2017 Brian Resnick and National JournalA Second Gettysburg Address, 50 Years After the Civil War.Theatlantic.com Retrieved February 03, 2022.

Maro, Publius Vergilius, https://www.idlehearts.com/88715/come-what-may-all-bad-fortune-is-to-be-conquered-by-endurance Retrieved February 03, 2022.

Quintenz, D. (February 1, 2018), Edward S. Curtis and the Really Big Dream. Retrieved February 7, 2022, from Cowboys & Indians.com Website: https://www.cowboysindians.com/2018/02/edward-s-curtis-and-the-really-big-dream/.

Quintilian & Russell, D. A. (2001). The orator's education. Cambridge, Mass: Harvard University Press.

Quintilian. (2006). Institutes of oratory. L. Honeycutt, Ed., (J.S. Watson, Trans.). Retrieved February 9, 2022, from Rehetori.byu.edu website: http://rhetoric.byu.edu/Primary%20Texts/Quintilian.htm / (Original work published 1856).

Quote by Plato: "Necessity is the mother of invention."

Quotespedia. https://www.org/authors/a/abraham-lincoln/give-me-six-hours-to-chop-down-a-tree Retrieved 2 Feb 2022.

Radar Staff (Aug 4, 2019). American Media Inc., — 'NO ONE REALLY KNEW HIM': Accused Walmart shooter Patrick Crusius described as taunted 'loner' with 'short temper Retrieved February 7, 2022, Canoe.com Website: https://canoe.com/news/crime/no-one-really-knew-him-accused-walmart-shooter-patrick-crusius-described-as-taunted-loner-with-short-temper

Randall, Kate (7 June 2017) Fired worker, an army veteran, kills five in workplace rampage in Orlando, Florida www.wsws.org, Retrieved 2021-01-31.

Regehr, Cheryl (2001-09-01). Crisis Debriefing Groups for Emergency Responders: Reviewing the Evidence. 2001 Oxford University Press

Retrieved February 8, 2022, from The Conversation.com Website: https://theconversation.com/why-leonardo-da-vinci-was-a-genius-54207.

Reuters Staff: Reporting by Bill Tarrant in Los Angeles; Editing by Steve Gorman: Retrieved February 16, 2022: https://www.reuters.com/article/us-illinois-shooting-gunman-idUSKCN1Q5052 Gunman in Aurora, Illinois, shooting described as 'loner'.

Rice, E. (1995) Idea Tasting. Needham Heights, Mass: Simon & Schuster Custom Publication.

Riley, J. W., & Humphrey, H. E. (1915). Out to old Aunt Mary's. Orange, N.J: Edison Blue Amberol.

Riley, J. W., & Humphrey, H. E. (1915). Out to old Aunt Mary's. Orange, N.J: Edison Blue Amberol.

Risen, C. (2019). The Crowded Hour. Place of publication not identified: Scribner.

Robb, G. (1999). Victor Hugo. W.W. Norton & Company.

Robert Louis Stevenson (n.d.), quote: "Keep busy at something: a busy person never has time to be unhappy." Retrieved February 7, 2022, from Quotefancy.com Website: https://quotefancy.com/quote/992977/Robert-Louis-Stevenson-Keep-busy-at-something-a-busy-person-never-has-time-to-be-unhappy.

Robert W. Service (1907) "The Cremation of Sam McGee". Retrieved February 7, 2022, The Poetry Foundation Website:
 https://www.poetryfoundation.org/poems/45081/the-cremation-of-sam-mcgee.

Robinson, Alex (November 20, 2017) Jim Shockey Goes Home: The Legacy of Modern Hunting's Most Influential Celebrity. https://www.outdoorlife.com/the-legacy-of-jim-shockey/

Robson, David (24th June 2014) Neuroscience: The man who saw time stand still bbc.com/future Retrieved February 1, 2022.

Rogers, C. R. (2016). On Becoming a Person: A Therapist's View of Psychotherapy. London: Robinson.

Rogers, C. (2011). On Becoming a Person. London: Constable & Robinson.

Rohn, J. Quotes (n.d.) Quotefancy.com. Retrieved February 7, 2022, from Quotefancy.com Website: https://quotefancy.com/quote/837558/Jim-Rohn-Always-be-willing-to-look-at-both-sides-of-the-argument-Understanding-the-other.

Ronayne, K. (July 31, 2019). Associated Press FBI: California festival killer a 'loner,' motive a mystery. Retrieved February 7, 2022, ABCNewsGo.com Website: https://abcnews.go.com/US/wireStory/california-festival-killers-motive-mystery-64673284

Roosevelt, T. (1927). The wilderness hunter. New York: Putnam.

Rozsa, M. (December 23, 2018) Revisiting Adam Lanza and autism, six years after Sandy Hook. Autism activists saw some backlash after the Sandy Hook shooting, but the public's attitude is shifting. https://www.salon.com/2018/12/23/revisiting-adam-lanza-and-autism-six-years-after-sandy-hook/

Rudyard Kipling (1910) Rewards and Fairies; Poem "If",Doubleday, Page & Company. en.wikipedia.org/wiki/If%E2%80%94 Retrieved February 03, 2022.

Rule 5122-29-10 Crisis intervention service". Retrieved February 10, 2022, from Ohio Laws and Administrative Rules Legislative services website.https://codes.ohio.gov/ohio-administrative-code/rule-5122-29-10.

Saddle Up Magazine   chase age

Sagan, C. (1985). Cosmos: Carl Sagan. New York, New York: Ballantine Books.

Sagan, Carl (1977). The Dragons of Eden: Speculations on the Evolution of Human Intelligence New York: Random House.

Sagan, Carl (1980) Cosmos - Heaven and Hell http://sirius.bu.edu/withers/media/bruno/ saganbruno.html. Retrieved February 5, 2022.

Seriously Science (Mar 16, 2017) "Study Shows Dogs Know How to Lie". discovermagazine.com/planet-earth/study-shows-dogs-know-how-to-lie? Retrieved: May 10, 2022.

Scheil, K., & Holderness, G. (2020). Shakespeare & biography. New York: Berghahn Books.

Schlessinger, L. D. (1996). Now Go Take on The Day: Harper Perennial.

Schmidt, Samantha (April 14, 2017) After years and hundreds of suicides off the Golden Gate Bridge, a new net could save lives.
https://www.washingtonpost.com/morning-mix

Schoenberg, Harris O. Combating Terrorism: The Role of the United, Center for UN Reform Education 2003

Schultz, Isaac (24 October 2019). "The World's Most Famous Ghost Ship Is an Enduring Symbol of Empire". Atlas Obscura. R
https://www.atlasobscura.com/articles/the-flying-dutchman-explained Retrieved 4 February 2022.

Schwantes, M. (n.d.) "Warren Buffett Says 4 Choices in Life Separate the Doers from the Dreamers".
https://www.inc.com/marcel-schwantes/warren-buffett-says-4-choices-in-life-separate-doers-from-the-dreamers. Retrieved May 31, 2022,
Scott Peck (n.d.), BrainyQuote.com. Retrieved February 11, 2022, from BrainyQuote.com web site: https://www.brainyquote.com/authors/m-scott-peck-quotes#:

Serving People with Disabilities in the Most Integrated Setting: Community Living and Olmstead" U.S., Department of Health & Human Services. Retrieved February 10, 2022, from HHS.gov website: https://www.hhs.gov/civil-rights/for-individuals/special-topics/community-living-and-olmstead/index.html#:

Shakespeare, W. (Hamlet, act 2 scene 2) Pub., 1604 public domain.

Shannon, C. E. (1950). Programming a computer for playing Chess. London: Taylor & Francis.

Sharma,Sumer (June 2016). You won't believe these 17 celebrities were bullied as kids. https://yourstory.com/2016/06/celebrities-bullied-as-kids/amp. Retrieved February 5, 2022.

Sheehan, Krista (September 30, 2017). At What Age Is the Human Brain Fully Developed? https://healthyliving.azcentral.com/at-what-age-is-the-human-brain-fully-developed-12310557.html.

Sheeran, E. (2015). Thinking Out Loud Sheet Music. Hal Leonard. http://www.myilibrary.com?id=912713.

Shields, M. (1997). J.P. McCarthy: Just Don't Tell 'Em Where I Am. Detroit, Sleeping Bear Press.

Shimshock, Rob (August 13, 2017) Dr. Jordan Peterson Talks Personality Differences Between Liberals and Conservatives [VIDEO] Retrieved February 8, 2022, from Daily Caller News Foundation Website: https://dailycaller.com/2017/08/13/dr-jordan-peterson-talks-personality-differences-between-liberals-and-conservatives-video/.

Silverman, H., Waldrop, T. Benjamin Keough, grandson of Elvis Presley, dies at 27

Sir William Osler Quotes (n.d.) QuoetsWiki.com. Retrieved February 10, 2022, from website: https://www.quotes.wiki/when-schemes-are-laid-in-advance-it-is-surpris/.

Smith, B., & Quindlen, A. (2018). A Tree Grows in Brooklyn. New York: Harper Perennial Modern Classics.

Smith, Betty (1943) A Tree Grows in Brooklyn. HarperCollins Publishers. ISBN: 0061120073, ISBN 13: 9780061120077.

Spector, J. (June 27, 2016) Paulo Coelho is A Person You Should Know. https://medium.com/a-person-you-should-know. Retrieved 6 February 2022.

Spencer, Herbert (1864). Principles of Biology, Volume 1. Williams and Norgate. p. 444. But this survival of the fittest, implies multiplication of the fittest.

Stanford News (November 12, 2018) Benjamin Franklin as the social network genius of his time? Yes, says one Stanford scholar. Retrieved February 8, 2022, from Website:https://news.stanford.edu/2018/11/12/benjamin-franklin-social-genius-18th-century/

State v. Soto, 2021-Ohio-3859.Court of Appeals No. L-21-1011 October 29, 2021. supremecourt.ohio.gov. Retrieved February 1, 2022.

Stekel, Wilhelm (1868-1940) inspirationalstories.com/quotes/wilhelm-stekel-anxiety-is-fear-of-ones-self/ Retrieved 2 Feb 2022.

Steven, Emma (February 8, 2019) Meet the Determined Woman who invented Duct Tape. https://www.jnj.com/our-heritage/vesta-stoudt-the-woman-who-invented-duct-tape.

Strauss-Kahn, Dominique Gaston André. (n.d.) The Columbia Electronic Encyclopedia®. (2013). Retrieved

February 16, 2022, from
https://encyclopedia2.thefreedictionary.com/Strauss-
Kahn%2c+Dominique+Gaston+Andr%c3%a9

Sullivan, Glenn (June 30, 2019) Divorce Is a Risk Factor
for Suicide, Especially for Men. Psychologytoday.com.
Retrieved February 1, 2022.

Susan S. Lang (April 25, 2002) Hungry young people
are more likely to attempt suicide, suffer from
depression and do poorly in school, Cornell Chronicle.
news.cornell.edu

Swansburg, J. (March 26, 2013) The Passion of Lew
Wallace. Retrieved February 7, 2022, from Slate.com
Website:
http://www.slate.com/articles/life/history/2013/03/ben_h
ur_and
_lew_wallace_how_the_scapegoat_of_shiloh_became_o
ne_of_the_best.html.

Tanushree, D. (16 April 2019). "Lara Dutta became Miss
Universe with this epic answer". Archived from the
original on 19 August 2019. Retrieved 2 February 2022.

Taylor, Dick (May 8, 2016) Real Possibilities Retrieved
February 8, 2022, from DickTaylorBlog Website:
Retrieved 2 February 2023.

Temperton, R., & Heatwave (Musical group). (1976).
Always and forever. London: Rondor Music.

The ABCs of Human Instincts
https://exploringyourmind.com/the-abcs-of-human-
instincts/

Terrace, H. (October 2, 2019).
https://www.psychologytoday.com/gb/blog/the-origin-words/201910/why-chimpanzees-cant-learn-language.

Terao, N., Yoshida, S., Wakasugi, M., World Presentations, Inc., & Contemporary Films/McGraw-Hill. (1969). Skinny and fatty. Japan: Educational Film Exchange and Mingei Eiga Sha.

The Declaration of Independence: A History". The U.S. National Archives and Records Administration. January 17, 2010. Archived from the original on August 17, 2008. Retrieved February 03, 2022.

The Fire Tetrahedron (A pyramid). "Information about the Fire Triangle/Tetrahedron and Combustion." www.firesafe.org.uk/information-about-the-fire-triangletetrahedron-and-combustion/ Retrieved 31 May 2022.

The Maritime Aquarium, Neighbor, (August 27, 2013). School Offers Many Advantages for Fish Too. https://patch.com/connecticut/norwalk/school-offers-many-advantages-for-fish-too

The National Suicide Prevention Lifeline and your organization (January 16, 2018) Retrieved February 10, 2022 from Website:
https://www.preventsuicidepa.org/wp-content/uploads/2018/02/PA-Office-Mental-Health-and-Substance-Abuse-Services-and-the-National-Suicide-Prevention-Lifeline-webinar-1-16-18-.pdf

The Outlaw Josey Wales. (2014). Place of publication not identified: Warner Home Video.

Therapy the Game, In July, 2014, the Pressman Toy Corporation was bought by Goliath Games

Thomas A. Edison Quotes. (n.d.). BrainyQuote.com. Retrieved February 6, 2022, from BrainyQuote.com Web site: https://www.brainyquote.com/quotes/thomas_a_edison_104931

Thomas Anthony Harris (1967), I'm OK – You're OK written, Harper & Row.

Thomas, D. (2004). Dylan Thomas. New York: Caedmon.

Thompson, P. D. G. J., & OverDrive, Inc. (2013). *Verbal Judo*. S.I.: HarperCollins.

Those who pray, those who work, those who fight. Retrieved February 8, 2022, from Medievalists.net website: https://www.medievalists.net/2016/01/those-who-pray-those-who-work-those-who-fight/.

Tickell, R. H. (2020) Kiss the Ground, documentary. Kisstheground.com.Retrieved 2 Feb 2022.

Todd, J. T., & Morris, E. K. (1994). Modern perspectives on John B. Watson and classical behaviorism. Westport, Conn: Greenwood Press.

Torrey, Edwin (November 14, 1918). "Six Suffrage Campaigns In South Dakota". The Saturday News. Watertown, South Dakota. The United Press.

Trinidad & Tobago News, Trinidad teen kills herself after mother took away phone The Trinidad Express

(Feb. 4, 2019) stabroeknews.com Retrieved January 31, 2022.

Trussell-Cullen, A., & Stevenson, P. (2002). Archimedes: The mystery of the king's new crown. Carlsbad, Calif: Dominie Press.

Twain M. (n.d.) "I am an old man and have known a great many troubles, but most of them never happened.." Retrieved February 16, 2022: https://www.brainyquote.com/quotes/mark_ twain_108600.

Twain, M. (1952). Huckleberry Finn: T. 1. Frankfurt, M. Rudl

Twain, M., & Center for Literary Review. (1978). Huckleberry Finn by Mark Twain, a review of the novel. Wilton, Conn: Current Affairs Films.

Twain, M., Gerber, J. C., Baender, P., Williams, T., & Bancroft Library. (2021). The adventures of Tom Sawyer. Oakland, California: University of California Press.

Twain, Mark (1896) The Adventures of Tom Sawyer. Public domain in the USA

Twerski, A. (Oct 29, 2017) Rabbi Twerski on Anger, Rage, and Resentment. aish.com Retrieved 2021-01-31.

University of Wisconsin - Madison. (2007, November 9). How Well Do Dogs See At Night?. ScienceDaily. Retrieved December 31, 2022 from www.sciencedaily.com/releases/2007/11/071108140336. htm

Updated 1:58 PM ET, Mon July 13, 2020.
https://www.cnn.com/2020/07/12/us/benjamin-keough-elvis-presley-grandson-death/index.html retrieved February 19, 2020.

Vaillant, J. (2005). The Golden Spruce, W.W. Norton & Co.

Valpy, Michael (June 25, 2004). "The universe is unfolding as it should". The Globe and Mail. Retrieved 7 September 2021.

Värnik, P (March 2012). "Suicide in the world". International Journal of Environmental Research and Public Health. 9 (3): 760–71. doi:10.3390/ijerph9030760. PMC 3367275. PMID 22690161.

VideosSubscribe Words of Wisdom — October 23, 2014 https://bigthink.com/words-of-wisdom/alice-walker-people-give-up-their-power-by-thinking-they-dont-have-any-2. Retrieved February 5, 2022.

Vince Lombardi (n.d.) BrainyQuote.com. Retrieved February 10, 2022, from BrainyQuote.com Web site: https://www.brainyquote.com/authors/vince-lombardi-quotes

Virgil quotes (n.d.) thinkexist.com (Ancient Roman Latin Poet and Author of the epic, Aeneid. 70 BC-19 BC).

Vonnegut, K. (2020). Hocus pocus. London: Vintage

Wagner, J. P. (2021). Enneagram Spectrum of Personality Styles: An Introductory Guide.

Walker A. (n.d.): "People give up their power by thinking they don't have any." https://www.brainyquote.com/quotes/alice_walker_385241

Wallace, L. (April 6, 2020) The Fair God or, The Last of the 'Tzins: "When people are lonely, they stoop to any companionship" Publisher: Horse's Mouth ISBN: 978-1839673443

Wallace, Lew (1998). Ben-Hur. Oxford World's Classics.

Wallas, Graham. (2018). Art of Thought. Place of publication not identified: SOLIS Press.

Watson, J. B. (1997). Behaviorism. New Brunswick, N.J: Transaction Publishers.

Weebly. https://allaboutconfucius.weebly.com/exile-and-return-home.html Retrieved 2 Feb 2022.

Wegner, D. M. (2004). Précis of the illusion of conscious will. Behavioral and Brain Sciences, 27(5), 649-659.

Weisman, Mary-Lou (1999), "The History of Retirement, From Early Man to A.A.R.P.", The New York Times, retrieved December 23, 2016

Westfall, Stacy Championship Bareback & Bridleless Freestyle Reining with Roxy. May 13, 2010 Retrieved February 7, 2022, from YouTube.com Website: https://www.youtube.com/watch?v=TKK7AXLOUNo

Wheat-ear tiara Maison Chaumet, May 2021 (ed./trans. PH) www.napoleon.org. Retrieved 2 Feb 2022.

White, E. (December 4, 2021), "Few parents charged when children use their guns in school shootings", https://www.latimes.com/world-nation/story/2021-12-04/explainer-how-unusual-to-charge-parents-in-school-shooting. Retrieved 4 January 2023.

Whorf, M., Beckmann, F., & WJR (Radio station: Detroit, Mich.). (1995). A tribute to J.P. McCarthy. Detroit: Producers?

Wiesel, E. (1991). The accident. Hill & Wang Publisher.

Wikipedia. Klondike Gold Rush - https://en.wikipedia.org/wiki/Klondike_Gold_Rush

Wikipedia. List of artists who have covered Bob Dylan songs- https://en.wikipedia.org/wiki/List_of_artists_who_have_covered_Bob_Dylan_songs

Wilcox, Manon (2019) https://colors-newyork.com/what-are-the-four-types-of-love-according-to-ancient-greek/

Wilde, O., Holland, M., & Hart-Davis, R. (2000). The complete letters of Oscar Wilde. London: Fourth estate.

William Congreve Quotes. (n.d.). BrainyQuote.com. Retrieved February 8, 2022, from BrainyQuote.com Web site: https://www.brainyquote.com/quotes/ william-congreve-quotes

William Shakespeare, Jr., Fishing

Willing Screenplay by Simone Yehuda

Wilson, J. Q, Kelling, G. (March 1982), "Broken Windows: The Police and Neighborhood Safety." Atlantic. www.psychologytoday.com/us/basics/broken-windows-theory. Retrieved May 29, 2022.

Wilson, P. F. (1993). Root cause analysis: A tool for total quality management. Milwaukee, Wisconsin, EU: ASQC Quality Press.

Wilson, R. E. (September 23, 2009) The Most Powerful Motivator: How fear is etched into our brains. psychologytoday.com Retrieved 2021-01-31

Winfrey, Oprah (n.d.) "Turn your wounds into wisdom" by https://www.osmquote.com/quote/oprah-winfrey-quote-a8f9a5.Retrived February 4, 2022.

Wiseman, R. (April 20, 2007), "The truth about lying and laughing" theguardian.com/science/2007/apr/2. Retrieved May 10, 2023.

Worster, D. (2014). Dust Bowl: The southern Plains in the 1930s. New York, NY: Oxford University Press.

Wu, S. (January 3, 2019). "How To Tell If Someone Is Lying to You In 5 Seconds". blinkist.com/magazine/posts/spot-liar-5-seconds. Retrieved: May 10, 2022.

Younge, Gary (August 21, 2003). "I have a dream". The Guardian. Archived from the original on August 27, 2013. Retrieved February 03, 2022.

Zane, Betty (n.d.) https://www.encyclopedia.com/women/encyclopedias-almanacs-transcripts-and-maps/zane-betty-c-1766-c-1831. Retrieved 6 February 2022.